THE QUEST FOR IMAGINATION

THE QUEST FOR IMAGINATION

ESSAYS IN TWENTIETH-CENTURY AESTHETIC CRITICISM

EDITED BY

O. B. HARDISON, JR.

1971
THE PRESS OF
CASE WESTERN RESERVE UNIVERSITY
CLEVELAND & LONDON

Cleveland, Ohio 44106

Printed in the United States of America.
International Standard Book Number: 0-8295-0207-6
Library of Congress Catalogue Card Number: 70-145425

Contents

Contents

Preface

IN 1781 IMMANUEL KANT INITIATED what he called a "Copernican revolution" in European philosophy. The *Critique of Pure Reason* shook the foundations of traditional thought concerning the relation of the mind to nature. It also pointed the way to a transformation of the theory of aesthetics. The implications of Kant's position were spelled out in the *Critique of Judgment*, published in 1790. This work remains the decisive event in the history of modern aesthetics. Its seminal concepts include the theory of the creative imagination, the "purposiveness without purpose" of works of art, the disinterestedness and subjective universality of judgments of taste, the definition of genius as the capacity to create without prescriptions or models, the analogy between art and play, and at least a suggestion of the essentially symbolic nature of art. These concepts furnish the coordinates which, in varying combination with other ideas, and with varying terminology and coloration, have remained basic in the aesthetic tradition from Kant's day to the present.

Kant's ideas were applied to literary theory in Germany in Schiller's *Letters on the Aesthetic Education of Man* (1793–95). They were imported into England (and thence to America) in Coleridge's *Biographia Literaria*, published in 1817. Coleridge spoke for an entire generation of authors and literary critics when he exclaimed,

> The writings of the illustrious sage of Königsberg, the founder of the Critical Philosophy, more than any other work, at once invigorated and disciplined my understanding. The originality, the depth, and the compression of the thought; the novelty and subtlety, yet solidity and importance of the distinctions; the adamantine chain of logic; and I will venture to add (paradox as it will appear to those who have taken their notion of Immanuel Kant from Reviewers and Frenchmen) the *clearness* and *evidence* of the *Critique of Pure Reason*; of the *Judgment*; of the *Metaphysical*

> *Elements of Natural Philosophy*; and of the *Religion within the Bounds of Pure Reason*, took possession of me as with a giant's hand. After fifteen years' familiarity with them, I still read these and all his other productions with undiminished delight and increasing admiration.

By the end of the nineteenth century, the Kantian revolution had permeated philosophy and had profoundly influenced disciplines as diverse as political science, history, and literary criticism, while providing the rationale for such movements in the area of the creative arts as art for art's sake, symbolism, and impressionism. It was not, of course, unopposed. The Philistines expressed alarm, the Utilitarians attacked, the scientists (or their popularizers) ridiculed. In the field of literary criticism, the popular journals continued to advocate the moral theory of literature inherited from Plato and Horace—what Poe was to call "the heresy of the didactic." In various ways they asserted that the value of literature is its ability to profit the reader while delighting him at the same time. Unfortunately this didacticism placed the literary journals in the curious position of decrying most of the significant literature of the age; but it was occasionally given depth by writers like Matthew Arnold, whose lapses as a critic—his belief, for instance, that literature could replace religion—are to be balanced against his sensitivity to the very real shortcomings of his age.

Meanwhile, formal literary scholarship as practiced in the universities took a direction different from both the aestheticism of the artists and the didacticism of the popular journals. The scholars aspired to make literary study a form of *Strengwissenschaft*—exact science—through the use of philology, or of adaptations of Darwin's theory of evolution to historical and artistic phenomena, or through sociological theories which sought to "explain" historical epochs and literary works by resolving them into various sources and influences, much as a compound is resolved by chemical analysis into its constituent elements. Most of these theories look more than a little bizarre today, but they had immense prestige in the late nineteenth century when the modern curriculum for humanistic studies was being established. Having undergone numerous updatings and modifications, they continue to be influential. Witness the frequency with which the charge of "scientism" is leveled against the ideal of literary scholarship taught in American graduate schools.

In the United States an effective critique of scientism in literary study was offered by the "new critics" of the nineteen-thirties and forties. The new critics were generally and quite consciously in the aesthetic tradition. They were heavily influenced by Coleridge and they agreed, though not unanimously, in regarding the literary work as valuable for its own sake (i.e., having unique ontological status), as characterized by organic unity, and as something to be experienced rather than analyzed into historical, biographical, psychological, and literary influences.

The new critics popularized several key ideas of aesthetic criticism. In spite of their effective defense of literary values and their extremely salutary effect on the teaching of literature, however, they were at their best in the practical business of analyzing specific works, and at their worst when attempting to generalize. Their achievement remains somewhat narrow. Typically, they published their ideas in the form of essays rather than sustained works. They touched on many of the implications of the aesthetic position, but they failed to develop them into a general theory of culture.

The major spokesmen for the aesthetic tradition in the twentieth century are familiar to most English-speaking readers, but they are talked about far more often than they are read. In the first place, the aesthetic tradition is international. Its full dimensions are visible only to those who are willing to venture beyond the boundaries of English and American literature. Yet the study of English and American literature is notoriously parochial, and English and American readers are likely to prefer third-rate products, if they are homegrown, to first-rate imports. In addition, the works themselves are difficult. Throughout its history the aesthetic tradition has been closely affiliated with formal philosophy. Many of its foremost advocates—writers like Jacques Maritain, Jean-Paul Sartre, and Ernst Cassirer—are philosophers first and aestheticians and literary theorists second. This is a major source of their strength in comparison to the new critics, but it creates obstacles for readers unfamiliar with the kinds of problems the aesthetic tradition seeks to examine, not to mention its characteristic vocabulary.

In retrospect, it seems proper to date the proximate origin of twentieth-century aestheticism in the period between 1890 and 1910. This period witnessed the publication of a series of important restatements of questions inherited from Kant and the Kantian tradition. It is all the more remarkable because the authors involved worked independently. They inherited elements of the same tradition—most of them were specifically indebted to Hegel—but there was little or no contact or cross-fertilization among them. They remained diverse in personality, tone, style, problems treated, and conclusions reached. The important figures are Croce, Bergson, Husserl, and Santayana. Bergson appeared on the scene in 1889 with his *Essai sur les donnés immediates de la conscience,* followed in 1900 by the famous essay on comedy, *Le Rire,* and in 1907 by *Evolution créatrice.* Santayana, the least typical of the group, published *The Sense of Beauty* in 1896, but this work is a compromise, an apprentice piece, and he did not find an authentic voice until *Interpretations of Poetry and Religion* (1900) and *The Life of Reason* (1905–6). Croce's *L'Estetica* appeared in 1901; and the two volumes of Edmund Husserl's *Logische Untersuchungen,* which marks the beginning of modern phenomenology, appeared in 1900–1.

Because each of these authors is highly idiomatic and because each influenced a significant group of successors, it is possible to speak of "schools" of twentieth-century aestheticism. Labeling, however, cannot be taken too seriously, because members of the schools are themselves independent thinkers who resist simple classification. Wallace Stevens was deeply impressed by Santayana, but no one who has read Santayana would confuse either his style or his ideas with Stevens' *The Noble Rider and the Sound of Words.* Susanne Langer's major works on aesthetics are directly indebted to Cassirer, but she was also influenced by Whitehead and Wittgenstein, among others. Maritain was influenced by Bergson, but in a negative way. He criticized Bergson in his first published work, *La Philosophie Bergsonienne* (1914), and from *Art et scholastique* (1920) to *Creative Intuition in Art and Literature* (1953) his effort has been directed to healing the breach which aesthetic theory opened between art and the moral imperatives of Catholic theology. If Sartre was influenced by Husserl and Heidegger, he was also influenced in his postwar writing by Marxist political thought, so that a striking change, almost a *volte-face,* is observable between *L'Imaginaire* (1940) and *Qu'est-ce que la littérature?,* published in 1947.

The tension between the idea of responsibility and the idea of disinterestedness in the thought of Maritain and Sartre illustrates an important point. In spite of the cultural lag evident in current literary discourse, scientism has pretty well run its course. Since the nineteen-thirties, the major pressure on serious aesthetic thought has come not from would-be Darwins or Taines but from an urgent and progressively worsening cultural crisis. The social trauma of World War I was not followed by the era of stability and progress forecast by allied propaganda. Instead, the trauma was intensified by further shocks that included the Russian Revolution, the rise of Fascism, the Great Depression, the Second World War, and the dismal and all too familiar record of the events that followed. The result among artists and students of culture has been an intensified sense of social responsibility, bordering in recent times on obsession. If the ship is sinking, goes the argument, what right do artists and scholars have to remain detached from the struggle to save it? Should they not be manning the pumps; or, to use Sartre's term, should they not become "engaged"? This is not a matter of writing with one hand and waving the appropriate banner with the other. It is a matter of basic alterations in the concept of art, the definition of humanistic education, and the objectives toward which scholarship is oriented. It results in calls for the writer to become a revolutionary in the literal sense of subordinating his work to the imperatives of revolutionary politics. On a more personal level, it threatens to change the writer's image of himself. Aesthetic criticism regards individuality as an absolute good and the corollary of this position is its insistence on absolute freedom for the artist and "disinterestedness" for the scholar. Utilitarian criticism sees the artist as the servant of a cause. He does not have autonomy, and if he fails to conform to appropriate standards, society has the right to censor or even punish him. When the artist accepts this position, his self-image changes, producing a complementary change in the nature of what he creates. Art is valued not as art but as it expresses approved doctrine—often in an approved style, such as "socialist realism."

Naturally, complementary changes occur in the areas of education and scholarship, where the didactic impulse generates programs to revise the canon of the classics—the list of works normally studied in the curriculum. Works are selected on the basis of their political orthodoxy. Or they are chosen on a quota system, each sub-group within a culture being assigned a number of works proportionate to its share of the total population. Or standard curriculum authors are attacked as "irrelevant" —either in political terms (Keats versus Shelley), or because they had the misfortune not to live in the twentieth century, preferably in an urban environment. As this happens, scholarship tends increasingly to disguised polemic, to attacks on artists for their political or social views, to defenses or revivals of minor propagandists, to charges of irresponsibility, escapism, fascism, and the like.

The degree to which this view has permeated current thought about literature is indicated by a recent speech by John Hurt Fisher, Executive Secretary of The Modern Language Association, to a meeting of Chairmen of Departments of English in the summer of 1969. Among other things, Mr. Fisher makes the blanket accusation that English departments are "inextricably bound in with an elitist principle." He adds that if the "elitist principle" is not accepted, "the English department may be worse than useless. It may be the dead hand of the past inhibiting the development of the attitudes and ideas of a new society." Later he adds that "The subject of English in this country has been used to inculcate a white, Anglo-Saxon, Protestant ethic," and concludes "My own feeling is that the game is just about played out."

One may question all of Mr. Fisher's assertions. From the aesthetic point of view, what he calls "the elitist principle" is nothing more ominous than the belief in cultivating the highest potentiality of each individual, whatever his race or socio-economic status, with the corollary that each student deserves the best that a humanities program can offer and nothing less. The notion that the past is a "dead hand," not to mention the idea that to teach the traditional curriculum authors is to inculcate a "white, Anglo-Saxon, Protestant ethic," is best understood as rhetoric. But what is evident is that such rhetoric has replaced serious thought at an extremely influential level of humanistic education. Clearly if the point of view suggested by this rhetoric prevails, the literary and artistic values that are at the heart of the humanistic curriculum today—the cultivation of individual taste, the sense of enlargement and discovery that come precisely because the authors we read are *not* of our own generation or socio-economic group, the understanding of the present in terms of a vital past—are in jeopardy.

We can admit that the motives for the new didacticism are usually admirable without approving of the directions in which they lead. Most humanists despise intolerance, believe that war has outlived any use it may have had, and admit the need for sweeping social reform. Granted all this, the fact remains that the subordination of humanistic goals to moral or political imperatives has been shown time and again to be destructive of the very values that literature expresses. The demand that the humanities serve this or that cause is always made on what seem unexceptionable grounds to those making it. And a few years after the fact, the demand always looks absurd and often cruelly perverse. Flaubert and Baudelaire were attacked for undermining divinely sanctioned moral codes by Christians whose lives could have served as models for hagiographies. The personal difficulties that this caused are evident in their lives, but there is no way of estimating the cultural damage—which is damage to the individuals comprising the society—caused by informal and organized suppression of their work. During the First World War, Americans, caught up in a paroxysm of nationalistic fervor, persuaded themselves that teaching German literature was unpatriotic (and with commendable consistency advocated the extermination of dachshunds). In the twenties the Soviet Union felt that to save socialism, the Russian symbolist movement had to be crushed. In the thirties, English and American Marxists attacked James Joyce as "decadent" while extolling a group of "proletarian" writers so abysmally bad that the Party seriously compromised itself among intellectuals by the absurdity of its claims. The current revival of didacticism has the same liabilities.

We do not know much about art, but we know enough to recognize that some approaches are simply inadequate. They are like trivial solutions in mathematics. They do not do justice to the subject, and they lead nowhere. When used as assumptions in the analysis of living literature, they produce caricatures of criticism. When applied to curriculum reform in the areas of selection of materials (the canon of classics), of teaching methodology, and of definition of goals, they eliminate even the possibility of humane discussion of the humanities. The result is not understanding but confusion. Instead of supporting valid claims, the custodians of the humanities become their own worst enemies. Humanists abandon their subjects and the experiences that led them to the humanities in the first place in favor of clumsy political and sociological clichés. Professional organizations are drawn into endless, debilitating squabbles that are symptomatic of loss of a sense of their real function. Meanwhile, since the experience of art remains real and vital, it becomes painfully clear to those who continue to respond to artistic values that the descriptions offered by the authorities are beside the point. As this happens, the position of the humanities in the curriculum and in culture as a whole is weakened. If those who profess the humanities fail to speak for them, they will hardly be defended by sociologists, economists, and physicists.

The essays collected in the present volume are intended to serve two purposes. First, they are intended as a reminder that amid the sound and fury created by the new didacticism, the aesthetic tradition has continued to examine aesthetic and literary problems in ways that can be taken seriously. The authors who are examined are among the most important twentieth-century representatives of this tradition. They differ among themselves in many ways. Their conclusions are often contradictory. They have in common, however, an awareness of what can and cannot be done that comes from familiarity with the history of aesthetic thought. They also share the ability to distinguish between solutions that are trivial and those that are worth pursuing, and a fine sensitivity to the special problems posed for the critic and artist by twentieth-century experience. Together they provide a cross section of the ways in which the aesthetic tradition has been reinterpreted to offer viable contemporary answers to such questions as the nature of literary experience, the form and function of works of literature, the place of literature in culture, and its relation to ethics and politics. Above all, they share a concern for the nature of the imagination—how it functions, its relation to the data it receives, and its expression in art. If the answers are not simple, they have the virtue of respecting the complexity of the questions. If they are not all "right," they are all significant. They deal with their subjects in a fruitful way, and each has claims to consideration by anyone seriously interested in the humanities in the twentieth century.

The second purpose follows from the first. Each author is examined in an essay that outlines the basic structure of his thought and illustrates this structure by reference to one or more of his major works. There has been no attempt to impose additional uniformity on the essays by suggesting that they follow a standard pattern or that they be slanted to illustrate a general thesis. If a method runs through them, it is the method of treating each author on his own terms. The resulting studies are both fresh contributions to the understanding of the authors included, and useful introductions to their work. The notes provide guidance for the reader who wishes to move from the essays to the authors themselves. The first essay discusses background. The final essay is speculative; it seeks to identify some of the implications of modern aesthetic thought for the future of humanistic culture.

The idea for this collection grew out of a seminar in contemporary criticism offered several years ago at the University of North Carolina in Chapel Hill. All members of the seminar contributed to the excitement which was the inception of this volume. A teacher learns from his students, and in this case the students were very good teachers. Several members of the seminar, now teachers and scholars themselves, are represented here. To them and to the other authors who gave generously of their time and knowledge I express my sincere thanks. Although the variety of opinion represented in the present volume should be obvious from the essays themselves, I will add that the opinions expressed in this preface are my own and do not necessarily reflect the opinions of the contributors, all of whom speak for themselves with quite sufficient eloquence.

O. B. H.
Washington, D. C.

THE QUEST FOR IMAGINATION

Nineteenth-Century Backgrounds of Modern Aesthetic Criticism

KEVIN KERRANE
UNIVERSITY OF DELAWARE

TWENTIETH-CENTURY AESTHETIC CRITICISM encompasses an extremely broad range of questions and answers about the art of literature. This range is so broad, in fact, that the term "aesthetic" may sometimes appear to be only a convenient label for a diffusion of critical attention into such areas as the dynamics of the creative process, the psychology of audience response, the nature of language itself, the ontological status of poetry, and the relations of literature to the other arts, to science, to religion, to myth, to history, and to humanistic education.

There are, of course, principles of order and continuity uniting these diverse inquiries. The aesthetic position has an inherent logic that underlies the frequent repetition (even among opposed critics) of such key terms as "imagination," "intuition," "freedom," "purposiveness," and "disinterestedness." Confusion concerning aesthetic criticism is in part a corollary of its long history. Its essential (though not always self-conscious) unity can best be seen when its modern varieties are placed against the basic assumptions laid down by Kant and Schiller and developed by nineteenth-century followers, whether rigorous and philosophic or impressionistic and contentious.

I

One of the many reasons why Immanuel Kant's *Critique of Judgment* (1790) is the seminal document of modern aestheticism is that its brief remarks on art constitute the completion of a philosophical argument. In effect, Kant raised art to philosophical status: he was the first modern critic to make aesthetics an integral part of a total system.[1] He was by no means the last. For Hegel, Schopenhauer, Santayana, Cassirer, and Sartre, the noun "aesthetic" has continued to signify art criticism as part of a larger theoretical inquiry. Moreover, for them as for Kant, this inquiry has been essentially epistemological. One of the most obvious distinguishing traits of aesthetic criticism is that it has traditionally attempted to justify its approaches to literature by reference to the noetic constitution of the human mind. Samuel Taylor Coleridge's statement of methodology is typical: "I labored at a solid foundation, on which permanently to ground my opinions, in the component faculties of the human mind itself, and their comparative dignity and importance."[2]

Kant's own aesthetic position clearly reflects the "Copernican revolution" he claimed to have effected in epistemology—a change from the Lockean view of the mind as a *tabula rasa*, a passive receiver of sensory data, to a view of the mind as an active and constructive instrument, partly constitutive of the world which it knows. In *Critique of Pure Reason* (1781) Kant had set forth the grimness of the human condition in epistemological terms: certain knowledge of the noumenal realm, the external world of *Dinge an sich*, is impossible. The mind does not receive a ready-made, dependably "objective" reality; the mind itself always enters into that which it perceives and understands. Thus, "seeing" is "seeing *as*." Kant's point is vaguely analogous to Heisenberg's Principle in quantum physics: the observer, in the act of "measuring," alters what he is trying to measure. Hazard Adams has suggested another analogy: Kant seems to be saying that it is as if each human being from birth wore spectacles which could never be removed.[3]

These spectacles might be identified as the categories of space and time, which for Kant are not objective properties of external reality, but rather the pre-conditions of perception itself, functions within the knower. For perception to be possible, Kant says, these categories must be applied by an "active faculty for synthesis"—*Einbildungskraft*, or "imaginative power":

> Psychologists have hitherto failed to realize that imagination is a necessary ingredient of perception itself. This is due partly to the fact that that faculty has been limited to reproduction, partly to the belief that the senses not only supply impressions but also combine them so as to generate images of objects. For that purpose

something more is undoubtedly required, namely, a function for the synthesis of them.[4]

In the act of perception, imagination *creates*: the "chaos" of sense data is given "order." (It is this insight that lies behind Coleridge's highly rhetorical definition of "primary imagination" as "the living Power and prime Agent of all human Perception, . . . a repetition in the finite mind of the eternal act of creation in the infinite I AM."[5]) What imagination creates is the world of "phenomena" or "appearance" (*Erscheinung*), a realm of sensory images which are now "manageable" in being discrete in space and time, capable of clarity, fullness, and immediacy. It is with these "intuitions" (*Anschauungen*) that the higher operations of the mind proceed; phenomena are interpreted by being predicated of such a priori categories as substance, quality, quantity, and relation.[6] In the Kantian scheme, however, the discontinuity between the knower and the external world remains absolute. The term "intuition" suggests the immediacy of the phenomenal rather than insight into the noumenal. And the phenomenal world, the product of imagination, is in effect "reality" or "Nature" for us.

Given such premises, it was only natural that Kant would eventually come to an exploration of aesthetic activity, that he would pass from an account of "knowing" to an account of "making." In Kant's epistemology knowing *is* a kind of making. As Hazard Adams explains,

> With objective nature reduced to mental creation, it was possible to consider artistic fictions as perhaps in their own way just as significant as objective fictions. To put it in another way, if the mind constructs its reality, or all the reality it can know, then *all* the activities of the mind take on a new importance.[7]

The link between Kant's epistemology and his aesthetics is, of course, the concept of imagination. He argues that the "active faculty for synthesis" operates in aesthetic creativity in much the same way as in perception: the imagination, as the term *Einbildungskraft* suggests,[8] is a *unifying* power, imposing order on a formless medium. Kant distinguishes the two operations of *Einbildungskraft*, however, by noting that whereas imagination is determined in the act of perception, in aesthetic activity it is free. In other words, we cannot choose *not* to order sense data in perception, and our linking of phenomena (e.g., in memory) is governed by laws of association. On the other hand, the processes of creative imagination are unfettered by associative patterns; Kant goes so far as to define art as "production through freedom."[9]

Kant's frequent use of this notion of freedom emphasizes the extent to which aesthetic criticism is fundamentally at odds with reductive psychologies. For example, although modern aesthetic critics sometimes rely on Freudian concepts and terminology, they invariably reject Freud's general theory—for the same reason that their spiritual forefather ultimately rejected the mechanism of Hartley and Hume. Kant admits that most mental operations proceed according to one or another kind of "law," but this admission only serves to elevate further the status of art as a liberating experience which "expands" and "strengthens" the mind.[10] The mere exercise of creative imagination, the sense of what Kant calls "play" (*Spiel*), is a way of asserting our humanity, or of recapturing the humanity we lose in mechanized mental processes.

Kant insists that the ways in which works of art are created cannot be explained rationally, much less reduced to a series of formulae or rules. Thus he identifies the operations of creative imagination with the term "genius." According to Kant, genius

> is a *talent* for producing that for which no definite rule can be given; it is not a mere aptitude for what can be learned by a rule. Hence *originality* must be its first property. . . . It cannot describe or indicate scientifically how it brings about its products, but it gives the rule just as nature does. Hence the author of a product for which he is indebted to his genius does not know himself how he has come by his ideas.[11]

Kant here provides a rationale for much expressive, avant-garde, and "romantic" art. Genius renders irrelevant such commonplaces of neoclassical criticism as genre requirements, decorum, and extrinsic prescriptions. Each imaginative construct is unique and follows its own laws.

Kant's use of the term "genius" does not conflict with his argument that creative imagination is universal throughout mankind, permanent and normal; *all* men possess some degree of imaginative genius. Indeed, proper aesthetic response requires the audience to exercise this faculty, to partake in some measure of the *artist's* genius. "Genial criticism"—which might be taken as a synonym for aesthetic criticism itself—is the name Coleridge gave to this effort "to judge in the same spirit in which the Artist produced, or ought to have produced."[12] In other words, Kantian aestheticism encourages the audience to focus on the animating principle of a work of art, to respect this *donnée*, and thus to experience the work sympathetically, as much as possible from the artist's point of view. The word "genial" is not only the adjectival form of "genius"; it also describes the tone of a poetic friendly to the artist. Aesthetic critics tend to be comprehensive rather than judicial, feeling little urgency about "grading" works of art. Though they often use as norms such concepts as unity, intensity, and complexity, they generally apply these with a minimum of prescription and give individual works of art the benefits of any doubt.[13]

For Kant, aesthetic response itself is, of course, a much more complex matter. Because he presents imagination as a mediating faculty between the senses and conceptual understanding (*Verstand*), he allows for a view of art as a special form of knowledge, a formulation of experiential particularity rather than logical universals. This insight has been crucial for modern aesthetic critics, most of whom wish to posit art as a counterweight to the claims of science to be the only valid form of knowledge. John Crowe Ransom, for example, uses a Kantian rationale to argue that art opposes the abstracting force of science by returning the "world's body" to us. Asserting that "most of the time we are not human, so far as it is a mark of the human dignity to respect and know the particularity by which we are so constantly environed," Ransom praises the faculty of imagination, "by which we are able to contemplate things in their rich and contingent materiality"; the creative imagination can provide us with especially clear intuitions, "images so whole and clean that they resist the catalysis of thought."[14] Ransom's point is similar to Ernst Cassirer's neo-Kantian description of art as "a continuous process of concretion," or Susanne Langer's elevation of the "presentational" immediacy of intuitions in art.[15] Because the spatial and temporal "coordinates" of phenomena are given with special precision and fullness within a work of art, the work is truly cognitive.

Kant calls attention to the cognitive status of art by defining creative imagination as "the faculty of presenting aesthetical ideas."[16] These ideas are not theses or "messages"; indeed, Kant's view contains implicit prohibitions both against the pretensions of crude didacticism to aesthetic status and against the critical "heresy of paraphrase." A work of art does have content, but this content is ineffable in discursive terms; its only adequate expression is the work itself. Kant defines an aesthetical idea as "that representation of the imagination which occasions much thought, without however any definite thought, i.e., any *concept*, being capable of being adequate to it." He continues by observing that "imagination (as a productive faculty of cognition) is very powerful in creating another nature, as it were, out of the material that actual nature gives it."[17] These brief remarks, as Frank Lentricchia has recently pointed out, may be taken as "the germinal source" for modern contextualist theory.[18] Moreover, Kant's comments are rife with humanistic implications. The successful artist, preserving the richness of phenomenal intuitions within boundaries which he himself has set, is imposing a semblance of necessity on pure contingency, creating *meaning* where none existed before. In the ability of imagination to create "another nature," there is an assertion of the human spirit's striving to master the facts of experience, to "remold" the world through artistic fictions.[19]

To understand fully the humanistic significance of art in the Kantian scheme, it is necessary to explore his treatment of "judgment" (*Urteilskraft*), the mind's "interpretation" of phenomena. A judgment of "Pure Reason" tends toward scientific explanation, relating a phenomenon to its supposed causes. A judgment of "Practical Reason" tends toward moral evaluation, relating a phenomenon to its hypothetical effects. Both of these judgments are "teleological"; that is, they interpret a given phenomenon by predicating it in terms of something beyond itself. But Kant argues that it is possible to form a judgment which is "aesthetic" rather than teleological—a judgment in which the phenomenon is considered in, of, by, and for itself.[20]

The implications of this argument cannot be emphasized too strongly. If "aesthetic judgment" is the proper mode of considering a work of art, then art has its own ontology. On epistemological grounds Kant is reestablishing "Beauty" in the classical triad, parallel to "Truth" (Pure Reason) and "Goodness" (Practical Reason). The aesthetic realm again assumes great importance as an area in which man fully asserts his humanity.

Kant calls aesthetic judgment "disinterested."[21] He means that nothing—no logical concept, no utilitarian impulse—comes "between" (*inter-esse*) the work of art and an aesthetic apprehension of it. Aesthetic judgment always reverts to the direct consciousness of the object *as given.* (Kant here presages a key insight of modern phenomenological criticism. In fact, the aesthetic experience, as Kant describes it, involves a kind of phenomenological "reduction" or "bracketing": shutting everything else out, the mind is open to the immediate experience of the object.)

Thus considered, a work of art is its own reason for being; its existence requires no justification on scientific or moral grounds. The freedom of art from the constraints of Pure Reason is so complete that Kant invalidates any version of Plato's representational theory and instead approximates Aristotle's insight: a work of art cannot properly be judged on the basis of its one-to-one fidelity to the factual world it imitates. In considering Homer's *Iliad*, for example, we cease to judge aesthetically if we begin to concern ourselves with the poem's historicity. Similarly, an aesthetic consideration of Leonardo's *La Gioconda* requires total disinterestedness about the existence of the real Mona Lisa. In judging aesthetically, "we do not want to know whether anything depends or can depend on the existence of the thing." We must remain "indifferent" about the reality of what is represented: "We must not be in the least prejudiced in favor of the existence of things, but be quite indifferent in this respect, in order to play the judge in things of taste."[22] The freedom in art from the constraints of Practical Reason is also emphatic in the Kantian argument. Coleridge gives a clear presentation of Kant's meaning in an amusing drama of ideas:

> Let us suppose Milton in company with some stern and prejudiced Puritan, contemplating the front of York Cathedral, and at length expressing his admiration of its beauty. . . . –P. Beauty; I am sure, it is not the beauty of holiness. –M. True; but yet it is beautiful. –P. It delights not me. What is it good for? Is it of any use but to be stared at?–M. Perhaps not! but still it is beautiful. –P. But call to mind the pride and wanton vanity of those cruel shavelings, that wasted the labor and substance of so many thousand poor creatures in the erection of this haughty pile. –M. I do. But still it is very beautiful. –P. Think how many score of places of worship, incomparably better suited both for prayer and preaching, and how many faithful ministers might have been maintained, to the blessing of tens of thousands, to them and their children's children, with the treasures lavished on this worthless mass of stone and cement. –M. Too true! but nevertheless it is *very* beautiful.[23]

Aesthetic judgment, by definition, vitiates the "teleological" aspects of a work of art. "Purpose" (*Zweck*) is negated: the work is considered as self-justifying and irreducible to logical concepts. But "purposiveness" (*Zweckmässigheit*) is affirmed: the work does appear to have been made in "conformity to law of the Understanding *in general*."[24] In other words, a work of art offers satisfaction through formal *unity*: because it is a product of the unifying imagination, it may be considered as a system of closely-knit internal relationships.

Even though Kant's general theory seems to militate against extensive "explication" of literary works,[25] his emphasis on "purposiveness" has encouraged later aesthetic critics to develop methods of practical analysis based on the concept of unity. The most famous of these, of course, rely on an analogy between a work of art and a living organism. It is noteworthy that Kant influenced modern biological theory by recommending that biologists adopt, as a problem-solving premise, the complete purposiveness of any living organism. A living being should be initially considered as an entity "*in which every part is reciprocally purpose and means.* In it nothing is in vain, without purpose, or to be ascribed to a blind mechanism of nature."[26] This insight has been adopted as a heuristic principle by many practical aesthetic critics, beginning with Coleridge:

> The spirit of poetry, like all other living powers, must of necessity circumscribe itself by rules, were it only to unite power with beauty. It must embody in order to reveal itself; but a living body is of necessity an organized one; and what is organization but the connection of parts in and for a whole, so that each part is at once end and means?[27]

The rules Coleridge speaks of are not extrinsic laws to which each poem must conform; instead, they are innate, self-generating, discoverable only in the poem itself, and applicable to no other poem. Thus, when an aesthetic critic looks for the principles of order in an individual poem, he is implicitly acknowledging that the poem constitutes a unique and coherent universe of its own. In short, the concept of "purposiveness," whether or not it is interpreted in organic terms, is another indication of aesthetic criticism as genial criticism: it yields practical approaches which respect the "integrity" of both the poet and the poem.

Aesthetic criticism, as we have seen repeatedly, is resolutely on the side of the artist. It raises his status, allows him autonomy (and even eccentricity), encourages critical "geniality," and supplies him with ammunition he can use against his Philistine enemies.[28] It is only natural that modern artists—increasingly alienated from the mass audience, and continually challenged by utilitarian tenets—have been so powerfully attracted to the premises of Kantian aestheticism. Practicing poets have in fact rivaled professional philosophers as proponents of aesthetic criticism. Of course, the dimensions of aestheticism have always been enlarged whenever a particular critic has been able to combine methodological rigor with experience as an artist. Among contemporary aesthetic critics John Crowe Ransom, Wallace Stevens, and Jean-Paul Sartre come immediately to mind. And from a twentieth-century perspective the work of the first aesthetic poet-critic, Johann Friedrich von Schiller, is still powerful and suggestive.

In the early 1790s Schiller interrupted his endeavors as a dramatist in order to pursue a number of "philosophical" problems he believed to be relevant to his literary work. He became a careful student of the *Critique of Judgment*, using Kant's epistemology to explore fundamental questions about the role of art in human life. In *Letters on the Aesthetical Education of Man* (1793–95) Schiller's poetic sensibility gave life to Kant's abstract premises. The result was an illuminating series of discussions on three main topics: art as play, aesthetic humanism, and the significance of aesthetic semblance.

In *Critique of Judgment* Kant often used the word "play" (*Spiel*) to describe the spontaneous freedom of creative imagination; at one point he defined poetry as "the art of conducting a free play of the imagination as if it were a serious business of the understanding."[29] Schiller extended Kant's insight by taking the metaphor of play more literally. He suggested, for example, that the beauty of Greek sculpture is a result of the same human impulse that delighted in "the bloodless athletic contests of boxing, racing, and intellectual rivalry at Olympia."[30] Schiller's concept of play does not trivialize art; "play" does not mean "playing around." Quite the contrary: Schiller's notion is humanistically rich. "Play" connotes the liberation of imagination in art, as well as a joy in life itself that Schiller identifies as a by-product of aesthetic activity.[31] In addition, Schiller's use of *Spiel* as a technical term advances the Kantian argument by calling attention to properties that works of art have in common with certain kinds of games: lack of intellectual or moral "purpose," and a balance between free movement and formal limits.

Schiller's discussion proceeds on epistemological grounds, using the term "play-instinct" (*Spieltrieb*) as an equivalent for Kant's "imagination." The difference in vocabulary indicates that whereas Kant emphasizes art as a kind of cognition, Schiller tends to emphasize it as a kind of value. In other words, the play-instinct is presented as a health-giving faculty which harmonizes the psyche—uniting the sensuous instinct (*Stofftrieb*), which binds man to matter and time, to the formalizing instinct (*Formtrieb*), which characterizes man as rational. *Stofftrieb* and *Formtrieb* are united in the "living form" of a work of art.[32] The dissociation typical of so many human activities is mended in aesthetic play: "All other forms of perception divide a man, because they are exclusively based either on the sensuous or on the intellectual part of his being; only the perception of the Beautiful makes something whole of him, because both his natures must accord with it."[33]

Schiller sees art as a harmonious force not only within the individual psyche, but throughout society as a whole. This concern for art as a civilizing influence, and for "aesthetical *education*," raises several issues of contemporary humanistic significance—similar to those treated by Ernst Cassirer (*The Logic of the Humanities*), Jacques Maritain (*Education at the Crossroads*), Herbert Read (*Education through Art*), and Northrop Frye (*The Educated Imagination*). Moreover, Schiller varies the strict Kantian approach by relating imagination to its cultural milieu, gauging the historical forces favorable or debilitating to man's capacity for free imaginative play. (Here he anticipates the efforts of many modern aesthetic critics—especially those who were writing on the eve of the Second World War—to deal with the modern "cultural crisis" in Western society.) According to Schiller, the cultural health of his own era was immediately endangered by "an all-dividing understanding," manifested in intellectual specialization, the division of labor, and increasing class tensions.[34]

Much of Schiller's humanistic emphasis derives from his insistence on the disinterestedness of man's delight in sheer "appearance" (*Schein*). In a work of art the determinate quality of ordinary life is absent: anything can happen. The realm of semblance is the realm of contingency, and hence of freedom. Schiller's insight is surprisingly modern: as René Wellek has pointed out, Jean-Paul Sartre sounds very close to Schiller when he claims that the ultimate aim of art is "to recuperate this world as if it had its source in human liberty."[35] Similarly, Susanne Langer recognizes Schiller's originality, even while acknowledging his debt to Kant:

> Schiller was the first thinker who saw what really makes "Schein," or semblance, important for art: the fact that it liberates perception—and with it, the power of conception—from all practical purposes, and lets the mind dwell on the sheer appearance of things. The function of artistic illusion is not "make-believe," as many philosophers and psychologists assume, but the very opposite, disengagement from belief—the contemplation of sensory qualities without their usual meanings of "Here's that chair," "That's my telephone," "These figures ought to add up to the bank's statement," etc.[36]

II

Nowhere in his aesthetic theory did Kant assign a metaphysical role to art. In the Kantian view the realm of *Dinge an sich* is as closed to the poet as to the philosopher: the discontinuity between the mind and the noumenal world remains inviolate. By contrast, aesthetic criticism in the first part of the nineteenth century was dominated by a romantic ethos which exalted the poet as a visionary who penetrates to the essence of reality. This new emphasis is perhaps typified by the changing use of the term "intuition," which came to refer more often to mystical insight than to the immediacy and precision of the phenomenal image.

The most emphatic spokesman for the new monism was Friedrich von Schelling, propounder of a vaguely pantheistic *Naturphilosophie.* Schelling attempted to vitiate the dualism between Mind and Nature by positing Nature as *natura naturans,* "the holy, ever-creative original energy of the world, which generates and busily evolves all things out of itself."[37] The aesthetic act, according to Schelling, is an act of inspiration in which this "ever-creative" force finds a special outlet. Art for Schelling is the embodiment of the infinite in finite form—giving us not the Kantian "world's body," but the "world's soul" itself. Art is thus enshrined as the highest form of knowledge, assuming an even greater significance than that accorded by Kant and Schiller. This is one reason why so many romantics, Coleridge in particular,[38] were attracted to Schelling's aesthetic. But as René Wellek observes, this aesthetic has its pitfalls:

> When in 1796, F. W. J. Schelling . . . drew up his program of a new philosophy, he completely ignored Kant's distinction between epistemology, ethics, and aesthetics. He put forward the grandiose claim that the idea of beauty, taken in the Platonic sense, "unites all other ideas." "I am convinced," he says, "that the highest act of reason is the aesthetic act embracing all ideas, and that truth and goodness are made kindred only in beauty." While Kant was at great pains to distinguish between the good, the true, and the beautiful, Schelling enthrones beauty as the highest value. But his beauty is actually truth and goodness in disguise.[39]

Wellek seems to say that Schelling's position is "counterrevolutionary," in that it negates Kant's basic insight into the indivisibility of form and content in art. Schelling implicitly rejects the concept of "disinterestedness," and encourages a variation of the didactic view: the poem becomes less important than the spiritual truth it supposedly represents. Moreover, Schelling's theory, and the related theories of such radical idealists as Shelley and Emerson, seem to constitute a debasement of the concept of imagination. First, creative imagination is no longer "free" if it is merely a channel for an external force (e.g., the "Over-Soul"). In addition, this theory emphasizes the work of art as a psychic event for the artist, implying that the "real" poem exists in the poet's mind *before composition*, and that it is then simply "expressed."[40] Imagination's creative activity, the actual process of "making" (what Coleridge called secondary imagination) is effectively ignored by being equated with perception (Coleridge's primary imagination). Finally, perception itself is likely to be treated mystically: if imagination is posited as a faculty which grasps the infinite, then it is working outside the categories of space and time, and it appears to be serving no basic *unifying* function.

With a few notable exceptions (e.g., Herbert Read), modern aesthetic critics have reacted against Schelling's poetic. Neo-Kantians and existentialists have reaffirmed the discontinuity between Mind and Nature, often expressing impatience with the simplistic aspects of romantic theory. This impatience is perhaps most evident in the writings of T. E. Hulme, who posited an aesthetic of the finite in opposition to Schelling's aesthetic of the infinite. Attacking the romantic tendency to fly away "into the circumambient gas," Hulme focused on the poet's "struggle" with his medium, language.[41] For Hulme a poem exists only *after composition*, and its value resides in the precision of its delineation of phenomenal experience.

This is not to suggest that the idealistic poetics of the nineteenth century are totally irrelevant to modern aesthetic criticism. For example, even though most contemporary inquiries into the nature of literary symbolism are non-idealistic, they owe a debt to the romantic ethos which, for the first time in the history of literary criticism, elevated the symbol as a non-discursive means of expressing the inexpressible.[42] In addition, because the rhetoric of idealistic criticism has been so affirmative in speaking of the resolution of dualisms, it has contributed indirectly to techniques of practical criticism; when a "new critic" like Cleanth Brooks examines a literary work as a "reconciliation of opposites," he is translating into formalistic terms a principle initially developed under the aegis of Schelling's thought.[43]

Perhaps the most valid claim to contemporary relevance that idealist aesthetics can make is in the continuing influence of G. W. F. Hegel, whose monistic philosophy might be construed as the inverse of Schelling's. Whereas Schelling had identified ultimate reality with the processes of Nature, Hegel identified it with the processes of Mind: "What is real is rational; what is rational is real."[44] A corollary of this foundational principle is, of course, that reality can be rationally known by the human mind. Thus Hegel departed from Kant's "critical" philosophy, and ambitiously attempted to build a system of thought encompassing "everything that is"—including even the *concreteness* of things.

One of Hegel's key concepts, both for his general system and his aesthetic theory, is "concrete universality" (*concrete Allgemeinheit*). Hegel's Mind or Spirit, like Schelling's Nature, is a dynamic force continually seeking embodiment. But Mind, trying always to render itself more intelligible, operates rationally, according to a dialectic; as a result, it is progressively particularized, becoming ever more determinate. For Hegel, Nature (matter) is the dialectical antithesis which Mind (spirit) has posited in striving to realize itself "objectively."[45] But a synthesis of spirit and matter is logically demanded, and it is precisely here that the crucial philosophical importance of art lies for Hegel. The concept of art is the completion of a dialectic, the resolution of a basic dualism—and individual works of art serve as new, more concrete embodiments of Mind: Hegel defines beauty as "the sensuous semblance of the Idea."[46]

As Hegel's definition suggests, he, like Schelling, assigns a metaphysical role to art. Even though Hegel praised the Kantian philosophy as "the starting point for the true conception of artistic beauty," he complained of Kant's failure to allow for the transmission of theoretical knowledge through the work of art: "It is the spirit of Kant's philosophy to have a consciousness of this highest idea, but always to eradicate it again."[47] Nevertheless, Hegel's claims for the metaphysical significance of art are much more modest than Schelling's, and his position more nearly resembles those of Santayana or Cassirer. Art is only one of three modes (religion and philosophy being the other two) in which Mind realizes itself fully. Nor is art the highest form of knowledge: some truths cannot be completely expressed in art because no "sensuous semblance" could be adequate to them. Art is limited to the manifestation of the Idea in its "immediacy."[48]

Because Hegel conceives of Mind as an active force which develops and concretizes itself through *time*, he identifies it with historical process. Thus, "philosophy" necessarily entails an analysis of history—and "aesthetics" necessarily entails an analysis of the history of art. Hegel's best known application of the dialectical method to art history is his distinguishing of three "stages" of art—symbolic, classical, and romantic

—illustrating a progressive dominance by the Idea of its aesthetic medium.[49] It is significant, however, that Hegel's account often treats myths and religious conceptions as if they were art. His remarks are obviously meant as part of a larger inquiry: *Geistesgeschichte*, the history of the human spirit.

The basis for such an inquiry is given in Hegel's *Phenomenology of Mind* (1807), an attempt at a "Science of the Experience of Consciousness." Hegel examines the historical stages of human consciousness, emphasizing man's status as a being who creates *value* and who thus steps out of mere animate nature and into history. In the last part of the *Phenomenology* he considers art, in relation to religion, as illustrative of "social life." With particular reference to ancient Greek culture, Hegel establishes a dialectic of epic-tragedy-comedy. The historical dominance of each genre signifies a distinct socio-religious ethos, a distinct cultural consciousness. In comedy, for example, the gods are usually ignored, vitiated by the "negative force" of the individual self; the norm is a kind of ironic but comfortable self-consciousness.[50]

From Hegel onward, the aesthetic discipline of *Geistesgeschichte* has been a means of dealing with the social and humanistic dimensions of art without compromising the integrity, the purposiveness, of individual works of art. *Geistesgeschichte* has taken many forms, all of them opposed to the "scientific" emphasis and reductive tendencies of pure historical criticism. The nineteenth century saw the rise of a literary scholarship professing linguistic and historical "objectivity," conceived on the model of the *Strengwissenschaften* (the strong and precise natural sciences). By contrast, aesthetic criticism, using methods at least partly subjective, concerned itself with what Wilhelm Dilthey called the *Geisteswissenschaften* (probably best rendered as "the cultural sciences" or "human studies"). Dilthey, though profoundly influenced by Hegel's thought, left aside the Hegelian method of a priori historical analysis. He insisted that the cultural historian must rely in part on his personal "lived experience" (*Erlebnis*) in order to understand the interiority of a culture, to comprehend man and his works in a fully human way.[51] History for Dilthey, and for any aesthetic critic, is not a collection of facts; it is spiritual action—thinking, feeling, willing.

Geistesgeschichte and the *Geisteswissenschaften* have continued to be central concepts in twentieth-century aestheticism. Georges Poulet provides an apologia for a literary history that, "in the highest and deepest sense, . . . is a history of human consciousness."[52] In true aesthetic fashion, Poulet is able (in *Studies in Human Time*, for example) to balance a sense of the epochal *Zeitgeist* with a respect for the unique consciousness expressed in the work of each writer he examines. Similarly, Ernst Cassirer traces in *Rousseau, Kant, and Goethe* a movement of the human spirit that no quasi-scientific historical method could ever delineate. Most of Cassirer's other work indicates the extent to which a commitment to the *Geisteswissenschaften* has permeated modern aesthetic criticism, encouraging inquiries into such "human studies" as depth psychology, myth, and language. In *An Essay on Man* Cassirer moves beyond Hegel even while echoing him: "Our objective is a *phenomenology of human culture*."[53]

III

The subjectivity necessarily entailed in the study of *Geisteswissenschaften* should not be confused with the "impressionism" that dominated aesthetic criticism in the latter part of the nineteenth century. Hegel had gone to an extreme in asserting the need for comprehensive rational analysis of art: "in works of art, mind has to do with its own."[54] At the other extreme, impressionistic critics—typified by Anatole France —adopted a position more radical than Kant's. In *La Vie littéraire* (1888) France argued for the total subjectivity of beauty, proclaiming an aesthetic that rendered criticism impossible, except as a record of the critic's sensitive feelings. But as O. B. Hardison has observed, "impressionism results from the exaggeration of one element of the aesthetic position at the expense of all the rest."[55] If the weakness of the idealistic poetic is its metaphysical inflation of the status of art, the weakness of the impressionistic poetic is its trivialization of art, its blindness to the humanistic implications of aesthetic theory.

Impressionistic criticism makes no attempt to provide a coherent view of man as man; it is "grounded" in nothing—hence its inherent relativism. And aesthetic criticism arrived at this dead end only by abandoning its philosophical heritage and foregoing its characteristic methodological rigor. The term "imagination," for example, had become much abused, often associated merely with the exotic and vague.[56] Any revitalization of aesthetic criticism, therefore, had to offer a philosophical framework, a sense of system. Needless to say, no one system transformed aesthetic criticism suddenly into the twentieth century—although it might be argued that a major turning point was the development of the phenomenological movement, and that Franz Brentano's *Psychology from the Empirical Standpoint* (1874) and Edmund Husserl's *Idea:*

General Introduction to Pure Phenomenology (1913) are the seminal documents for modern aestheticism. In the brief space remaining, however, it would be well to sketch the lines of influence emanating from two philosophers whose contributions to contemporary aesthetic criticism are rarely discussed: Aristotle and Henri Bergson.

In 1895 S. H. Butcher published *Aristotle's Theory of Poetry and Fine Art*, the first English edition of the *Poetics* in one hundred years. As such, it represented an attempt to return Aristotelian criticism to favor by proving its essential compatibility with romantic aestheticism. As Butcher's title suggests, Aristotle was being presented as the first aesthetic critic. Even though the *Poetics* is grounded in a survey of the materials of poetry rather than a theory of the human mind, it adumbrates Kant's postulation of an aesthetic category: "To Aristotle we owe the first clear conception of fine art as a free and independent activity of the mind, outside the domain of both religion and politics, having an end distinct from that of education or moral improvement."[57]

Butcher argues that Aristotle was not prescriptive but descriptive, the practitioner of a genial criticism distinct from the neo-classical tradition. Using the full weight of philological scholarship, Butcher banished the notion of the "three unities" and, more importantly, equated Aristotle's concept of "probability" with aesthetic "purposiveness"; probability, Butcher showed, refers not to verisimilitude, but rather to "the internal structure of the poem; it is the inner law which secures the cohesion of the parts."[58] Many of Butcher's other conclusions appear less justifiable as an account of what Aristotle really meant. Butcher admitted that Aristotle seemed so modern to him that "we may, almost without knowing it, find ourselves putting into his mouth not his own language but that of Hegel."[59] It was on the strength of his own idealistic premises that he attributed to Aristotle a romantic theory of organicism (with the work of art a concrete universal) and a concept of the "nature" that art imitates as *natura naturans*.

Nevertheless, Butcher was on firm ground in treating "imitation" as the differentia of fine art, and he succeeded in reconciling Aristotle's concept with aesthetic "imagination."[60] This insight has been supported by a host of modern aesthetic critics. Susanne Langer notes that "'Imitation' is used by Aristotle in much the same sense in which I use 'semblance.'"[61] To the phenomenologist Roman Ingarden, "It seems probable that Aristotle had in mind the same thing that in my book, *Das literarische Kunstwerk*, I called 'objective consistency' [*gegenständliche Konsequenz*] within the framework of the world presented in the work."[62] John Crowe Ransom argues that imitation can be defined as "the use of language to denote natural objects as given, contingent, today as 'existential'; to be received in their fullness, which is their givenness; to be distinguished from those abstract or working objects that we employ in practical operations."[63] Northrop Frye equates imitation with the fictive imagination, speaking of "the transmutation of experience into mimesis, of life into art, of routine into play."[64]

These statements suggest that aesthetic criticism has generally abandoned whatever commitments it once had to the anti-mimetic tenets of romantic expressionism. Several modern aesthetic critics, in fact, have found Aristotle's essential tough-mindedness a valuable counterweight to the idealistic tendencies within their own theories. Northrop Frye, for example, grounds his romantic concept of "myth" in a generic approach to aesthetic fictions, using Aristotle's term *mythos* ("plot") to refer to "archetypal narrative."[65] Similarly, Jacques Maritain's concern with the "movement of spirit," the *action* within a literary work, balances the *praxis* of Aristotle against the *élan* of Henri Bergson's dynamistic philosophy.[66]

Bergson's importance to Maritain, and to aesthetic criticism in general, results from his development of a dualistic epistemology that expresses many of the insights of Kant and Schiller in a new way. Bergson's "intelligence" and "instinct" are analogous to Schiller's *Formtrieb* and *Stofftrieb*—with one significant difference: Bergson, as a philosopher of vitalism, is biased in favor of "instinct."

This bias is evident in the definition of his mediating concept, "intuition," as "disinterested instinct."[67] Both words in the definition require explanation. In itself, instinct, like *Stofftrieb*, unites man with matter and time: it deals with things rather than relations, works through concrete images, and is capable of apprehending the "mobile and continuous."[68] Instinct that becomes "disinterested" or "detached" is aesthetic: it is a capacity for perceiving objects *as given*, without any interest in their utility.[69]

Like Kant's *Anschauung*, then, Bergson's "intuition" refers to clarity and immediacy of perception. But it also carries a new meaning: Bergson emphasizes the duration of lived experience, the continuity of the knowing consciousness. Intuition is an expression of the *moi fondamental*, the "self which endures"; through intuition objects are grasped in their "rhythmic motion" as part of a *durée*, rather than being "frozen" into discontinuous impressions.[70] To put it another way, intuition allows for a special knowledge of the individual object through a union of mind and feeling, an "intellectual sympathy," by which "one places oneself within an object, in order to co-incide with what is unique in it and consequently inexpressible."[71]

Bergson's rhetoric is the rhetoric of an idealist, but his meaning is distinctly modern and basically phenomenological. He is not arguing that intuition gives us the noumenal world, but merely that it gives us duration. As Maurice Merleau-Ponty points out, Bergson's aim was "not to fly above perception but to penetrate it." Speaking of "a sort of Bergsonian 'reduction' which reconsiders all things *sub specie durationis,*" Merleau-Ponty pays tribute to Bergson's pioneering insight:

> He does not say that all things are, in the restrictive sense, images, mental or otherwise,—he says that their fullness under my regard is such that it is as if my vision took place in them rather than in myself, as if to be seen were only a degradation of their eminent being, as if being "represented" . . . far from being their definition, resulted from their natural profuseness! Never before had anyone established this circuit between being and myself, which has the result that being is "for me," but that in return the spectator is "for being." Never before had anyone thus described the brute being of the perceived world.[72]

The extension of Bergson's principles into poetics is likewise a venture in phenomenology. When Bergson says that art reveals "nature" to us, that it brings us "face to face with reality itself," he is not echoing Schelling. Instead, he is anticipating critics like Gaston Bachelard, for whom aesthetic experience is a direct apprehension of matter.[73] Significantly, Bergson also adumbrates Bachelard's position by occasionally comparing aesthetic contemplation to an hypnotic trance or a dream-state: "Our soul, rocked and put to sleep, forgets itself as in a dream, to see and think with the poet."[74] Bergson is obviously not referring to a sense of passivity, but rather to a heightened awareness and finely "focused" consciousness (like Bachelard's "reverie"), in which there is freedom from practical considerations.

Bergson's emphasis carries two other significant implications. The first is humanistic. In treating aesthetic activity as a specially immediate, full, and precise kind of perception, Bergson relates art to the rest of human life, and the poetic image becomes an epistemological norm. As Paul De Man observes, Bergson's theory amounts to a "poetization of human experience," in which poetics become "a vital source for theoretical psychology."[75] Secondly, the Bergsonian view is more than compatible with the modern, anti-expressionistic commitment, typified by Paul Valéry, to the poetic *medium* as the true area of poetic value. And if, as Hazard Adams and Frank Lentricchia suggest, Hulme "ushered in" modern criticism through his efforts toward a contextualist theory, then it is important to recall that Hulme was explicit in acknowledging a debt to Bergson for his epistemological premises.[76]

It would be tempting to try to gauge the full range of Bergson's aesthetic influence—from his indirect justification of imagistic poetry, stream-of-consciousness fiction, and theories of cinema to the humanistic "rescue" of his students (especially Hulme and Jacques Maritain) from a despair engendered by the mechanistic view of life. But the greatest significance of Bergson's position is its reformulation of the aesthetic postulates of Kant and Schiller. Bergson was one of those who helped aesthetic criticism return to the sources of its own power—to recapture, maintain, and diversify its own fundamental tenets. The subsequent development of modern aestheticism, as the following essays will show, has been both productive and exciting.

NOTES

1. See Monroe Beardsley, *Aesthetics from Classical Greece to the Present* (New York, 1966), p. 210.
2. Samuel Taylor Coleridge, *Biographia Literaria*, ed. J. Shawcross, 2 vols. (London, 1907), I, 14.
3. Hazard Adams, *The Interests of Criticism* (New York, 1969), p. 71.
4. Immanuel Kant, *Critique of Pure Reason*, trans. Norman Kemp Smith (London, 1929), p. 165.
5. Coleridge, *Biographia Literaria*, I, 202.
6. See especially Kant's "Analytic of Concepts" in *Critique of Pure Reason*, pp. 103–75.
7. Adams, *The Interests of Criticism*, pp. 71–72.
8. George Whalley, in *Poetic Process: An Essay in Poetics* (Cleveland, 1967), p. 62, quotes one of Coleridge's early notebook entries: "How excellently the German *Einbildungskraft* expresses this prime and loftiest faculty, the power of coadunation, the faculty that forms the many into one—in-eins-bildung! Eisenplasy, or esenoplastic power, as contradistinguished from fantasy, or . . . mirrorment."
9. Immanuel Kant, *Critique of Judgment*, trans. J. H. Bernard (New York, 1951) p. 145 (Section 43).
10. Ibid., pp. 170–71 (Section 53).
11. Ibid., pp. 150–51 (Section 46).

12. Coleridge, "On the Principles of Genial Criticism," reprinted in *Biographia Literaria*, II, 222.

13. The best example of the genial aesthetic critic is probably Coleridge himself. The reason for the general "perniciousness" of contemporary reviews, he argued (*Coleridge's Shakespearean Criticism*, ed. T. M. Raysor [Cambridge, Mass., 1930], II, 57–58), was that "the writers determined without reference to fixed principles," encouraging people "rather to judge than to consider, to decide than to reflect." Chapter 17 of the *Biographia*, Coleridge's reflections on Wordsworth's poetry, is a good example of genial criticism in practice: even Wordsworth's "characteristic defects" become avenues of approach to his "characteristic beauties."

14. John Crowe Ransom, *The World's Body*, 2nd ed. (Baton Rouge, 1968), pp. 211, 116, and 118.

15. Ernst Cassirer, *An Essay on Man* (New Haven, 1944), p. 144; Susanne Langer, *Feeling and Form* (New York, 1953), especially Chapters 3 and 4.

16. Kant, *Critique of Judgment*, p. 157 (Section 49).

17. Ibid.

18. Frank Lentricchia, "Four Types of Nineteenth-Century Poetic," *Journal of Aesthetics and Art Criticism*, XXVI (1968), 360: "As the contextualists read this passage, the poetic object is an organic affair, a closed system of linguistic relations, a verbal universe, a 'nature,' whose meaning cannot be translated for the reason that it inheres in the peculiar context or formal structure of the poem itself. . . . The autonomous literary imagination, bound to the meaning in which it chooses to express itself, makes meaning *in* the medium. Language ceases to function as transparent form *through* which we are given access to meaning and value. The poem, by being autotelic, becomes opaque."

19. See *Critique of Judgment*, p. 157 (Section 49), and the discussion of Aristotle's concept of "imitation" in Part III of this essay.

20. See especially pp. 10–17 and 26–29 in Kant's Introduction to *Critique of Judgment.*

21. Ibid., pp. 38–39 (Section 2).

22. Ibid.

23. Coleridge, "On the Principles of Genial Criticism," reprinted in *Biographia Literaria*, II, 242.

24. Kant, *Critique of Judgment*, p. 78 ("General Remark on the first Section of the Analytic").

25. See Kant's discussion of "subjective universal validity" in Section 8 of *Critique of Judgment*, pp. 48–51, and the brief discussion of impressionistic criticism in Part III of this essay.

26. Ibid., p. 222 (Section 66). See Charles W. Hendel's discussion of Kant's influence on biological thought in the Introduction to Ernst Cassirer's *Philosophy of Symbolic Forms* (New Haven, 1965), I, 25–27.

27. Coleridge, *Shakespearean Criticism*, ed. Raysor, II, 223–24.

28. The best example of an aesthetic counterattack may be Théophile Gautier's Preface to *Mademoiselle de Maupin* (1835), a witty indictment of moralistic and utilitarian critics.

29. Kant, *Critique of Judgment*, p. 165 (Section 51).

30. Friedrich von Schiller, *Letters upon the Aesthetic Education of Man*, trans. anon., in *Literary and Philosophical Essays*, The Harvard Classics, Vol. 32 (New York, 1910), p. 266 (Letter 15).

31. Ibid., p. 267 (Letter 15), and pp. 305–13 (Letter 27).

32. Ibid., especially p. 263 (Letter 15).

33. Ibid., p. 311 (Letter 27).

34. Ibid., especially pp. 230–39 (Letters 5 and 6).

35. René Wellek, *A History of Modern Criticism: 1750–1950*, Volume I: *The Later Eighteenth Century* (New Haven, 1955), 255; cf. Sartre's *Situations II* (Paris, 1948), p. 106.

36. Langer, *Feeling and Form*, p. 49.

37. "Concerning the Relation of the Plastic Arts to Nature," trans. Michael Bullock, reprinted by Herbert Read, *The True Voice of Feeling* (New York, 1953), p. 325.

38. Hazard Adams, in *The Interests of Criticism*, p. 93, discusses the "two Coleridges." On the one hand, there is "a Coleridge who sees the poem in a Kantian way as having no exterior object to which it refers, only an interior aesthetical idea that it creates by its own nature and which is untranslatable from it." On the other hand, there is "a Schellingean Coleridge who sees the poem as a linguistic representation of the highest spiritual act, the poet's marriage of mind and object. (The poem is not the act itself, apparently.)" The clearest indication of Coleridge's attraction to Schelling's poetic is "On Poesy or Art" (1818) which echoes "Concerning the Relation of the Plastic Arts to Nature."

39. Wellek, *A History of Modern Criticism, 1750–1950*; Volume II: *The Romantic Age* (New Haven, 1955), p. 74.

40. See Lentricchia, "Four Types of Nineteenth-Century Poetic," p. 356.

41. See, for example, "Classicism and Romanticism," in *Speculations*, ed. Herbert Read (New York, n. d.), p. 132: "The great aim is accurate, precise and definite description. . . . But each man sees a little differently, and to get out clearly and exactly what he does see, he must have a terrific struggle with language, whether it be with words or the technique of the other arts."

42. A good example is Coleridge's famous definition of the symbol in *The Statesman's Manual*; while Coleridge was apparently most concerned with the symbol as "characterized by a translucence . . . of the eternal in and through the temporal," he made the crucial distinction that the symbol "always partakes of the reality which it renders intelligible, and while it enunciates the whole, abides itself as a living

part in the unity of which it is the representative." See Coleridge's *Works*, I, ed. W. G. T. Shedd (New York, 1844), p. 437.

43. See Brooks' *The Well Wrought Urn: Studies in the Structure of Poetry* (New York, 1947), p. 27. Cf. Alice D. Snyder, *The Critical Principle of the Reconciliation of Opposites as Employed by Coleridge* (Ann Arbor, 1918).

44. See Hegel's *Logic*, trans. William Wallace (London, 1892), pp. 10–11.

45. See Hegel's *Philosophy of Fine Art*, I, trans. F. P. B. Osmaston (London, 1920), pp. 14–16.

46. Ibid., I, 53.

47. *Introduction to Hegel's Philosophy of Fine Art*, trans. Bernard Bosanquet (London, 1886), pp. 151–52. Cf. René Wellek, *A History of Modern Criticism*, I, 231.

48. Hegel, *Philosophy of Fine Art*, I, 8–9 and 138–40. Hegel views art as constantly striving to reveal deeper truths than its medium can circumscribe; when it succeeds most fully, therefore, it has ceased to be art: it becomes a form of religion. This theory seems to look toward an eventual historical "death" of art; see René Wellek's discussion in *A History of Modern Criticism*, II, 321–22.

49. This schema is worked out in great detail in Volumes II, III, and IV of the *Philosophy of Fine Art*. For example, symbolic art (dominance of the Idea by the medium) is associated with architecture, classical art (equilibrium of Idea and medium) with sculpture, and romantic art (dominance of the medium by the Idea) with poetry. But the category of "classical" can also be applied to poetry, thus suggesting a norm of *concrete universality*: the total interpenetration of form and content. An extension of this concept would corroborate the Kantian argument that the "meaning" of a poem cannot be isolated from its "concretion"; ultimately, the meaning is the poem itself.

50. See *The Phenomenology of Mind*, II, trans. J. B. Baillie (London, 1910), pp. 754–58.

51. See especially "Lived Experience, Expression, and Understanding," "The Basis and Methods of Psychology," and "The Limits of Generalization in History," trans. H. A. Hodges, in *Wilhelm Dilthey: An Introduction* (London, 1944), pp. 117–18 and 133–38.

52. Georges Poulet, "Réponse," *Les Lettres nouvelles*, June 24, 1959, p. 12.

53. Cassirer, *An Essay on Man*, p. 52.

54. *Introduction to Hegel's Philosophy of Fine Art*, p. 22.

55. O. B. Hardison, Introduction to *Modern Continental Literary Criticism* (New York, 1962), p. xii.

56. See A. S. P. Woodhouse, "Imagination," in *Encyclopedia of Poetry and Poetics*, ed. Alex Preminger, Frank J. Warnke, and O. B. Hardison (Princeton, 1965), p. 374.

57. *Aristotle's Theory of Poetry and Fine Art*, 4th ed. (New York, 1951), p. 162.

58. Ibid., p. 166.

59. Ibid., p. 114.

60. Ibid.; see especially pp. 121–62.

61. Langer, *Feeling and Form*, p. 352.

62. Roman Ingarden, "A Marginal Commentary on Aristotle's *Poetics*—Part II," *Journal of Aesthetics and Art Criticism*, XX (1962), 282.

63. John Crowe Ransom, "The Literary Criticism of Aristotle," in *Lectures in Criticism*, ed. Elliot Coleman (New York, 1949), p. 21. See also Ransom's essay on "The Mimetic Principle" in *The World's Body.*

64. Northrop Frye, *Anatomy of Criticism* (Princeton, 1957), p. 113; Frye defines imitation (p. 113) as "an emancipation of externality into image."

65. Ibid., pp. 162 and 366–67.

66. See especially *Creative Intuition in Art and Poetry* (New York, 1954), pp. 250–64.

67. Henri Bergson, *Creative Evolution*, trans. Arthur Mitchell (New York, 1911), pp. 176–79.

68. Ibid., 165–76.

69. Ibid., p. 177. Cf. Bergson's description of philosophical method in *Matter and Memory*, trans. Nancy Margaret Paul and W. Scott Palmer (London, 1911), pp. 239–45.

70. Henri Bergson, *Time and Free Will*, trans. F. L. Pogson (New York, 1910), pp. 117–37.

71. Henri Bergson, *An Introduction to Metaphysics*, trans. T. E. Hulme (London, 1913), p. 41.

72. "Remarks at the Bergson Centennial at the Sorbonne," in *The Bergsonian Heritage*, ed. Thomas Hanna (New York, 1962), pp. 137–38.

73. See Bergson's remarks in "Laughter," reprinted in *Comedy*, ed. Wylie Sypher (Garden City, N. Y., 1956), pp. 161–62.

74. Bergson, *Time and Free Will*, trans. Pogson, p. 11.

75. "Modern Poetics, II: Twentieth-Century French and German," in *Encyclopedia of Poetry and Poetics*, p. 519.

76. See especially "Bergson's Theory of Art" in *Speculations*, ed. Read, pp. 141–69; and "Notes on Bergson," in *Further Speculations*, ed. Sam Hynes (Minneapolis, 1955), pp. 28–62. Cf. Adams' *The Interests of Criticism*, p. 89; and Lentricchia's "Four Types of Nineteenth-Century Poetic," p. 359.

Reason and Imagination in Santayana's Theory of Art

JEROME ASHMORE
CASE WESTERN RESERVE UNIVERSITY

SANTAYANA'S VIEWS OF ART AND ITS CRITICISM can be separated into three distinct classifications: (1) those concerned with beauty; (2) those concerned with "rational" art; and (3) those concerned with criticism. He offers no principle or central concept by which these varied perspectives may be arranged as a system of aesthetics. Yet, despite their appearance of diversity, they interpenetrate and may be seen as a single body of doctrine attaining unity by mere cogent relationship, by pervasive telic values of happiness and freedom, and by a natural alliance of feeling, seeing, and doing. His view of beauty is in the context of empiricism; his view of art as rational emphasizes utility; and his view of criticism rests on the assumption of an essential identity of poetry and religion that is used as a basis for constructing a standard by which to rank literary achievement.

In the history of aesthetic theory Santayana stands in the interval representing the transition from the nineteenth century to the twentieth. In paying his debt to his time he was limited to the use of the analytic, functional, and introspective version of psychology, of which he was a serious and competent student. By the time that the psychoanalytic schools, the behaviorists, the *Gestalt* perspective, and other species of approach to the life of mind had become established, Santayana had ceased to write in a major way about either beauty or art. But twentieth-century innovations in the field of psychology have not dislodged the kind Santayana used as a foundation for his aesthetics. It remains traditional and reputable despite alternative trends.

Santayana's theory of rational art, although dominated by the Hellenic Greek view of reason, also embodies the nineteenth-century views of Spencer and Darwin. Like Spencer, Santayana accepted as one goal of evolution a vital equilibrium between an organism and its environment. With Darwin, he affirmed that the course of evolution is characterized by progress. In the twentieth century a concept of progress still occupies men's thoughts, and as long as it does, Santayana's theory of rational art will be alive and current.

About his position relative to poetry and to criticism, let Santayana speak for himself. In a letter of December 13, 1928 to Thomas Munro he wrote:

> . . . we were not very much later than Ruskin, Pater, Swinburne, and Matthew Arnold: our atmosphere was that of poets and persons touched with religious enthusiasm or religious sadness. Beauty (which mustn't be mentioned now) was then a living presence, or an aching absence, day and night; history was always singing in our ears; and not even psychology or the analysis of works of art could take away from art its human implications. It was the great memorial to us, the great revelation, of what the soul had lived on, and had lived with, in her better days. But now analysis and psychology seem to stand alone: there is no spiritual interest, no spiritual need. The mind, in this direction, has been *desiccated*: art has become an abstract object in itself, to be studied scientifically as a *caput mortuum*; and the living side of the subject—the tabulation of people's feelings and comments—is no less dead.

I

In *The Sense of Beauty*, which Santayana characterizes as an outline of his aesthetic theory, he presents a clear exposition of the subjective self as a vehicle of aesthetic dynamics. In this work he accepts as foundational assumptions both hedonism and mechanism. Pleasure is good and pain is bad, while one of the chief objectives in mapping the field of aesthetics is to distinguish aesthetic pleasures from other kinds. In the steps toward this delimitation Santayana assumes that feelings are derived entirely from the physiology of the human organism and therefore that feeling has a spatio-temporal location and a physico-chemical base responsive to laws of physical bodies and also that, because of such a subjective origin, one man's feelings do not duplicate another's.

Santayana reaches the sphere of aesthetic behavior by a series of exclusions from an original large and general domain: the entire universe seen under mutually exclusive categories of mechanism and consciousness. When the universe is considered as entirely physical it is *ipso facto* entirely mechanical and will have no consciousness. But, by being devoid of consciousness, the physical world is devoid also of value, for, as Santayana sees it, value occurs only within consciousness. However, within consciousness itself there is a portion that will contain value and one that will not. In the portion of consciousness denoted as intellectual, value cannot be located. Santayana says of this intellectual content that in it "every event would . . . be noted, its relations would be observed, its recurrence might even be expected; but all this would happen without a shadow of desire, of pleasure, or of regret. . . . We might have a world of idea without a world of will" (SB, 18).[1] The intellectual processes of consciousness must be decanted and that step will leave a residue of feeling that is inseparable from vital impulses and is likewise the home of values.[2]

But even with the location of values isolated, the aesthetic values cannot become objects for examination until they are discriminated from moral values. This required discrimination is made by limiting moral values to the characteristics of negation and instrumentality, leaving a remainder of pure aesthetic value. Santayana is affirming a doctrine that both emotions and impressions of sense are capable of "objectification" (*v.* SB, 47), an act which is familiar in the case of colors, which appear to be qualities on the surfaces of external things, whereas their true location is in human psychology and physiology. Pleasure undergoes a similar kind of objectification and such an occurrence is an aesthetic perception and the point of origin of the value—beauty. Santayana consistently maintains that activity of a physiological mechanism is required before a psychic sublimation can occur.

The elements of our nature which make us sensible of beauty and the constitution of the physical thing toward which our experience of beauty is directed are exclusive of each other. The physical thing definitely is not a container of beauty and beauty definitely is not something noumenally objective. The experiencing organism is the source of beauty, while aesthetics concerns itself with the perception of values. Santayana states emphatically that the external thing toward which the self's impulses react does not share the value character of the reaction.[3] Yet it cannot be concluded that he implies the external thing is "nothing" or that he believes it insignificant in the aesthetic sensing.[4] What he contends is that the external thing of nature or art or other order is quite different from the subject's appreciation of it as beautiful, on the ground that a value does not have the constitution of a thing.[5]

In Santayana's outlook values are individualistically human, not superimposed by the authority of any well-informed person or of any arbitrary scale. When we affirm value as human, we deny one value cutting across many selves,[6] just as we would deny that there is one toothache that everyone should seek and experience. There is a multiplicity of feeling and also of sensing and of valuing. These multiplicities do not have any unity transcending them. Beauty is relative and pluralistic and otherwise does not exist either as an ideal or as a principle.[7] If there are laws of beauty, they are in the world of physiology and psychology, not in outer things.

After identifying beauty as "pleasure regarded as the quality of a thing" (SB, 49), Santayana explains how the senses contribute to the pleasure that is transformed into beauty. The transformation of organic apprehension into beauty occurs under three aspects: material, form, and expression. Basically and for the most part, the materials of beauty are developed from the physiological and psychic acts relating to the eye or to the ear. Nevertheless Santayana mentions that the generation of beauty may be influenced by other sources of a more organically diffuse nature, including love as a passion and social instincts (*v.* SB, 58–59). By reason of its own operations the human organism is a beauty-making machine. Placed in contact with a colorless, odorless, tasteless, textureless, silent, mysterious, resistant outer domain, it manufactures phenomenal objects, pleasure, and aesthetic values. Each of the five senses participating in this process has the aptitude to contribute to beauty.[8] Yet even with all the attributions that the senses make to the nonsensuous external world, there are situations in which the organism may lack a response of charm or delight and thereby be denied an aesthetic tone. It is quite conceivable that outer things may be experienced in a predominantly observational and intellectual mode, void of desire, pleasure, pain, or regret, that is, the outer world may be experienced with values absent. Such a world seems to be the kind which science constantly seeks to construct.

In the manner of the Greeks Santayana proclaims sight and hearing as the aesthetic senses, as differentiated from taste, smell, and touch, which he designates as nonaesthetic. His criterion for the differentiation is quite simple. Sight and hearing have the rank of aesthetic senses because they afford physically measurable phenomenal objects having structure and an identifiable location; the remaining senses do not. Therefore sight and hearing are readily adaptable to the objectifying activity of the understanding; the remaining senses are not. The relation between the aesthetic and nonaesthetic or lower senses is not one of exclusion but rather one of relative importance in consummating the value of beauty.[9]

According to Santayana the next element contributing to the occurrence of beauty is form. The effects of form, although enhanced by sensuous surface, are not traceable to it, but rather to certain ideal relations that accompany the object being apprehended. Form lies between two poles, one the simple delight in sensuous surface, the other a field entirely excluding the senses—that of attention to ideas associated with the object, apart from the idea of the object itself. Within this intermediate zone there is a collection of sensible units, which, if considered singly, are indifferent with respect to a sense of beauty. But the same units in combination may be a correlate of pleasure in the subject and thereby become an occasion relative to beauty. The combination may be given or it may be composed with the assistance of apperceptive types. Beauty through form, then, is the combination of discretely indifferent elements that pleases and depends on whether the organism is aware of the elements in the totality it is perceiving. If not, it is experiencing a sensation, not a perception of form.[10]

Pleasure, then, may arise from a synthesis of elements either already determined when given or entirely undetermined. Where the synthesis is not given as determined, for example, in clouds, in water, or in a hazy landscape, beauty will depend on how abundantly an individual's mind is stored with apperceptive types and what skill he possesses in applying these types to outer things which structurally are indeterminate. To these kinds of things the mind will assign some unstable form derived from some apperceptive type.[11] This step is not required when a determined combination of elements is given. In either case simultaneous objectification of the synthesis is a value from form, providing pleasure is present.

Santayana's third means contributing to the arousal of beauty is expression. In this aspect value is correlated with some experience other than what nature, some work of art, or some other datum literally suggests. The basis for beauty from expression is the mental process of association, not the intrinsic status of what is before the percipient.

In distinguishing value through expression the impulse to pleasure is again basic but directs itself to something outside of the object's material and formal properties, and the value forthcoming requires the extra step of association. Expression, in Santayana's sense of the term, is a quality acquired by objects through association, a meaning and tone characteristic of other objects, but merged in a given object which is otherwise independent (*v.* SB, 193). Nevertheless, the pleasure objectified by association remains an immediate feeling.

Value from material and from form occur with reference to only one object, whereas in expression there are two—the given and the associated—plus an emotional effect provoked through the associated object. Further, expression has the capacity of acting in two ways: it "may make beautiful by suggestion things in themselves indifferent, or it may come to heighten the beauty which they already possess" (SB, 193).

But again, expression is not based on a theory of association by external relation.[12] It differs from such a theory by being restricted to acts within an individual mind,[13] which through imagination must supply one of the terms used in the association. There is no public presentation of the associated object. Nor is there a demand that it be something aesthetic. It may be or it may not. Instances of nonaesthetic association could be utility, cost, economy, fitness, evil, or pain.

In the essay "The Mutability of Aesthetic Categories," published about thirty years after *The Sense of Beauty*, there is a long and important footnote revealing that Santayana had modified his thinking about the character of objectification of pleasure.[14] One of the main points of the emended view is that pleasure is not intrinsically subjective and therefore does not need to be objectified. This conclusion follows from a belief that terms of thought are something distinct from particulars of existence and that most of the universals used in discourse are a result of the organism's contact with the particulars of existence and are signs and names remaining after that contact and standing for inscrutable substances. Pleasure is an example of such a name. So is color. As names they are neither subjective nor objective but are neutral. As neutral they could not participate in objectification. Here Santayana is viewing pleasure as a universal of discourse standing for some dark substance. Pleasure is found in experience, but the experience is of discourse and its medium of universals.

Other points in this fertile footnote are that beauty is a visionary essence and as such is indefinable; that "objectified pleasure" is a phrase which indicates the conditions and manner in which the apparition of beauty arises and vanishes and which is not presented as a definition of beauty. He adds that now he might say beauty is a vital harmony felt and fused into an image under the form of eternity. In this remark he is suggesting that the pleasure characterizing beauty must transport the subject to the realm of essence. Elsewhere he remarks: "the beautiful is itself an essence, an indefinable quality felt in many things which, however disparate they may be otherwise, receive this name by virtue of a special emotion, half wonder, half love, which is felt in their presence" (RB, 8).

Another difference between the earlier and the later approaches to beauty rests on the distinction between looking to understand and looking to see. In looking to understand one is preoccupied with practical considerations and assumptions of mechanical causation. In looking to see one escapes from a utilitarian context and whatever confronts him is sublimated into an essence. In looking to understand, beauty is absent; in looking to see, beauty has the opportunity to exhibit itself.

In spite of these unexpected qualifications to his doctrine of beauty, three of his early convictions remain unaffected: first, that beauty is an illusion of a quality of an external thing; second, that beauty depends primarily on individual psychology;[15] and third, that to be a value, beauty must be interpolated with a moral objective, that is, it must be an element in some harmonious combination with other interests, a combination which serves as a guide for living and offers happiness as a reward.

II

Confusion in interpretation of what Santayana designates as rational art may be averted if attention is directed to the unusual sense in which he employs the terms "reason" and "art."

For Santayana reason is not a given psychological faculty, nor is it associated with any syllogistic or other discursive procedure seeking assurance for a sound conclusion. His reason has two aspects. The first is that it is a "method of imaginative thought" (DP, 463) which, with no prior prescription, can survey all of an individual's interests at once, perceive how they check and support each other, and place the ones auguring happiness in a balanced, harmonious, and coherent relationship[16] while rejecting those which do not. In its other aspect reason is the formal organization[17] which results from this method and "signifies a conjunction and mutual modification of impulses in a man or in a society" (DP, 307). Reason, in this aspect, is the map in man's quest for happiness. In addition, Santayana elaborately acknowledges how the Greeks provided the foundation for his conception of reason (*v.* LR, I, 14–28).

There also is a departure from verbal convention in Santayana's version of the term "art." It does not signify fine art. For him fine art is suspect and much of it is denied membership in the field of art. At least three criteria mark his discrimination of art from fine art: first, fine art lacks the utility of art; second, fine art is without a moral commitment; and third, fine art, being predominantly involved with imagination, makes an abstraction from the physical things of the environment and art does not. Fine art is not art in the best sense, for in the best sense art is an element in a rational program of living and fine art almost never is. The fine arts may be decorative, may arouse value, beauty, and sometimes may be superimposed on utility, especially in the case of architecture. But in themselves the fine arts are not useful, not rational, not conducive to human progress, and not one of the elements ideally represented in the moral goal of a human individual. In distinction from fine art Santayana calls his kind of art "rational art." It is much closer to *techne* than to *mimesis*. In this essay wherever the term art appears, it will signify Santayana's rational art. "Fine art" will be denoted by using the full phrase.

Art is a natural activity of man dependent on the presence of an organism and its environment, with each having the property of plasticity. The two interact with a twofold result upon the organism: it impresses itself on its environment, but reciprocally, it is impressed by its environment.[18] Of these two results, the activity of the organism upon its environment pertains to art; the effect of the environment on the organism does not.

In the impress that the organism makes on its environment there is, within each, a specific constitutent which is primary to the transaction. In the case of the organism that constituent is instinct; in the case of the environment it is the given material, both physical and nonphysical. Instinct and material are the bare components out of which art develops, but although necessary for this development they are not sufficient to assure it. The interaction of the organism's impulse and the environmental material will leave a product, but the product may belong in either of two categories: it may have utility or it may not. If it does not have utility it is disqualified from classification as art; if it has utility it is eligible to become art. The product will assume the full status of art when it meets the further condition that the impressing organism, in other words, the maker or doer, is at times conscious of the utility of what he is doing. If the maker or doer is sometimes conscious of the utility of what he is doing, the product is art; if he is completely unaware of utility in his product, even though it has potential utility, the product is not art.

Art, then, involves the action of an organism upon its environment leading to a result recognized by the organism as useful. It is an approved function; that is, some rational activity, which began at random, chanced to have utility, and became a habit amenable to being transmitted to companions of the innovator and to following generations. In a subsequent historical stage, when man exercised reflection to project an ideal moral program, art served as a vehicle by which the ideal might be approached. Art is any making or doing judged meritorious by its part in a general advance toward realization of a rational ideal. Art is not limited to interaction with the physical world. Various fields of human endeavor, such as science, religion, or politics, serve equally well as an environment. Arts are methods by which man meets the difficulties and predicaments of his diversified life, methods which assist him in survival within the environment in which he finds himself. Santayana's view is veritably an economist's view of art. In his eyes the arts are definitely means of producing wealth.[19]

However important instinct may be in the origin of art, Santayana makes the equally important point that art never remains confined by instinct, but soon breaks away from this inner source to become an outward product subserving the formal conditions of reason. The direction of the process culminating in art is from an inward state to an outward form, not the reverse. And to qualify as art the movement and the product must represent reason.

Another fundamental relation within art is that between utility and structure. One of the attributes of art is acknowledged utility; but unless this utility can be used to carry on human progress, the art product is nullified. In this impasse structure becomes of vast consequence, for through its instrumentality innumerable repetitions of the art act may be assured and rational artists may continue in their ways. The structure of an art product has two loci: one in the artificer and another in the material he impresses. In the artificer, structure is the basis of skill and perseverance; in the art material, structure implies plasticity to the active skill.

All art has a rational end. The initial urge of the organism feels this end, which appears as some ideal goal that represents a good and, if reached, guarantees happiness as a by-product. Santayana speaks literally when he calls the structure in art which assists reason "a happy organization" (LR, IV, 11). There is a second by-product of art seen as a consequence of the force through which it acts on the totality of man's environment. Not quickly, but slowly and relentlessly, the continuous impression on the environment by the organism registers a change in the environment. It is to the very activity of art and the changes wrought by the expression of man's mind on matter that human progress may be traced.[20] But art is even more than an environmental ladder to human amelioration. Art also is a preserver and carrier of rationality over future generations and, on its own terms, moves toward ideals whose attainment advances human interests physically, cognitively, and affectively.[21]

Santayana's well-known concept, the Life of Reason, presupposes that diverse impulses of an individual are to be balanced and harmonized in an ideally composed program which will serve as a goal for action. The prime characteristic of reason is the formal organization of such a program. When attending to interaction with its immediate environment and simultaneously maintaining an interest in the ideal future harmony, life may be called "reason in operation." In both principle and practice the Life of Reason is art. Both arise from a human operation. Both are identified with a goal consciously used to guide this operation. In both, the method or technique that constructs the product is teachable. Both embody a creative idea. Both demand liberal genius and a favorably plastic environment. Both have natural sources and use natural materials. Both enlist ideas that must be practical. Both supply evidence that the natural world is a fitting home for the human individual.

Rational art lends itself to division into two stages, one designated industrial, the other liberal. Industrial art is also called mechanical or economic. An assumption of continuity is implicit between the two stages. Industrial art carries on a more direct struggle with the materials of nature than liberal art and is more mechanical, servile, and repetitious. Yet there cannot be liberal art without industrial art. In fact, there is no such thing as liberal art as a separate activity identifiable in isolation. Liberal art is rather an epiphenomenon or transcending of industrial art. When the industrial artisan, by having used environmental material to progress toward an ideal, feels an enlightened freedom, he has arrived at the point where he may witness spirituality within himself. A "liberalized" psychic condition is then present, and it favors the injection of creativity into the product of the moment. Under these conditions the individual is engaging in liberal art.

It is clear that, for Santayana, fine art in general lies outside of the domain of art and, by the standards of the Life of Reason, commands no great respect. He often could not hold back his disdain: "'fine arts' grow pale and empty as well as ugly when they are altogether separated from economic and moral uses, and express only caprice, luxury, and affectation" (DP, 91); "there is no lack of folly in the [fine] arts; they are full of inertia and affectation and of what must seem ugliness to a cultivated taste . . . the [fine] arts may die of triviality, as they were born of enthusiasm" (PGS, 21); "in my own case, aestheticism blew over with the first mists of adolescence; I very soon tired of aesthetic affectations and archeological pedantry: nor has my love of the beautiful ever found its chief sustenance in the [fine] arts" (PGS, 501). To be sure, Santayana allows fine art to represent an interest of the human organism, but for him this interest does not integrate easily with other interests and acts required for successful advance toward the moral ideal. And, if works of fine art are disregarded and aesthetic values, as they accompany rational activity, are the only concern, Santayana will say that "life is, in one aspect, always a fine art . . . an aesthetic sanction sweetens all successful living; animal efficiency cannot be without grace, nor moral achievement without a sensible glory" (LR, IV, 188).

Santayana does not follow the modern assumption that literature, music, architecture, sculpture, and painting are on the same theoretical level and, while each is granted to be unique, all are viewed as responsive to the same principles. In his references to the fine arts he betrays a preference for the bifurcation among them that prevailed in ancient Greece. In the ancient view, poetry and music in its various denotations held a high place, whereas architecture, sculpture, and painting were somewhat degraded. A bit of evidence that the Greek dichotomy influenced Santayana is offered in *Interpretations of Poetry and Religion* and in *Three Philosophical Poets*, where the highest achievements of art are granted to poetry. Yet nowhere does he allude to music, architecture, sculpture, or painting as capable of a comparable performance. Doubtlessly his own position as a poet influenced his high opinion of the corresponding fine art. He also was theoretically committed to approval of architecture, since it embodied the utility so essential to his moral theory. Sculpture could be granted the oblique merit that it might be decorative within architecture; but painting seems to have nothing to recommend it, and implicitly it is toward painting that much of Santayana's negation of fine art seems to be directed.

In *Dominations and Powers* Santayana is quite conscious of the negative and destructive powers of the mechanical and industrial arts,[22] an aspect he slighted in the five-volume work, *The Life of Reason.* He also becomes aware of a consequence he neglected totally in the earlier work, which is that the mechanical and industrial arts conflict with each other, in the sense that the producers of one art product are disposed to crush the producers of another, whether similar to the first or unlike it. The basis of hostility among the producers is traced to their motivation by interests and desires. It is the counter stresses and irrationality of the activities of impulse that precipitate clashes and curses on men. In the practice of an art some of the organism's interests will reach outside of itself and this condition is likely to arouse proprietary passions. In fact, such interests may be so strong that they overrun the field of art entirely and extend to viciousness, destruction, and most of the other human woes. The will involved may be one, not only to devour, but to gather, hold, and guard everything devourable. Arts, which formerly were depicted only as objects of respect, now are not invariably a kind of rational industry; they may be pernicious deviates from rationality.[23]

Santayana's qualification of his opinion of the arts seems to correlate with one regarding human progress. Thus, he speaks of two kinds of progress, one denoted temporal, the other, true. Temporal progress is the advance of everything toward death, true progress relates to a degree of perfection sought within life. Previously, human progress for Santayana was something *sui generis*, which, though it might have moral ambiguity, did not divide itself into kinds. But altogether *Dominations and Powers* is a modification rather than a rejection of *The Life of Reason.*

III

Despite his prose artistry, his poetic genius, and his concern with beauty and with criticism, Santayana possessed an aversion to the ordinary view of aesthetics. This disposition seems to revert to two factors. First, in his zeal for a rational program of interests he would not recognize aesthetics as separable from moral philosophy and what carried the name of philosophy of art he called "sheer verbiage" (PGS, 20). It was his conviction that to abstract a so-called aesthetic interest from other interests "is to make the aesthetic sphere contemptible" (OS, 38). But his attitude changes totally and aesthetics is approved if it is held in unity with moral philosophy and rational art,[24] and any aesthetic theory attributed to him must include that qualification. The second factor tending to alienate him from an independent aesthetics can be found in his declaration "I didn't have and haven't now a clear notion of what 'aesthetics' may be" (MS, 156).

Part of what perplexed Santayana when considering aesthetics as a particular discipline is set forth in his essay, "What Is Aesthetics?"[25] He does not settle the question he proposes in the title, but is willing to view it as insoluble and vexatious, since its very terms "dislocate the constitution of things" (OS, 32).

The first dilemma arises when identity between aesthetics and some distinct activity is sought. It cannot be found: an art student carries on aesthetic activity, yet so does a psychologist in a laboratory. If activity is construed as thinking, the result is no better: a dialectician seeking the relation of the beautiful to the rational or to the absolutely good is speculating aesthetically; so is a theologian treating the emanation of the Holy Ghost from the Son and from the Father, when the Holy Ghost signifies a fullness of life realized in beauty.

An approach through aesthetic experience also fails. It leads to a broad field containing countless miscellaneous occasions appealing to diverse individual consciousnesses. Within these experiences no common and specific aesthetic quality is discoverable and they invite widely divergent interpretations without indicating whether the foundation of an aesthetic experience is to be found in nature, in a sense organ, or in human spirit.

Reasoned knowledge is another blind path. It contains a choice between two implements—observation or dialectic. Observation produces natural science; dialectic produces ideal science. Aesthetics cannot be put exclusively into either of these divisions of science, but has a character amenable to both. The phenomena of art and taste are factual and belong within natural science; creative effort and critical interpretation move in the realm of value and so belong within ideal science. Again aesthetics is recalcitrant to comprehension.

Under the terms of his analysis Santayana decides that aesthetics is neither part of psychology nor of philosophy, and further, that neither the history of man nor of art isolates "any such block of experience as aesthetics is supposed to describe" (OS, 36).

IV

The failure to find a unique region of human experience to which aesthetics corresponds does not exclude a more favorable outcome in the realm of ideal expression. Although in the ideal realm an unequivocal aesthetic science is not conceivable, a respectable substitute is found in the art and function of criticism. Criticism is "a reasoned appreciation of human works" (OS, 37), and in this sense it extends to all kinds of products and is not at all restricted to the fine arts. Moreover, criticism functions within certain categories of reference: beauty, propriety, difficulty, originality, truth, and moral significance.

There is a place in criticism for the moral philosopher. He serves to combine into an harmonious ideal all the categories used in critical appraisal and thereby establishes a standard for the relative estimation of the products, which must have the additional property of being a goal influencing human effort. The composition of the standard must be rational, which signifies that it will represent both aesthetic and nonaesthetic interests and that these will form a harmonious balance with each other. In respect to criticism, then, Santayana is normative and at the same time naturalistically teleological; moreover his theory demands a continuity between things empirical and things rational. He is not impressed favorably by criticism as he finds it. He says that generally it is "something purely incidental—talk about talk—and to my mind has no serious value except perhaps as an expression of *philosophy* in the critic" (LGS, 195). He adds that he has never written criticism for any other reason. Elsewhere he claims: "Criticism . . . is a serious public function; it shows the race assimilating the individual, dividing the immortal from the mortal part of the soul" (LR, IV, 151).

The central and most comprehensive treatment of Santayana's theory of criticism is the collection of essays published under the title *Interpretations of Poetry and Religion.* Arbitrarily considered, with the objective of extracting a theory of criticism contained in this volume, the subject matter of the essays roughly falls into three divisions: the first concerns the establishment of the interrelation of poetry and religion; the second outlines the psychological functions pertinent to poetry and religion; and the third exhibits the components and the scope of poetry together with a normative hierarchy for critical judgments. The total theory has a structure consisting of three interlocking elements: (a) a specified psychology of understanding and imagination; (b) a doctrine of kinship of poetry and religion; and (c) a schema for measuring poetic accomplishment.

(a) Santayana's virtual identification of poetry and religion is dependent on his account of understanding and imagination. Under the kind of psychological terms he accepts, poetry and religion may be identified and their common character used for the ends of literary criticism; with another kind of psychology this overlapping of the two might not happen.

Within the psychology he endorses, Santayana distinguishes two kinds of imagination—one denoted by the imagination itself and the other by understanding. He denies any exclusive disjunction between these two psychic functions; they are continuous and his differentiation of them is nominal.[26] His convictions follow from a carefully wrought theory of mental organization in which only two of the five senses—hearing and sight—produce understanding. Of these two, sight plays the dominant role. It is visual apprehension that activates the mind's powers of "synthesis, abstraction, reproduction, invention" (IPR, 2). These powers Santayana takes to be equivalent to understanding. However, understanding has a companion faculty in the form of the imagination, which asserts itself almost as soon as the understanding begins to function. At this point the mind "turns from the frigid problems of observation to its own visions" (IPR, 2). The understanding interprets the senses but the imagination always overlays that interpretation.

The assumption that in mental processes the imagination inevitably joins forces with understanding becomes the premise which allows Santayana to conclude that the imagination does the work of the intelligence and to assert that "imagination and intelligence do not differ in their origin but only in their validity" (IPR, 5). Under these terms there is a relationship among common sense, science, and imagination. They are alike in source, in character, and in motivation and differ only in respect to validity. The distinction among them is not material or efficient, but solely ideal. It is only under the abstractions of logical discrimination that independent functions may be assigned to common sense, science, and imagination. In their dynamic state of functioning they are inseparable. Santayana now may proclaim a distinction most useful to his doctrine of poetry and religion and to other of his literary views: "Those conceptions which, after they have spontaneously arisen, prove serviceable in practice, and capable of verification in sense, we call ideas of the understanding. The others remain ideas of the imagination" (IPR, 5).

After assuring himself of the kinship of understanding and imagination and of the differentiation of the two by means of the criteria of utility and verification by sense, Santayana reaches the point where he may impose a ranking on various individual minds. The norm for this ranking is susceptibility to imagination as it relates to the large questions of life and the universe. The highest order of mind is that wherein imagination envisions states of affairs that are beyond the scope of the understanding. In this kind of metavista feeling and passion are also present, providing further distinction from the process of ordinary understanding. This elite territory, open to imagination but beyond the limits of understanding, is the ground from which religion and metaphysics develop. Both of these disciplines, as well as poetry, require apprehension of forms, which being supersensible, are not available to understanding. Paradoxically, the intuitions which science cannot embody remain as the inspiration of poetry and religion.

With regard to the function of being prophetic, imagination and understanding are definitely homogeneous,[27] but they differ in verification and use of their prophecies. Prophecies of the understanding are verifiable within the operation of ordinary sense perception; prophecies of the imagination may not be. Also prophecies of the understanding often may be a warrant for fulfillment in practical action, whereas prophecies of the higher imagination carry no such warrant.[28] The prophecies of the understanding relate to established kinds of experience shared within most human communities and verifiable within the sense experience of the given community, and hence frequently are put to use in the advancement of general welfare. But the prophecies of imagination functioning singly overreach the level of common experience and accordingly are not quickly or readily verified or applied. However, the imagination, when freed, may bring larger benefits to man than when it is united with understanding.[29]

Santayana sees imagination as having a continuity divisible into two segments, higher and lower, which, although distinguishable for purposes of exposition, are not operationally exclusive. Imagination, in its lower segment, is a primary force in the exercise of understanding. In its higher segment it reaches beyond the province of rote utility and linguistic verification indigenous to understanding. Only imagination can meet the unknowable outer world and transform each piece of its varied furniture into a symbol.[30] Yet, as agents of vision, both segments and the ideas of each are one unit.

When imagination is free of direct outer reference it is "the true realm of man's infinity where novelty may exist without falsity and perpetual diversity without contradiction" (IPR, 20). Nevertheless "highly imaginative things . . . express real events, if not in the outer world, at least in the inner growth or discipline of life" (SELS, 249). Santayana sometimes speaks of a dramatic aspect of imagination and considers it "one of the richest endowments of the human psyche . . . the faculty of acting out a part, working out a motive, finding words and gestures and actions that express it. This is the faculty that creates dreams in sleep and genius in natures that are wide awake and simultaneously aware of many circumstances" (ICG, 132). Technically, imagination is a region between sensation and abstract discourse, "where more is seen at arm's length than in any one moment could be felt at close quarters, and yet where the remote parts of experience, which discourse reaches only through symbols, are recovered and recomposed in something like their native colours and experienced relation. This region . . . has pleasures more airy and luminous than those of sense, more massive and rapturous than those of sense, more massive and rapturous than those of intelligence" (LR, IV, 15). On the other hand, Santayana warns that imagination may be irresponsible and treacherous, may be an obstacle to the perception of fact, and may cloud science with passion, with fiction, and with sentimental prejudice (*v.* IPR, 10–11).

(b) The psychological foundation prescribed by Santayana and his discrimination within the sphere of imagination enable him to defend a belief in the essential identity of poetry and religion, which is the most important single idea in all of his literary philosophy and criticism. Poetry and religion are ideal constructions that make the facts of nature and history morally intelligible and practically important, thereby fulfilling the supreme function of the imagination.

In basic texture, poetry and religion are substantially one and acquire different names according to whether they intervene in life or merely supervene upon it.[31] The term "religion" is preferred when the reference is to a principle used in the conduct of life; when there is no such pragmatic association, the term "poetry" is chosen. But the presence or absence of moral objectives has no effect on the imaginative content of either of the two directions it takes. It is understood that all manifestations of religion are not of equal moral significance; the same is true with all manifestations of poetry. At its highest power poetry "is identical with religion grasped in its inmost truth" (IPR, 290). In this eminent identity poetry is without frivolity and religion is without delusions and deception. The intuition of each has attained its maximum comprehension of ultimate reality and they are together as one.

In *Interpretations of Poetry and Religion* Santayana appears to be influenced primarily by Matthew Arnold, John Stuart Mill, and William James. In his *Literature and Dogma* Arnold had presented religion as "morality touched by emotion," and in *Culture and Anarchy* he viewed the best Greek art, religion, and poetry as one and the same. Such an identity was most congenial to Santayana and was reinforced by John Stuart Mill, who, in *Three Essays on Religion*, stated that "religion and poetry address themselves . . . to the same part of the human constitution: they both supply the same want, that of ideal conceptions grander and more beautiful than we see realized in the prose of human life."[32] This was precisely Santayana's own point of view. Clinical support for his theory of the interpenetration of understanding and imagination came from James' theory that the subjective difference between imagined and felt objects is less absolute than supposed, that cortical processes underlying imagination and sensation are not definitely discrete, and that the imaginative process differs from the sensitive process by intensity rather than by locality of neural processes.[33]

(c) With poetry and religion conceived as alternative representations of an identity, Santayana has a ready-made standard for literary criticism. The highest ranking poetry will be that which achieves a religious mode in scope, refinement, and profundity. Other poetry, perforce, must accept a lower rank. In the scale for judging poetry there are three levels of analysis, containing four stages of ascending rank—the lower level has two of these, the intermediate and upper level one each.

The two stages found on the lower level are those of euphony and euphuism. Euphony is the lower of the two and as a criterion asks only that the sound of poetry be pure, pleasing, and fluid. At the next higher stage, euphuism, there is a demand for coherence in imagery together with associations in memory and suggestions for imaginative constructions from elliptical phrasing, with all these elements forming a harmonious unity. The third stage occupies the intermediate level, and to qualify for this rank the poet must inject himself into his poetry. In so doing he will be classed as romantic and will be free to disregard categories that maintain purely rational order. At the fourth stage, or highest level, reason must be reintroduced and the scope of the imaginative outlook extended so that the subject matter selected may be treated on a cosmic scale (*v.* IPR, 287–88). The poetry of the lowest level is dominated by sensuous surface and purveys pleasantness merely in response to demands of the ear. The poetry of the intermediate level has the additional feature of romantic deflections of the self or idealizations of episodes in human existence. The poetry of the highest level is rational over a background of universal proportions and derives its beauty from its religious response to demands from the soul.

Besides the bare structure of levels designed for grading poetry, there are some characteristics found in all poetry regardless of its rank. These characteristics are what might be called poetic content, and this distinctive kind of content may be viewed in terms of its origins, its substantial nature, and its function. Poetic content, or stuff, has its source in emotional experience. Viewed in the light of the self's experience, the real world is only an outline, superimposed, as it were, on the dreamlike state of the soul—perpetually one of chaos and unrest. There are two sides to the contact between the soul and the other world, and these sides are different in kind. One resembles a top surface characterized by a logical and intellectual order; the other is an under surface of dreaming, generating, amorphous becoming that makes no use of logical methods in its thought products, yet always has discursive reason imminent above it. This subrational layer of experience is the soil of the emotional expression required in poetry. In the case of the ordinary man this obscure region may be the source of merely insignificant utterance; but in the case of the poet it is the basis and effective cause of his art.

The substance of poetry, however, is gleaned from an interaction between the mind's emotional and intellectual divisions. Left to itself it is the nature of the intellect to cast out any emotion that tinges a perception. The intellect strives to arrogate control and to impose its own conditions on perceptual material. In many cases it succeeds. But the poet will not tolerate this kind of usurpation. He retains the emotion that the intellect would have banished and allows it to permeate his ideas while he gives them imaginative interpretation, under the stimulation of his sense of beauty and his impulse to harmony. Within this poetic act the substance and chief ingredient is emotion. It takes him out of the province of discursive reason and it acts as a common bond on all his creation. For the poet those things hold together that adhere to the same emotion. This principle which enlists emotion for coloring the constituents of poetry with the same tone distinguishes poetic thought from the practical kind which holds together through some given interest and from the scientific kind which holds together on account of spatio-temporal relations or identity of theoretical formulation (*v.* IPR, 261–63).

Besides indicating the source and substance of poetry, Santayana mentions its function. The poet's creations are not merely diversion or whimsy; they have an established function. As might be expected this function is moral in character.[34] To grasp its import one must imagine a bidirectional movement on the part of the poet's creative faculty. In one phase the movement abandons the level of common perceptual experience and goes beneath it to embrace the raw stuff of sensation with unfettered imagination. In the other phase the movement transcends these depths of indefiniteness and forms novel compositions that lift it above the dead level of plain, uninspired experience. Here there are two essential steps traversed by the poet: the going downward into a state of unintellectualized sensation where the poet has for companions what literally might be called madmen and the going upward into a state of reason and the company of enlightened prophets. The first step is for the objective of obtaining materials to be converted to higher ends; the second is to form those ends in a structure of symbols representing the truest aims and finest achievements of the soul (*v.* IPR, 270).

Although he is willing to construct levels of gradation for the poetic product that serve as standards for its criticism and as categories determining its type, Santayana never confuses this normative attitude toward poetry with the factual data of the human poetic matrix. In principle all poetry is alike, regardless of whether after the fact it is separable into graded compartments. All poetry evolves out of the same substance, which is emotion, and from the same center, which is the passions, although the result will differ according to individuals. All poetry, too, is supported by sensation and cognition of natural environment, and on that account, fits the world and practical living.[35] On the respective questions, then, of inclusion under a principle, of the context of origin, of fundamental substance, and of relevance to outer nature, all poetry is one. It is on questions of critical judgment of the finished poetic product of individual artists that poetry is diverse.

In *Three Philosophical Poets* the general tendency is more toward philosophy than toward poetry, yet there are passages of definite significance for criticism. The principles advocated in *Interpretations of Poetry and Religion* are maintained without alteration, but the emphasis on the identity of poetry and religion is replaced by emphasis on the relation between poetry and philosophy. The chief question Santayana raises is: "Are poets, at heart, in search of a philosophy? Or is philosophy, in the end, nothing but poetry?" (TPP, 8). The implications of this question bring forward several interesting topics, including the accommodation of poetic brevity to philosophy, the potential of philosophy as a source of inspiration, the emotional metaphysics of philosophical poetry, philosophical theory as poetic content, and finally diversity in modes of art as they affect the relation between poetry and a moral life. Lucretius, Dante, and Goethe offer excellent examples for these topics. Lucretius is an example of the identity of poetry and naturalism, Dante of poetry and supernaturalism, and Goethe of poetry and romanticism.

As Santayana construes the terms "poetry" and "philosophy" they are not two things but one. In such a light the presence of philosophical theory in poetry is commendable rather than objectionable.[36] Poetry's highest attainment is the exhibition of the organization of all things as a value occurring in the imagination; this is the condition by which the presence of theory elevates poetry to its highest level.[37] Poetry without theory is doomed to be minor. Lucretius could "see the world to be one great edifice, one great machine, all its parts reacting upon one another, and growing out of one another in obedience to a general pervasive process or life" (TPP, 4). Dante "covers the whole field from which poetry may be fetched, and to which poetry may be applied, from the inmost recesses of the heart to the uttermost bounds of nature and destiny" (TPP, 133). Goethe's magical medley "is full of images, passions, memories, and introspective wisdom" (TPP, 207). He knows admirably the multiformity and intricacy of things of the universe and makes of them a natural concert, "all the more natural for being sometimes discordant, sometimes overloaded and dull" (TPP, 207). Great poetry is indeed difficult to measure. The perfect poet will contain and transcend the genius of Lucretius, Dante, and Goethe, but he has not yet appeared in this imperfect world.

V

It seems perverse to consider ending remarks about Santayana's theory of criticism without mentioning his early and compressed article, "Walt Whitman: A Dialogue."[38] With all its brevity this work affords an exceptionally penetrating and illuminating treatment of fundamental issues within literary criticism, and particularly within criticism of poetry. The dialogue takes place between two fictional participants, Van Tender and McStout. Van Tender roughly corresponds to the protagonist and McStout to his antagonist.

Van Tender is liberal and romantic. He proposes a theory in which individual interpretation is a prime factor in poetry. The poet's own feeling tones and purely sensuous expression are sufficient sanction for poetic merit, and freely imaginative expression of the unique and the momentary without reference to any accepted external standard is entirely proper. McStout is fashionably conservative. He opposes his friend with an academic and even puritanical version of the classic imitation theory according to which the poet must represent or reproduce some generally accepted truth. However, in McStout's conception, the truth does not happen to be an *arche* but is merely what is believed to be best according to the prescriptions of convention.

The two men are immersed in a large issue that frequently has arisen in the history of criticism. In a way they are reviving the old conflict over fine art according to nature or fine art according to rules, another statement of which may be the question "Is fine art an imitation or an interpretation of life; is it fundamental to fine art to depict the instinctive, immediate flux, or to be guided by the integrating force of rational discipline?" Throughout the discussion the poetry of Walt Whitman is merely a convenient medium through which to consider the principles in dispute. There are much larger issues at stake than whether or not Whitman is adequate as a poet.

Actually the main issue of imitation vs. interpretation is not explicitly pressed during the dialogue but rather is implicit in the examination of a number of subissues. These, if resolved, would assist in partially resolving the more comprehensive question of which they are a part. These smaller explicit issues, all germane to poetry, include questions regarding linguistics, conformity to convention, necessity of illusion, communication of feeling, communication of an outer beauty, variation in the intrinsic beauty of objects, standards of valuing, and moral consequences.

By an examination of contrary viewpoints, the dialogue seeks to discover the scope and nature of poetry. Instead of a solution Santayana offers a thorough deliberation about both sides of each issue. Underlying the contentions of the characters is an attitude of dispassionate inquiry. Shall the classicist or the romanticist be awarded the laurels? Is poetic art an imitation or an interpretation of the universe and its constitution? Is the best poetry instinctive, passionate, and representative of the flux of existence or must poetry bring itself under some ideal discipline? Is fact or value to be the prior consideration? Is emotion to supersede thought? Is poetry to be seen as something liberal, passive, tolerant, and contemplative, or as something orthodox, selective, and judicial? The contents of *Interpretations of Poetry and Religion* and *Three Philosophical Poets* represent Santayana's resolution of the questions raised in "Walt Whitman: A Dialogue." But the questions remain fundamental in any study of poetry and its criticism and are a good example of the clear and enduring kind of thought in which Santayana engaged. It is considerations such as these which make *The Sense of Beauty* a standard reference for courses in aesthetics and *The Life of Reason* a continual inspiration to all who seek a civilized level in the art of living.

NOTES

1. Quotations from Santayana are from the following works:
   (SB): *The Sense of Beauty* (New York, 1896)
   (IPR): *Interpretations of Poetry and Religion* (New York, 1900)

(LR): *The Life of Reason* (New York, 1905 and 1906)
(TPP): *Three Philosophical Poets* (Cambridge, Mass., 1910)
(SELS): *Soliloquies in England and Later Soliloquies* (New York, 1922)
(OS): *Obiter Scripta: Letters, Essays and Reviews*, ed. J. Buchler and B. Schwartz (New York, 1936)
(RB): *Realms of Being* (New York, 1942)
(MS): *The Middle Span: Persons and Places*, II (New York, 1945)
(ICG): *The Idea of Christ in the Gospels* (New York, 1946)
(DP): *Dominations and Powers* (New York, 1951)
(PGS): *The Philosophy of George Santayana*, ed. P. A. Schilpp, 2nd ed. (New York, 1951)
(LGS): *The Letters of George Santayana*, ed. D. Cory (New York, 1955)

2. "... values spring from the immediate and inexplicable reaction of vital impulse, and from the irrational part of our nature." SB, 19.

3. "... there is no value apart from some appreciation of it." Ibid., 18.

4. ". . . there could be no beauty if there was no conception of independent objects." Ibid., 74.

5. "Beauty . . . is a value; it cannot be conceived as an independent existence which affects our senses and which we consequently perceive. It exists in perception and cannot exist otherwise." Ibid., 45.

6. "... no two men have exactly the same faculties, nor can things have for any two exactly the same values." Ibid., 42.

7. "It is unmeaning to say that what is beautiful to one man *ought* to be beautiful to another. If their senses are the same, their associations and dispositions similar, then the same thing will certainly be beautiful to both. If their natures are different, the form which to one will be entrancing will be to another even invisible." Ibid., 41 (Santayana's italics).

8. "There is no function of our nature which cannot contribute something to this effect [of beauty], but one function differs very much from another in the amount and directness of its contribution. The pleasures of the eye and ear, of the imagination and memory, are the most easily objectified and merged in ideas; but it would betray inexcusable haste and slight appreciation of the principle involved if we called them the only materials of beauty." Ibid., 53.

9. "Artists in life, if that expression may be used for those who have beautified social and domestic existence, have appealed continually to these lower senses. A fragrant garden, and savory meats, incense, and perfumes, soft stuffs, and delicious colors, form our ideal of oriental

luxuries, an ideal which appeals too much to human nature ever to lose its charm." Ibid., 66–67.

10. "... unity cannot be absolute and be a form; a form is an aggregation, it must have elements, and the manner in which the elements are combined constitutes the character of the form. A perfectly simple perception, in which there was no consciousness of the distinction and relation of parts, would not be a perception of form; it would be a sensation. . . . Form . . . does not appeal to the unattentive; they get from objects only a vague sensation . . . they do not stop to survey the parts or to appreciate their relation." Ibid., 96.

11. "Every cloud has just the outline it has, although we may call it vague, because we cannot classify its form under any geometrical or animal species; it would be first definitely a whale, and then would become indefinite until we saw our way to calling it a camel." Ibid., 113.

12. ". . . if expression were constituted by the external relation of object with object, everything would be expressive equally, indeterminately, and universally. The flower in the crannied wall would express the same thing as the bust of Caesar or the *Critique of Pure Reason.*" Ibid., 196.

13. "What constitutes the individual expressiveness of . . . things is the circle of thoughts allied to each in a given mind." Ibid.

14. *The Philosophical Review,* XXXIV (May, 1925), 284n.

15. Santayana accepts the functional, analytic, and introspective type of psychology as in William James, but thinks of James mainly as a stimulus for recognition of a sense for the immediate, unexplained, and instant fact of experience and expresses a preference for Hermann Ebbinghaus on technical questions. The work of Gustav Theodor Fechner provides the basis for treating aesthetic value from form. The distinction between looking to understand and looking to see is directly from Schopenhauer. The doctrine of essence was suggested by various representatives of idealism, although Santayana followed none of them explicitly.

16. ". . . reason and the ideal are not active forces nor embodiments of passion at all, but merely a method by which objects of desire are compared in reflection." LR, I, 265. ". . . reason in my philosophy is only a harmony among irrational impulses." MS, 85.

17. "Rationality is nothing but a form, an ideal constitution which experience may more or less embody." LR, III, 8.

18. "Man . . . not only needs plasticity in his habits and pursuits but finds plasticity also in the surrounding world. . . . Life is an equilibrium which is maintained now by accepting modification and now by imposing it." LR, IV, 3.

19. "Wealth is itself expressive of reason for it arises whenever men, instead of doing nothing or beating about casually in the world, take to

gathering fruits of nature which they may have uses for in future, or fostering their growth, or actually contriving their appearance. Such is man's first industrial habit, seen in grazing, agriculture, and mining. Among nature's products are also those of man's own purposeless and imitative activity, results of his idle ingenuity and restlessness. Some of these, like nature's other random creations, may chance to have some utility. They may then become conspicuous to reflection, be strengthened by the relations which they establish in life, and be henceforth called works of human art. They then constitute a second industrial habit and that other sort of riches which is supplied by manufacture." LR, II, 64.

20. "What makes progress possible is that rational action may leave traces in nature, such that nature in consequence furnishes a better basis for the Life of Reason; in other words, progress is art bettering the conditions of existence." LR, IV, 13.

21. "If art is that element in the Life of Reason which consists in modifying its environment the better to attain its end, art may be expected to subserve all parts of the human ideal, to increase man's comfort, knowledge, and delight. And as nature . . . is wont to satisfy these interests together, so art, in seeking to increase that satisfaction, will work simultaneously in every ideal direction." Ibid., 16–17.

22. ". . . the greater and swifter the power that mechanical instruments put in man's hands, the greater will be the occasional temptation that will assail him to put this power to the test. And this is socially and morally an omnipotent power, less to produce than to destroy." DP, 89.

23. "Economic arts in particular . . . deviate in all directions from rational industry, run into the opposite blind alleys of avarice and luxury, and equip militant egotism with instruments for its mad experiments. All this occurs because the motive force in economic labor always remains some offshoot of primitive greed and cupidity. The good to be attained is not seen or imagined; there is at bottom only an indiscriminate impulse to grasp, to keep, and to swallow." Ibid., 93.

24. "Aesthetic sensibility colors every thought, qualifies every allegiance, and modifies every product of human labor." LR, IV, 183. ". . . the pleasures of perception are not beauties, if they are attached to nothing with a right of citizenship in the natural or in the moral world." OS, 39.

25. *The Philosophical Review*, XIII, no. 3 (May, 1904), 320–27. Reprinted in OS, 30–40.

26. "Understanding, as we have defined it, is itself a kind of imagination." IPR, 7.

27. "Understanding . . . is . . . an imagination prophetic of experience, a spontaneity of thought by which the science of perception is turned into the art of life." Ibid., 7–8.

28. "Imagination is an irresponsible principle; its rightness is an inward rightness, and everything in the real world may turn out to be disposed otherwise than as it would wish." Ibid., 10.

29. "The imagination, even when its premonitions are not wholly justified by subsequent experience, has . . . a noble role to play in the life of man. Without it his thoughts would be not only far too narrow to represent, although it were symbolically, the greatness of the universe, but far too narrow even to render the scope of his own life and the conditions of his practical welfare." Ibid., 8.

30. Therefore, man's mental relation to his environment is a dream composed of the symbols supplied by the imagination. For Santayana man is a dreaming animal.

31. "Religion and poetry are identical in essence, and differ merely in the way in which they are attached to practical affairs. Poetry is called religion when it intervenes in life, and religion, when it merely supervenes upon life, is seen to be nothing but poetry." IPR, v.

32. J. S. Mill, *Three Essays on Religion* (New York, 1884), p. 103, quoted by G. W. Howgate, *George Santayana* (Philadelphia, 1938).

33. Cf. W. James, *The Principles of Psychology* (New York, 1950), II, 68–75.

34. In retrospect Santayana tempered his insistence on a moral end in poetry: "So anxious was I, when younger, to find some rational justification for poetry and religion, and to show that their magic was significant of true facts, that I insisted too much as I now think, on the need of relevance to fact even in poetry. . . . I maintained that the noblest poetry also must express the moral burden of life and must be rich in wisdom. Age has made me less exacting and I can now find quite sufficient perfection in poetry, like that of the Chinese and Arabians, without much philosophic scope, in mere grace and feeling and music and cloud-castles and frolic." SELS, 254.

35. But ". . . the function of poetry is not to convey information, not even to transmit the attitude of one mind to another, but rather to arouse in each a clear and more poignant view of its experience, longings, and destiny." RB, 111. "Poetry and religion discerned life in those very places in which sense and understanding perceived body." LR, I, 128.

36. "To object to theory in poetry would be like objecting to words there; for words, too, are symbols without the sensuous character of the things they stand for; and yet it is only by the net of new connections which words throw over things . . . that poetry arises at all. Poetry . . . is itself a theoretic vision of things at arm's length." TPP, 124.

37. "In philosophy itself investigation and reasoning are only preparatory and servile parts. . . . They terminate in insight, or what in the noblest sense of the word may be called *theory*—a steady contem-

plation of all things in their order and worth. Such contemplation is imaginative. . . . A philosopher who attains it is, for the moment, a poet, and a poet who turns his practised and passionate imagination on the order of all things, or on anything in the light of the whole, is for that moment a philosopher." Ibid., 10–11 (Santayana's italics).

38. *The Harvard Monthly*, X (May, 1890), 85–92.

Stevens on Imagination— The Point of Departure

JOSEPH N. RIDDEL
STATE UNIVERSITY OF NEW YORK AT BUFFALO

For Frederick J. Hoffman (1909–1967)

> The poet finds that as between these two sources: the imagination and reality, the imagination is false, whatever else may be said of it, and reality is true.

> If imagination is the faculty by which we import the unreal into what is real, its value is the value of the way of thinking by which we project the idea of God into the idea of man.

I

IN THE BEGINNING, Stevens discovered, was the world, the real, things as they are; and later came mind, the unreal. And yet, once mind was, the real could never again be itself.[1] In the human beginning, then, was the word. For only mind, the unreal, can name and thus conceive beginnings and the order and direction they imply. Only mind can speak of history and form, because mind has created history and form as the space of its being. The unreal is the necessity of the real, and its center. It is also the point from which the self begins, and therefore a point (unlike the center of the Romantic self)[2] where the self is nothingness. The imagination is false and unreal, because it too is at the center of the self. But it is a nothingness that is being, or at least the potentiality of being. The real, though true, cannot ultimately be material, for although materiality has its being, it is lacking a noetic center and thus it lacks, in Heidegger's term, fundamental Being. The real, then, must be human, and to be human it must be endowed with the unreal: the poet must discover the "unreal of what is real" (CP, 313); but he must also "create his unreal out of what is real" (NA, 58).[3]

Stevens' "theory of poetry," which he desired to be a "theory of life" (CP, 486), lies in his acts of poetry, the "act" of importing the unreal into the real. His theory of imagination presumes that the imagination is self-generative, an energy of being. We may call it "faculty," after the fact; but what we name as "faculty" we know only in its forms. Imagination is potentiality incarnating itself in the "world" of the poem. Unless it incarnates itself (in language, in the sound of words, in the "act of the mind"), it fails of being. It must be *in the world* by creating its own "world." It incarnates itself as "act," its being manifest in a "world of words . . . / In which nothing solid is its solid self" (CP, 345), where "Real and unreal are two in one" (CP, 485). The imagination, or that which we reflect on and nominate as the central human power, is at once our nothingness and the source of our being. It is a *point* at which our self begins, and like God, a mystery that must be reified and celebrated. It is truly the "subject of the poem" (CP, 176) in that it is what the poem is constantly bringing to form and therefore celebrating as essential (that is, the source of) being: the point "at the root of the tongue" (CP, 313).

The imagination, for Stevens, is "beginning." It is youth, and thus "ignorance." Like youth it is the potentiality of a future; and like ignorance it embraces the universal present. As Hillis Miller has suggested,[4] the birth of Stevens' imagination lies in the moment of the "annihilation" of the gods, in the moment following upon an utter skepticism, a "mortal no" which denied the transcendent self, yet brought happily to birth a "passion for yes" (CP, 320). In that moment occurred the "imagination's new beginning" (CP, 320), the discovery that even as nothingness, the imagination's being endured. It became human. Indeed, its destiny, its essence, like "a child asleep in its own life" (OP, 104, 106), is to become human:

> To see the gods dispelled in mid-air and dissolve like clouds is one of the great human experiences. It is not as if they had gone over the horizon to disappear for a time; nor as if they had been overcome by other gods of greater power and profounder knowledge. It is simply that they came to nothing. Since we have always shared all things with them and have always had a part of their

> strength and, certainly, all of their knowledge, we shared likewise this experience of annihilation. It was their annihilation, not ours, and yet it left us feeling that in a measure, we, too, had been annihilated. It left us feeling dispossessed and alone in a solitude, like children without parents, in a home that seemed deserted, in which the amical rooms and halls had taken on a look of hardness and emptiness. What was most extraordinary is that they left no momentoes behind, no thrones, no mystic rings, no texts either of the soil or of the soul. It was as if they had never inhabited the earth. There was no crying out for their return. They were not forgotten because they had been a part of the glory of the earth. At the same time, no man ever muttered a petition in his heart for the restoration of those unreal shapes. There was always in every man the increasingly human self, which instead of remaining the observer, the non-participant, the delinquent, became constantly more and more all there was or so it seemed; and whether it was so or merely seemed so still left it for him to resolve life and the world in his own terms. [OP, 206–7]

Within this passage is nearly the whole range of Stevens' maneuvers: the loss of a "full" world that is a prelude to human freedom; the "as if"[5] world of fiction which has replaced the incarnate gods; the metaphors of dislocation, hollowing out, and flattening of intersubjective space, those traditional "homes" of nostalgia we lived in before we became fully human or self-conscious and thus alone;[6] the poverty of the space in which we dwell, yet the potentiality for filling it with our own being; and finally, the nontragic, even comic, acceptance of the role of orphaned self, the freedom of the child gained out of the death of the parents. The gods are part of us because, in the end, we recognize them as the projections of our self as center, but in their death, wherein we too become unreal, we affirm ourselves as creator and center, both father and child, dreamer of our past and "maker" of our "world" (CP, 129). We thus regain our freedom or potentiality to be, to change, a freedom denied in the closed and changeless forms of the gods.

This end, indeed, lies in Stevens' beginning. "Sunday Morning," among the earliest of Stevens' mature verse, demands that one seize the day by seizing one's centrality in it. The poem's third stanza is a condensed "history" of the birth and the death of the gods, and the new beginnings of the self:

> Jove in the clouds had his inhuman birth.
> No mother suckled him, no sweet land gave
> Large-mannered motions to his mythy mind.

He moved among us, as a muttering king,
Magnificent, would move among his hinds,
Until our blood, commingling, virginal,
With heaven, brought such requital to desire
The very hinds discerned it, in a star.
Shall our blood fail? Or shall it come to be
The blood of paradise that we shall know?
The sky will be much friendlier then than now,
A part of labor and a part of pain,
And next in glory to enduring love,
Not this dividing and indifferent blue. [CP, 67–68]

"Sunday Morning" is a poem of Cartesian opposites: of man-woman; man-God; self-world; time-eternity; motion-permanence; light-dark; life-death. And yet it is a poem of partial resolutions, aggressively deliberate choices. The denial of infinite space returns to the self an intimate space. The horizons of color become, at least for the speaker, both a delight and a solace for the transcendence that is rejected—for the nothingness which the metaphors of transcendence and permanence cannot satisfactorily manifest. Eternity as knowable in words is a fixed image, visual and static; eternity at the end of time is silence at the end of sound, or blackness into which color shades. Time is a whirl of motion, sound, color, all measured against its inevitable opposite. In terms of the third stanza, to arrive at the self as center, after the old shapes have failed and been annihilated, is to find oneself in a definitely limited space, but a space made intimate in its mortal texture. It is a space of precise sensations, of particular images, a space into which one can expand without the anxiety of needing more. But more significantly, it is a space where lines shade into lines, sounds into other sounds, and each distinct thing lives in change flowing toward its opposite, depending on that opposite and on transience for its identity. Yet for the historical conscience, one desiring more, it is a horizon that divides, a mockery of permanence. The lady's desire for "imperishable bliss" is a nostalgia for the gods. To accept their annihilation, to make "Divinity . . . live within herself," is to accept the self as nothingness, seeking to harmonize itself with the ceaseless flux. It is also to accept the identity of the self with the darkness and silence, the end as well as the beginning.

As the previous long quotation suggests, Stevens does not think of this annihilation of the gods and the consequent dislocation of self as fixed in any specific historical time. It took place in the fall into self-consciousness ("Adam/ In Eden was the father of Descartes," CP, 383) but its particular relevance for modern man is that it has not provoked the old "nostalgias" (see CP, 321—the "nostalgias" is a name for old types or figures now dissolved into an emotion of loss or absence). That is, it has not thrust him toward new paradises but has moved him ever nearer to the center of himself: "And Eve made air the mirror of herself" (CP, 383). Consequently it has posed ever-increasing existential questions (even ones of pleasure) as the self is narrowed to a point, the center which might be anywhere and hence nowhere. The annihilation of the gods is the annihilation of the Ideal, of the still-point, leaving man not so much without identity as without place.[7] It has left him in a world that flows and changes, in which things are only what they are (real) and he is only what he is (unreal). His place is only relative to the things which move about him or amid which he moves; thus reality becomes his "inescapable and ever-present difficulty and inamorata" (OP, 241), the objective place which the imagination grasps in order to "realize" itself as subject.

That place, however, is never finally fixed, and it is always changing. Like the flow of words and sounds in a poem, it is marked by the silent interspaces. The place is not so much the location for an "act of the mind" as it is medium of the act. Setting words in motion (or sounds in circulation) within a controlled frame is Stevens' mode of catching the place of the self in its duration. "The Pleasures of Merely Circulating" (CP, 149) insists on a self that can enjoy pleasure; the contingency of motion, like the nonsense of words or sounds circulating, nonetheless implies a center where pleasure *is*. "It Must Change" is the central term of his poetic triad; and the change of abstractions ("It Must [also] Be Abstract") is that they flow in a controlled and framed space (linguistic space, artistic space) from a beginning toward some end that is not defined but nonetheless premised. The beginning and end may well be the same point, closing a circle which confirms a self at its center. A beginning, then, a point of departure, is necessary to every motion; a beginning is a search toward form, a movement toward filling out some abstraction.[8] The annihilation of the gods may have left the self an orphan in an emptied house, but it nonetheless left the space of the house to be refurnished.

At the center of the self is a point—what Georges Poulet calls the "point of departure"[9]—where the creation of a new form, or self, begins. For modern man, who lives as Poulet says in moments of time without coherent past or present and thus must be the architect of both his moment and his future, this point is at once his identity and his nothingness. To discover this point Stevens must rid himself of all phantoms and nostalgias, all parents, and thus accept the burden of a continuous creation that has no one place of beginning and no final end, only new beginnings. Stevens' poetry, from first to last, is a living presence of those beginnings, those points of departure and the projected possibilities they imply: "men make themselves their speech" (CP, 345). The point of departure, Stevens' unreal imagination, is the point of remotest interiority from which he launches his act toward the world, in an effort to make sure that the "sky will be much friendlier *then* than now" (my italics). Only in looking back, from the middle of the journey or the process of the act of the mind, does he see that point of departure, and in naming it "imagination" make it the "subject of the poem." Only in that act does he make the multiple and separate durations of his various acts continuous, thus creating a "time" from the "place" that his imagination locates itself in. The imagination names itself when it names the world.[10]

II

Stevens' eagerness in his prose to define the imagination (as value) has detracted somewhat from the fact that his poetry is more concerned with nominating than defining. His imagination is essentially nominal, not essential, for reasons previously adduced: because Stevens had to forfeit the kinds of transcendental "ground" from which a theory of a "shaping spirit" (literally) depends. More than once in his prose he attempts to distinguish between two kinds of romanticism: the idealistic and the experiential; the vatic and the human; the traditional and the modern; the false and the true (see NA, 61, 138). In every instance he opts for the latter, because the former is "obsolete." The myths and mystique of idealistic thought, which allowed it to deal with the world's dualism and contrariety as resolvable outside (before or beyond) experience and illusion, and hence as ultimately resolvable within the visions of the poet as seer, are no longer possible. But of course Stevens could only reject the old definitions; his own were, like all definitions, products of the imagination—metaphorical, "as if," fictional—and they only proved the self-sustaining nature of an unreality that could not be defined because it could not be fixed. The imagination escaped being fixed in essentiality because it was as mysterious as the life it initiated—as mysterious and as central as any "point of departure."

Stevens' rejection of Plato's metaphorical "idea" of the bipartite soul, in "The Noble Rider and the Sound of Words," as well as his deliberate rejection of Coleridgean theory ("a man who may be said to have been defining poetry all his life in definitions that are valid enough but which no longer impress us primarily by their validity," NA, 41)—these are rejections of definition itself. To be defined, he said of "nobility," is to be "fixed and it must not be fixed" because nobility, like an "external thing," "resolves itself into an enormous number of vibrations, movements, changes" (NA, 34). Platonic nobility took its absolute value from the Ideal. Modern nobility is relative, to person, place, and act; it *must* change, unlike the many rigid statues, representing a willed permanence, of Stevens' poems and prose.

It is no wonder then that Stevens' prose bemuses those looking for definitions, or that one can quote the poetry and prose against each other. Stevens shifts his allegiances constantly from imagination to reality and back again, as he admitted to one critic (L, 710, 747). These shifts are the "vibrations" of the subject becoming object. But the self is neither subject nor object. It *is* in the "vibrations, movements, changes" between two polarities that are at best hypothetical, or better fictional. And just as the vibrations and changes are caught in a form, like the "fluent mundo" in the "crystal" (CP, 407), they point both before and beyond themselves; so that the ultimate crystal, or supreme fiction, toward which they point suggests that the point reached is only a beginning, a "lesser poem" to some "essential poem" (CP, 440). For Stevens we "live beyond ourselves in air" (CP, 518) because we live in imagination, the unreal; yet the imagination seeks its ultimate shape within the shapes of the world and its words. The imagination thus lives off the annihilation of its old shapes; it lives in its negations.

Stevens, or his poetic voice, can state in a late poem that "We say God and the imagination are one" (CP, 524), a line that reverberates in its context as both direct assertion and tentative discovery. In the first place, saying it, it becomes so. God is a product of the imagination and hence a projection of it, the ultimate being we conceive to be our origin and thus not a shape at all. And the "We say" is an essential qualification, not ironic as some critics have argued, because in the saying we have named our "interior paramour," our point of departure that looks both back and forward at some "central mind." Naming it, it is; yet even the saying is tentative, though "enough." In the saying, we "project the idea of God into the idea of man" (NA, 150). I will return to this operative saying-act in Stevens' last poems; for now it is only necessary to keep it in mind when dealing with his evocations of a starting point that is indefinable but not unnamable. In the end, even the "absence of the imagination had/ Itself to be imagined" (CP, 503).

Being unreal, "the imagination never brings anything into the world but . . . on the contrary, like the personality of the poet in the act of creating, it is no more than a *process*, and desiring with all the power of our desire not to write falsely, do we not begin to think of the *possibility* that poetry is only reality, after all, and that poetic truth is a factual truth . . . ? . . . In consequence, when men, baffled by philosophic truth, turn to poetic truth, they return to their *starting-point,* they return to fact, not, it ought to be clear, to bare fact . . . but to fact *possibly* beyond their perception in the first instance and outside the normal range of their sensibility" (NA, 59–60, my italics). The "starting-point" is like the "rock" of reality, the "fact" which marries subject and object. This "fact" lies both before and after the act of the mind and is its origin and end, the imagination and the poem. The act itself, or "process," then becomes the "incandescence" of that point and a commentary on it.

So long as we see the poem and its language as a meditation on the "starting-point," the point is an incandescent past vibrating toward a transcendent future. But if we hear the silences passing between sounds, and thus the intersections of the unreal and the real, we experience the ever-presence of the point, where mystery informs fact, in the acts of the mind. There is no mystery in Stevens' world without fact; no interiority without exteriority; no past or future without present; no sounds of music without the mysterious nothingness of silence; and yet no "giant" without the "murderous alphabet" (CP, 179). There is no point of departure without the subsequent temporal position or positions (those points where the act of the mind comes to form) from which we reflect simultaneously upon our origins, our departure, our movement, and our prospective end. In singing "a tune beyond us as we are" (CP, 167), we sing of birth and death and of the poem. We sing in order to be.

For Stevens, then, the imagination and poetry had to be the "subject of the poem," a point from which the human issues and to which it returns (CP, 176). (One cannot help thinking of "subject" here in at least two of its meanings.) It is not too much of an oversimplification to say that Stevens' poetic search from first to last was for that point from which he and his words were constantly issuing and to which they sought to return. "Sunday Morning" was the discovery of the urgency of that starting-point, precisely because all other centers had been lost. The starting-point is not so much a past or a power to be discovered as a mode of being to be reconstituted: as one makes the self a center when the gods are annihilated, as "Hoon" creates a "Palaz" to encompass his own emptiness and make his ceremonies real (CP, 65). Near the end of his life Stevens would confirm it as the "rock," the "starting point of the human and the end"; that "starting point" is the "mind," the mind at its innermost moment, at one with body and the physical world, "point A." Yet it is, this "rock," the "gray particular of man's life," the "ground" which he must cover or "cure" with his "leaves" (CP, 525–28) that proclaim its ongoing vitality. At each point, "point A" or "B," the self "begins again." Between these early and late metaphors lie Stevens' incessant voyagings (east-west; north-south; sun-moon; Alpha-Omega), his "never-ending meditation," in short, his open-ended poems that are so much about the world because they are about his "makings" and unmakings of it. Between the two are the poem's (and the poet's) life, the work of the orphaned imagination adducing itself as origin and end, and thus filling up the space between the A and Z of reality with its unreal:

> Reality is the beginning not the end,
> Naked Alpha, not the hierophant Omega,
> Of dense investiture, with luminous vassals.
>
> It is the infant A standing on infant legs,
> Not twisted, stooping, polymathic Z,
> He that kneels always on the edge of space. . . . [CP, 469]

The dominant figures of Stevens' last poems, the "child asleep in its own life" and the old men seeking their fathers, come close to marrying Alpha and Omega in the mysterious revelation the poet had always sought.[11] Certainly this last poetry is, by virtue of its purity and control, a poetry of nearly completed space, a poetry of the "solitary home" (CP, 512), which, like the room where Santayana lies dying (CP, 508), has been refurnished in its minimum necessities and not of "dense investiture." In contrast to earlier opulence, it is ascetic, like a "sarcophagus" containing an "owl" (CP, 431). But then, it is not less elegant than Crispin's "cabin," only more ceremonious and appropriate for its occasion. It is a room of things of this world bathed in the "total grandeur at the end." The broader similarities of the two, Crispin's "cabin" and the "solitary home," might be a proper starting-point for examining the continuity of Stevens' response to the role he inherited when the gods were annihilated.

III

"It is one of the peculiarities of the imagination," Stevens writes in a well-known passage, "that it is always at the end of an era. What happens is that it is always attaching itself to a new reality, and adhering to it. It is not that there is a new imagination but that there is a new reality" (NA, 22). He is talking about the response of imagination to the "pressure of reality," the modern violence which he speaks of elsewhere, taking his phrase from Simone Weil, as "decreation": "Modern reality is a reality of decreation, in which our revelations are not the revelations of belief, but the precious portents of our own powers. The greatest truth we could hope to discover . . . is that man's truth is the final resolution of everything" (NA, 175). Stevens' special emphasis on "decreation," the "making pass from the created to the uncreated," is illuminated by a preceding remark in which he quotes Paul Klee on the artist's need to establish himself " 'there where the organic center of all movement in time and space—which he [Klee] calls the mind or heart of creation—determines every function' " (NA, 174). This is surely a point (not a still-point) of departure; decreation is for Stevens not so much the destructive act of a nihilistic age as the inevitable first gesture of the creative or initiating act—the new beginning.[12] It is the existential moment of rupture and renewal, where the new form emerges out of the death of the old: as stated in a late poem, the phrase "Farewell to an idea" is the transitional beginning of three of its parts, the renewed flashings of "The Auroras of Autumn" (CP, 411). The point of departure for the modern poet (it is significant that in this essay on the relations between poetry and painting Stevens is speaking of the modern as opposed to the traditional artist) is not in some remote past, or from some traditional a priori. It is a point continuously present, interior. The mind creates the gods, and the mind annihilates them. The old gods, the ancient forms, are the essential sacrifices to the life of the imagination.

"The Comedian as the Letter C" is the *summa* poem of *Harmonium*, itself a volume of the poet's middle years. But *Harmonium* is close enough to youth for Stevens to remember the innocence of his starting point, so that he is less preoccupied with mythologizing its loss than in exploring the poverty of its gradual disappearance. In the 1940s, as he passed sixty, Stevens would invariably return to the imagination's youth —to the "figure" of the "youth as virile poet"—just as in his very last years the figure would lose its form to become the essential point: "a blind thing fumbling for its form" (OP, 104). For the imagination as "virile youth" is the "imagination without intelligence," without memory: "still half-beast and somehow more than human, a kind of sister to the Minotaur. This younger figure is the intelligence that endures. It is the imagination of the son still bearing the antique imagination of the father. It is the clear intelligence of the young man still bearing the burden of the obscurities of the intelligence of the old" (NA, 52–53). This youth is the emergence of the "yes" after the "final no," a response upon which the "future world depends" (CP, 247); it is the "passion for yes" that survives the "mortal no" (CP, 320). And its "yes" is manifest in new "shapes" which are related to the old as the son's imagination to the father's. But these poems, like their complementary prose, have arrived at a point so distant from the self's origin that they must mythologize the original point by evoking its eternal youth, a "kind of sister to the Minotaur," within a tradition of types. Similarly, they must evoke a physical world and exhort one to his life there, whereas the earlier poems were more immediate engagements of the self's rapid departure from that ground.

The urgency of establishing that point is never more apparent than in "Le Monocle de Mon Oncle" (CP, 13–18), that comic vision of a man "at forty" who must affirm without nostalgia that there is "a substance in us that prevails." "Le Monocle" is a poem of changes and metamorphoses: on time receding from youth, once thought to be permanent, and on the necessity for achieving a new illusion of permanence. From the perspective in which the avuncular irony now speaks, change has a meaning only when seen to merge toward some "basic slate," some "one," not a beginning but an end. Yet that is no certain answer. "The honey of heaven may or may not come,/ But that of earth both comes and goes at once." How then to grasp a substance that prevails yet comes and goes? How to grasp an "ancient aspect touching a new mind"? The lover ages into the poet, the parabolist in search of "the origin and course/ Of love." It is an "origin" that impinges on his present. Thus his poems become the incarnate moment of change and form ("verses wild with motion, full of din"), in which is grasped a new beginning that nevertheless incorporates the old one, including the sexual origins that were his earlier acts of initiation. "Le Monocle" anticipates the later poems, in which poetry becomes its own subject because the subject is always the same: the "origin and course/ Of love," the self seeking itself in the other.

In this perspective "The Comedian" (CP, 27–46) takes on its autobiographical significance as a parable of the modern poet, whose Americanness is the condition of his modernism. The poem begins in a "World without Imagination" and courses a journey of the "imagination's new beginning." That the new beginning implies a reduction of self and a reorientation of the starting-point suggests one dimension of the parable. That it ends in Crispin's humble "cabin," the space of his own domesticated self and the true point of origin of his new vocation, indicates yet another. The journey from east to west and from south to north offers two other coordinates, which make the parable at once subjective and universal. For Crispin is the antecedent of imagination, the comedic self whose identity lies in the "part" (but necessary part) he plays. Undone, he has to improvise a new self, and in doing so, find a new place. The east-west, south-north movements in the poem suggest respectively the movements of time (the incessant westwarding of history that made American poets so self-conscious of being either the last link in a cycle or a new beginning for one) and of the self (from the primary sensuousness of youth to the primary intellect of maturity). "The Comedian," of course, arrives at only a relative north, the provincial Carolinas of a middle age. And his westward course, as James Baird suggests,[13] proves only that wherever men go, the imagination only repeats its role and responsibility: to abstract a living (intersubjective) space, to make new colonies not so much in the image of the old as in a continuum with them. History, as Levi-Strauss would put it, is both diachronic and synchronic. The place of Crispin's beginning, a "World without Imagination," is in a world of words which have lost touch with things, and hence in an elegance of sound that has no "ground." He is soon "at sea," with a language which no longer refers to a point of origin. His departure from Bordeaux, in other words, is from a point already denied—an *in medias res* beginning which, as Edward Said claims, is "a convention that allows a beginning to pretend that it is not one."[14] "An ancient Crispin was dissolved"—including all the established roles (from Saint Crispin the patron of travelers to his multiple roles in Italian and French comedy). And so his new beginning is a movement away from nothing and from the fatherland. His beginning, in other words, is born out of the negation of his previous role, which he must reconstitute on a new ground. It is as inevitable as history, and it demands a total regrounding of language. Not only does Crispin move from Bordeaux through Yucatan to the Carolinas (and thus from the quintessence of western aesthetic thought through a new exoticism to a place where the new idiom, restoring word to thing, is emerging in his acts toward that world), he moves historically from a closed or structured culture to an emerging one, from an end to a beginning. The exotic middle of the voyage provides a revealing interlude, in which the primitive strategy to avoid formlessness (and hence the direct question of origins) is to retreat into set rituals (sonnets which, like myths, structuralize change), another form of colony-making. The "cathedral" which Crispin rejects is the closed space of all myth. (Recall Stevens' insistence that he had written an anti-mythological poem, L, 778.)

The move to Carolina (an *approach*, one notes) is like a fluctuation between two elements (sun and moon; origin and image; object and subject), a movement of incessant new beginnings which composes a space that differs from Bordeaux and Yucatan only in its potential open-endedness, its commitment to change, its youthfulness if you will. Yet it is also a circular movement. Crispin's new colony demands its architecture of composed or aesthetic space (and hence is closed, a cabin), yet indicates that origins are what one is constantly leaving (and hence is open, capable of increase). Thus Crispin's "idea" of a colony, a "new" or "matinal continent," includes all the paradoxes of beginnings. He dreams empires and creates a colony; dreams "Loquacious columns by the ructive sea" but builds a cabin instead. In short, the space Crispin composes is the space of a beginning—a "nice shady home" that is not final as home might be (say, the "solitary home" Stevens seeks in his last poems) but open, social, and tentative as a beginning must be.

Crispin's domestication, his "return to social nature," is the beginning of himself as creative man. He produces four daughters with curls (definite and particular) rather than "diviner young." He is "clipped," yes, in that he discovers his beginning is only a repetition of other beginnings, his colony no more than the repetition of man's creative impulse itself, and not a true discovery. He is returned to the ground, made self-consciously aware that it is beginnings, not ends, questions and not answers, which compel the imagination. Crispin discovers that all "relations" (relatings? relationships?) are "clipped" (ended? cultivated?) and that they must have their end, as opposed to their consummation.

But implicit in Crispin's "Disguised pronunciamento" (as implicit as the "sure" answers of his daughters' questionings) are the beginnings which have led to that end and to new beginnings: the "Seraphic proclamations of the pure/ Delivered with a deluging onwardness." Crispin discovers his new beginning in social nature, and in the sexuality of his creative act; but his act has its economic exactions, the price he pays for cultivating, like Candide, his own garden. To affirm that "his soil is man's intelligence," Crispin has had to reject his earlier egocentrism, and hence commit himself to history and its price. He has had to locate the imagination in time then, and not in the ideal: in change and not in the "lex" and "principium"; in beginnings and not ends. For the imagination is not "lex," it is time itself, time as the initiating and protean impulse.

Stevens has not only returned the imagination to earth, he has established in the profuse elegancies of the poem its mortal colorations and sounds, the unreal of what is real. In defining Crispin's proper domain, as "magister of a single room," Stevens defined the limitations, and the beginning, of the modern imagination: that minimum of sound in the profundum of silences. Like Henri Focillon, an aesthetician whose work he came later to know, admire, and quote (NA, 46), Stevens discovers the "life of forms" in the internal urgency of the "relation": of relating, telling, making poems, and thus, in Jean Wahl's phrase, naming himself. Form is open, protean, always striving to transcend the limitations of its objectivity. The order Crispin arrives at, and his consequent reduction, gives him a precise identity—a life within an identifiable structure—and thus a unique and human imagination rather than a cosmic one. The reduction has its price; identity is its own exchequer. But more importantly, it always points beyond itself to a future identity, and thus anticipates its own negation, its own clipping. Such is the new "starting-point" Stevens had arrived at in *Harmonium.*

IV

If Crispin had to forfeit his "cloudy drift" or "mental moonlight" for a colony without definite "lex" and "principium," this reduction to the "prose" of a "still new continent" confronted him with the futility of dreaming beyond the moment and thus denying the moment. His "prolegomena" is "full of the caprice, inscribed/ Commingled souvenirs and prophecies." His planned colony, with himself as generative center, accepts its discrete horizons: an "island hemisphere." He forfeits the "hapless words" which are "counterfeits" of time past and time future, the "romance" that had driven him to his old "wanderings." "Preferring text to gloss," he establishes himself in the moment of immediacy, which is no less a solipsistic moment. In his "matinal continent" he finds himself not at the end but at the beginning, in a world that precedes the fully realized self. He finds himself, that is, at the point of his own nothingness. The "cabin" he builds upon that ground is a new space of human, not divine, presence. In this space questions and not answers are the mode of reality: a world in which "beginning with green brag,/ Concluding fadedly" is not so much "profitless" as necessary. The cabin is a "beginning," in the poverty of self; he engenders his own end, becomes literally the father who must be clipped.

The questions posed by Crispin's fatalism suggest that if one's end is in his beginning, perhaps the whole effort is profitless. The consequences for the man of imagination who made the choice of "Sunday Morning" come home most forcefully in a poem which celebrates beginnings that anticipate only their own exhaustion, or, like "Sea Surface Full of Clouds," evince an endless series of engagements of imagination and reality, beginning and end, without hope of resolution. The choice of "Sunday Morning" committed the self to its own nothingness: "Death is the mother of beauty." It compelled the imagination toward the ground of incessant flux, no less a threat for its being vital and substantial. Offering the imagination a place, it affirms the imagination's unreality. Just as the "listener" of "The Snow Man" (CP, 9) becomes "nothing himself" at the perfect moment of his knowing and "beholds/ Nothing that is not there and the nothing that is," so Crispin's colony is defined by its place and not by his initiative. Crispin concludes "benignly," at the point where his social nature begins.

Stevens' poetry of the thirties, following a half-decade's silence after *Harmonium*, inscribes another metaphor of the journey from south to north. It is a journey of the self, a reorientation of the imagination in terms of the discovery of Crispin that "his soil is man's intelligence." The voyage north reestablishes the imagination at the edge of things and at the center of "mobs of men" (CP, 122). The imagination has survived the dense sensuousness of the purely physical only to fall into the cold abstraction of an impoverished social world. Crispin's colony becomes masses of men; Carolina becomes a nearly polar north; his turnip the object, as in "Owl's Clover," of hungry men who desire a "duck for dinner."

Stevens' poetry of the thirties is committed to the challenges history poses to the imagination, and thus reasserts, in an anti-romantic time, the privileges of human subjectivity, of the self as center. Yet he must admit the imagination's unreality, its essential falseness. The "romantic must never remain" (CP, 120) and neither can the gods. The solitary self, like "Hoon" who "found all form and order in solitude" (CP, 121), is vanquished. The imagination becomes in its nothingness an irrelevancy to the mass, to the overwhelming necessity of the material. The subjective or fictional does not satisfy hungry stomachs, the "modes of desire." But in the very moment desire becomes most unappeasable, and the "epic of disbelief" accentuates the absence of the other, the self discovers a belief beyond belief, the greater hunger of the self's nothingness. Absence cries out for new "shapes" and "forms," "Requiring order beyond their speech." It is the cry of an "immense suppression" demanding freedom (CP, 122). The imagination is reborn in the moment of its annihilation, a "Will" to be that arises at the ultimate point of nothingness. It is the urgency of a "Mozart, 1935" to "Be thou, be thou/ The voice of angry fear" and thus to be (CP, 132); or it is the imagination of "Owl's Clover" that is equated with the "night" (OP, 71) and the "subman under all/ The rest, to whom in the end the rest return" (OP, 66).

The self is driven to the ultimate "point" where its own nothingness threatens the existence of the other. Its very absence initiates an action. The Mozart of 1935 begins to play again: "the voice that is in us makes a true response" (CP, 138). And the imagination takes on a "shape" without shape, becomes a point of departure from which a new order is projected. And thus out of its own nothingness the imagination is renewed. It can be named, can name itself. And the nothingness of self begins to fill up again:

> If ever the search for a tranquil belief should end,
> The future might stop emerging out of the past,
> Out of what is full of us; yet the search
> And the future emerging out of us seem to be one. [CP, 151]

The future may only be fiction, and like poetry a "finikin thing of air" (CP, 155), but false or not, it affirms the reality of imagination as point of departure. "Music is not yet written but is to be" (CP, 158). I imagine, therefore I will be, because the imagination points me beyond myself: "one of the motives in writing is renewal" (OP, 220). This remark, from an essay written to introduce a reading of part of "Owl's Clover," is followed somewhat later by an expansive passage on the "incessant desire for freedom in literature" as a "desire for freedom in life" (OP, 227) and hence for the "mysterious" which bathes being. And Stevens defines this mystery as an "unwritten rhetoric" that embraces his language, a rhetoric into which the effects of the written and spoken language are always shading. It is this "unknown" (OP, 228) into which the poet is always pushing; and it is this unknown which is the imagination's origin and end.

"Owl's Clover" rediscovered the nothingness of imagination as a point below and before shapes: as the night which is the origin of day, the death that precedes and follows life and thus is intrinsic to it, as change. The imagination, or its shape in poetry, thus becomes the "subject of the poem" in "The Man with the Blue Guitar," in the very sense that any act of life is definable as an act because it exists between a point of initiation and a culmination. The girl's song at Key West emerges as an order all its own, from the background roar of the sea, and descends to its own conclusion, forming a momentary whole, a "world" of which she is the "maker." The poet, observing, notes that it is the imagination he has literally seen. The imagination is namable in its arc, in the space of its illuminations which is the poem or "song." This fictive "arranging, deepening, enchanting," recognized for its falsity, is nonetheless real, our exploration of "our origins" (CP, 130). Like so many other makings of space, artistic and thus subjective space, the "world" of the girl's song is a composing of the self as imagination—as its own origin.

"The Man with the Blue Guitar" is the central poem in Stevens' rediscovery of his origins, in terms of the commitments and clippings of *Harmonium.* Its improvisational form, its circular yet disjunctive movement, the incompleteness of the parts and of the whole—these qualities of structure are revealing manifestations of the imagination imagining itself in a series of self-inventions. The self-reflexive form of "Blue Guitar," with its openendedness, is a triumph of a belief beyond belief, of an act sustaining itself. Like "Comedian," yet without the pseudo-narrative, the poem begins spontaneously without formal beginning, an improvisation that presumes a norm to improvise upon. And indeed this illusion of the beginning as continuation is essential discovery. The sounds of the guitar emerge from a silence without which the sounds would be immeasurable, from a nothingness without which consciousness would have no coordinates, no rhythm and texture. The beginning of "Blue Guitar" presumes an eternal "now," the now of the mind's act (of consciousness). But it is an immediacy which is known from the midst of time, reflectively and thus reflexively. The act of imagination must have a beginning and end, as the arbitrary sections have their beginnings and endings. Indeed, duration is marked by this succession of renewals, in one sense a repeated cycle, synchronic like the seasons. In yet another sense, it is a diachronic flow from past toward future. Stevens must maintain both these senses of time lest the imagination get lost in cosmic repetitions and be subsumed by its own dreams of self-transcendence.

The sixth poem of "Blue Guitar" is a good example of its composed moments of consciousness, the space or interval of the imagination giving itself shape in "tune" or time. The passage follows the famous imperative of the fifth poem wherein the "audience" insists that "Poetry// Exceeding music must take the place/ Of empty heaven and its hymns

. . . "—must, that is, spatialize the duration of its being, generate the ontological center from which all ontologies derive. The sixth poem goes as follows:

A tune beyond us as we are,
Yet nothing changed by the blue guitar;

Ourselves in the tune as if in space,
Yet nothing changed, except the place

Of things as they are and only the place
As you play them, on the blue guitar,

Placed so, beyond the compass of change,
Perceived in a final atmosphere;

For a moment final, in the way
The thinking of art seems final when

The thinking of god is smokey dew.
The tune is space. The blue guitar

Becomes the place of things as they are,
A composing of senses of the guitar. [CP, 167–68]

The poem emerges literally from the midst of the previous one, continuous with it yet a departure from it. Any close scrutiny would remark the puns on "as if," on "nothing," and "seems"—the fictional imperatives to create a "space" out of time, to compose a flow into a "moment final." The generative act is a "tune" which is converted into a "space," a "place," "beyond the compass of change" in a "final atmosphere," all of which are conditions of "as if" or "play." "Play" is both nominal and verbal; and "place" suggests the verbal act even as it locks that act in position or form. The "tune beyond us" is to be "nothing changed"; the fictional composing of "as if" space is only a transferring of flux into form, a "composing of senses" of the "guitar" or imagination. The imagination's "place" is its form, its fictional being. The nothingness of imagination assumes a shape or "place" when it is named as our source, and thus composed like a tune in space. The ambiguity of the concluding line reveals that the thing composed is the composing thing.

In another poem (the twenty-fifth), the act is imaged as a clown twirling the "world" upon his nose, the act that is a form which dissolves when the act ceases. "Blue Guitar" is a poem that takes its inspiration from a painting, presented as a musical improvisation. The desire for a "point of still" (CP, 181) becomes a desire for a new beginning (not Eliot's still-point), and thus for incessant new beginnings, confirming the imagination not as substance but as "absence" (CP, 176). It is an absence, however, which seeks a shape or manifestation, a space to compose itself and thus to be. "Blue Guitar" ends, literally, by declaring a starting-point, the right to "choose" (CP, 184).

Stevens, as is evident from a late essay, was no little concerned by the fact that to live in the mind was to live in mediacy: "we never see the world except the moment after. Thus we are constantly observing the past" (OP, 190). Our reality is the material become immaterial in the space of our mind's breaches of it: "What we see is not an external world but an image of it and hence an internal world" (OP, 191). Poetry is the "art of perception" and "the problems of perception as they are developed in philosophy resemble similar problems in poetry" (OP, 191). "Just as in space the air envelops objects far away with an ever-deepening blue, so in the dimension of the poetic act the unreal increasingly subtilizes experience and varies appearance. The real is constantly being engulfed in the unreal" (OP, 239–40). But skepticism need not obtain. This is the way things are. They are not unless played upon the blue guitar, and yet when they are, they are engulfed in nothingness, in a fiction: "We live in the center of a physical poetry, a geography that would be intolerable except for the non-geography that exists there—few people realize that they are looking at the world of their own thoughts and the world of their own feelings" (NA, 65–66).

This non-geography is the "space" of subjectivity which, without the structures of the other, would be only space as absence. The extreme "end" of imagination, then, is abstraction, in the sense that space itself, interior or exterior, is abstraction (NA, 139)—because space has its definitions, its beginnings and ends. The very experience of space, of forms and shapes in relation, is evidence of the imagination, whose "end" is abstraction. But its "end," its destined shape, exists, like the gods, to be annihilated. If the imagination is the power by which we "import the unreal into what is real" (NA, 150), it is also the "irrepressible revolutionist" (NA, 152). It not only creates space but, in its restlessness ("It can never be satisfied, the mind, never," CP, 247), it destroys ancient spaces or empties ancestral homes. Yet, if the imagination's ultimate end is abstraction, it can only be defined by change, its incessant renewals. As "revolutionist" it decreates the very abstractions which are its issue: "the mind destroys" (CP, 239). Modern reality is for Stevens a reality of decreation not, as for Simone Weil, because modern history is antithetical to order or system, but because the nature of reality, its generative impulse, denies essence. Stevens' fear of definition in "The Noble Rider and the Sound of Words" is a commitment to change as the vital form of initiation. Thus "It Must Change" is inseparable from "It Must Be Abstract" because they are coordinates of the imagination as "process."

If the world no longer rests, like Claude's, on pillars which support all its forms, it nonetheless must have a center—even if that center is an absence. What emerges from the improvisations of "Blue Guitar," which ends with the affirmation of a future that is open, is the dependence of the real on the unreal. The poet must "Take the place/ Of parents, lewdest of ancestors./ We are conceived in your conceits" (CP, 195). The "never-resting mind" discovers that the "imperfect is our paradise" (CP, 194); this is Stevens' resolution of the unresolvable, a poem which ends in a discovery of the mind's new beginnings. "After the final no there comes a yes/ And on that yes the future world depends" (CP, 247). The "yes" is a kind of incipient "form on the pillow humming while one sleeps" (CP, 247) or a "little owl within" (CP, 246). The intensely self-reflexive poems in Stevens' three volumes of verse after *The Man with the Blue Guitar* insistently name the imagination in its whole range from nothingness to incarnation, from subject to object. In that act of naming the self is affirmed as center, and its "world" as both subject and object: "Every poem is a poem within a poem: the poem of the idea within the poem of the words" (OP, 174). The search for the hero and the search for the central are of a piece. It is a search for the moment of innocence, wherein man might "mate his life with life" (CP, 222). Thus the mind must destroy.

This is the theme of "Man and Bottle" (CP, 238), and its companion piece, "Of Modern Poetry" (CP, 239)—the poem of the mind which cannot act by any old "script" but must assume the role of the *deus absconditus* reappearing as human center. "Of Modern Poetry" begins with a nominalizing phrase. The mind literally names itself as function: "The poem of the mind in the act of finding/ What will suffice." The phrase is both nominal and verbal, but it has no object. And it names that which has no antecedent, no history, except the "souvenir" of an anachronism. The poem's imperative, then, is to improvise its own "lex" and "principium" in the duration of its performance. It ends with another nominal phrase, this one neither verbal nor initiating. Between beginning and end, the "mind" is set in the midst of a number of objects, housed in an aesthetic space (the "theatre") which it composes by setting itself there. The act is the poem itself, "Sounds passing through certain rightnesses," like words flowing on a page, "wholly/ Containing the mind, below which it cannot descend,/ Beyond which it has no will to rise."

Stevens' great long poems of the forties and early fifties—"Notes toward a Supreme Fiction," "Esthétique du Mal," "Credences of Summer," "Description without Place," "The Owl in the Sarcophagus," "The Auroras of Autumn," and finally "An Ordinary Evening in New Haven"—are "events" of the mind in the act of finding what will suffice. And as "events" they are poems about first and last things (eschatological poems), not because they are about the course of life from birth to death but because they are about the rhythms of imagination from act to form, innocence to experience, silence to sound, chaos to order, origin to motion. But the act does not end in order or "final form." Forms dissolve into one another in the continuum of a performance that is a "never-ending meditation."

There is room here to deal with these poems only in terms of rhythm—like "Notes," which begins with the imperative "Begin" and moves verbally both away from and toward the "first idea" it seeks (CP, 380). For the "first idea" was not "to shape the clouds/ In imitation" (CP, 383); it was the beginning of the self in raw perception, subject and object at one in innocence. In this sense the reality "preceded us" (CP, 383), resting in things themselves; and as we come to make it within us, we lose the first idea by making a world of words. So the first idea which we can apprehend only in "ignorance" (and after "ignorance" only in the silences before speech, the sleep before waking, the stillness before action) is "refreshe(d)" in the poem because "It [the poem] satisfies/ Belief in an immaculate beginning" (CP, 382).

Wherever one touches "Notes" (and the title itself suggests a tentative beginning), he finds the poem turning in upon itself, evoking the pristine beginning away from which it moves, the innocence it seeks in its own end. Heavy with words, it would divest itself of naming; inevitably abstract, it would, "must," change. And thus it would refresh abstractions, until the ultimate abstraction would be that of beginning itself, the myth that supplants the myth of an "inventing mind as source" (CP, 381) and thus frees the imagination to be its own origin. The "first idea is an imagined thing" (CP, 387). Like its incipient form, arbitrarily named the "MacCullough," an "expedient," it is "Logos and logic, crystal hypothesis,/ Incipit and a form to speak the word/ And every latent double of the word,// Beau linguist" (CP, 387).

In "Notes," and in the self-reflexive poems of the self as center, Stevens had constantly to reiterate that the imagination is the act of imagination, "crystal hypothesis" (thus abstract) yet "Incipit and a form to speak the word" (and thus an origin). MacCullough, though an abstraction, is the imagination as both subject and object, both speech and the "form to speak." He is "major man," a "form" of man himself, which we must think of when we think of centers, the gods being annihilated. But the point is, we must think of centers. The "idea of man" is "More fecund as principle than particle," more powerful in the "abstract than in his singular" (CP, 388). Thus in thinking it, man embodies the "first idea" in himself as thinker. The poem circles back continuously to this origin, which is also the origin of change, change in turn denying every form or shape even as it confirms that to be is to have shape: as Nanzia Nunzio (nothing?) needs Ozymandias, a "fictive covering" (CP, 396). Change, then, confirms "beginnings": "Of these beginnings, gay and green, propose/ The suitable amours. Time will write them down" (CP, 398). The poem, transforming the world in metaphor, refreshes the world by catching the "freshness of ourselves." The poem of time and change celebrates beginnings.

"It Must Give Pleasure" thus offers an image of beginning married to end in the "poem" or "crystal," the "good" of which is its transformations, "the merely going round" (CP, 405). The poem confirms repetition, even as it offers the hope of an end in which "They will get it straight one day at the Sorbonne" (CP, 406). The "supreme fiction" is sustained in the dream of attaining a supreme fiction, the dream of the imagination transcending itself as act. But the poem can only offer itself as a formal repetition of that ideal act of transcendence. The "fluent mundo," the poet dreams, "will" come to revolve in the "crystal" of the poem, marrying abstraction and change in an endless repetition which does not exhaust itself. The poem gives pleasure because it holds out the possibility of achieving the purpose of its beginning, of rendering a "supreme fiction." But for the poet of time, he is involved in a "war that never ends," writing a poem about "faithful speech." (CP, 407–8). He is "always in the sun," always standing in change, the real, and participating in the search for the first idea that, ultimately, has being only in his words. Thus the poem ends not by delivering the supreme fiction or capturing the "first idea" but by celebrating the "freshness" of beginnings.

V

These new beginnings signify the circularity of the poetic act. The existential dialectic of "Notes" does not lead to a synthesis in pleasure. The poem's tripartite divisions are interdependent and, ultimately, simultaneous; the "time" of the poem is an interior time, the duration of an "act" incarnating itself in a form or "crystal." The poem as "crystal" reflects both interior and exterior worlds—the point of departure and the "fluent mundo." The poem's three parts, then, compose an aesthetic space, a series of self-reflexive mirrors. Yet the external form of "Notes" only seems to belie the openendedness of Stevens' other late, long poems, like "Esthétique du Mal" and "An Ordinary Evening in New Haven." It does so only if one accepts the poem as a self-contained image or "crystal," and not as a continuing reflection on the "crystal" as evolving form, the poem that "will" be. "Notes" is "notes toward." Reflecting inward to the center, like a crystal, it also reflects outward. It catches up the "fluent mundo" into a center, and casts it toward an expanding horizon. And the "crystal hypothesis," one recalls, is the "MacCullough," man made major. No wonder Stevens thought of writing a fourth part, to be called "It Must Be Human" (L, 863–64).

The essential discovery of Stevens' late "meditations" only confirms that being is choosing, choosing oneself, as at the end of "The Man with the Blue Guitar." Evoking the "supreme fiction," the "ultimate poem," the "central poem," they direct the "act of the mind" toward a possible end. And thus they name as being the poet's non-being, his many possible selves, his freedom. The hero of Stevens' late poems is the "seeker." He is a mind which would create itself either by discovering its beginning (the parent) or its end (the nothingness after death); and thus it is a mind fully conscious that it exists in its consciousness of itself.

"The Sail of Ulysses" is an interesting instance, a monologue of "*Ulysses,/ Symbol of the seeker*" reading "*his own mind*" as he rides under the "*shape of his sail*" (OP, 99). The poem is framed by the metaphor of Ulysses as mind and act, the two inseparable in their "shape" that is a "sail" or a form to ride with and redirect the energy of the cosmos. Ulysses' reflections, then, are upon his adventures of the mind, which begin in "human loneliness," the "space and solitude" of our "inner direction" (OP, 100). His meditations move toward a "knowledge" of the world. Knowledge is creation, the illuminating of the "shapes" of the world.

The "creator is a lamp" enlarging the "space on which it stands" (OP, 100). But the creator is also "unnamed" because at the "center of the self" he exists as "future man" (OP, 101). He names himself when he names the world, but he names himself as namer. In seeking a "final order" he creates the "beginning of a final order,/ The order of man's right to be" (OP, 101). The act of knowing becomes an act of life, anticipating a future knowledge of a future self:

> We come
> To knowledge when we come to life.
> Yet always there is another life,
> A life beyond this present knowing,
> A life lighter than this present splendor,
> Brighter, perfected, and distant away,
> Not to be reached but to be known. . . . [OP, 101]

The beginning opens up the end, and illuminates its own nothingness. It offers "no map of paradise" but only futurity, something beyond the "ancient symbols" (OP, 102). "The mind renews the world in a verse" (OP, 103), and thus begets itself. But only momentarily. Ulysses' reflections upon his own mind arrive at the self as center, as "sibyl," but a "sibyl" without a shape. The "sibyl" is "a blind thing fumbling for its form," the "old shape/ Worn and leaning to nothingness," and a "child asleep in its own life" (OP, 104). These metaphors catch the "shapes" before shape, which were the preoccupation of Stevens' last years. The "sibyl" is "our need," and thus the source of our self as future. From this point (the imagination or, if you will, the "child asleep in its own life") emerge the "Categories of bleak necessity" (OP, 104) by which we name the world and thus transcend ourselves. Naming is the imagination's role: "Just to name, is to create," by which we arrive at "another plane" (OP, 104).

"The Sail of Ulysses" ends by naming the mind as its own origin. In a variation on that poem, "A Child Asleep in Its Own Life" (OP, 106), the child is father to the man because its incipient shape holds the potential for creating still more old men. Like Santayana in "To an Old Philosopher in Rome" (CP, 508), the dying self clutches the particulars of its world in the faith that a still potential self may yet be born. One goes on making poems until the end, even when confronted by the "plain sense of things" and the "end of the imagination" (CP, 502). For that "end," too, that "absence of the imagination had/ Itself to be imagined." Stevens' last poems seek the father "at the head of the past" (CP, 501) not as consolation but as one seeks the possibility of self-renewal.

And yet, he does not foresee that renewal is any more than the possibility which sustains his present moment. The "life beyond" is "Not to be reached but to be known." Confronting the plain sense of things, his "grief" is that "his mother should feed on him" (CP, 507), that mother earth is his end. The only consolation is the poem as "solitary home," like the "poem that took the place of a mountain" (CP, 512). Each poem is a testimony to its moment; and the shape of that moment, like a mountain, will endure. "Ariel was glad he had written his poems," for in writing them he had named himself Ariel, made himself in his world; so that his poems compose a "planet on the table": "makings of his self" but no less "makings of the sun" (CP, 532). They are a world then—not "the" makings of the sun but acts of making it, naming it as source and preserving its shapes, becoming one with it. His poems are revelations not of past but of future being, disclosures of an "undetermined form" (CP, 531) which has the potential to move toward form.

Everywhere in late Stevens this incessant discovery of possibility confirms a future that makes present being at once a reality (substantial) and a nothingness (a potentiality for the future). What it really confirms, however, is the imagination as continuously present. It defines the self as the potential for self-transcendence, and thus as the "seeker" or "Wanderer" (CP, 522). And it defines poems as at once "shapes" or "icons" (thus abstract) and acts (thus forms of change), in which the reader may realize his own continuing consciousness in the poet's words. Poems are "the edgings and inchings of final form," (CP, 488) but not a "final form." Indeed they deny the attainability of "final form," except as they are instants of it (toward it) incorporated in words. Thus they marry self and other and in doing so adduce all we know of the mystery of the mind, "The starting point of the human and the end,/ That in which space itself is contained, the gate/ To the enclosure . . ." (CP, 528).

VI

The discovery of the "starting point of the human" is the discovery of the "instant moment" which precedes time and space and lies at the origin of being. It is a "moment" adduced in a late poem, "Prologues to What Is Possible" (CP, 515), which perhaps more fully than any other poem catches the total rhythm of Stevens' self-creative act of the mind.

"Prologues" is therefore the proper place to focus one's concluding observations on Stevens' theory of imagination, since that theory must, in the lines from another poem, assume that a "theory of poetry" is a "theory of life." "Prologues" catches in its titular metaphor Stevens' discovery of his beginning in his end, which for him is no different from affirming that his end lies in his beginning. Or in the words of another poem: "And yet this end and this beginning are one" (CP, 506). These are not paradoxes, but alternate ways of presenting the continuum of an act which can only define its action by defining a starting-point and end. The act is ultimately to be defined only as a "process," but a process, like a "Prologue," is necessarily previous to finality or ultimates, or supremes.

The poem opens by relaxing into a long line, an "ease of mind" that evokes a simile. The "ease of mind" is "like being alone in a boat at sea." But the simile becomes substance in that it is the action, a movement of the "boat carried forward by waves resembling the bright backs of rowers." The first half of the poem is a movement "toward" the interior center of the mind, a verbal movement effected in a language which becomes a figure within a figure moving toward a "moment" totally within time, space, and language. The "boat . . . built of stones" (no longer "like" a boat, but a verbal thing itself) thus casts off its materiality to become the vehicle of a motion of a solipsistic voyage into a purely verbal universe, itself centered upon silence. The self "traveled alone, like a man lured on by a syllable without any meaning." The movement is toward a point where all form is "shatter(ed)," a "point of central arrival, an instant moment, much or little,/ Removed from any shore, from any man or woman, and needing none."

This point is also the verbal center of the poem ("none"—no one? no thing?)—an ultimate interiority. It is the space of being as nothingness. And the second half of the poem begins: "The metaphor stirred his fear. The object with which he was compared/ Was beyond his recognizing." The "point" of arrival must be named, as beginning; and the movement of the poem is reversed, the "self" moving out from that "instant moment" through the "enclosures of hypotheses" to become an addition to the world. The poem both enacts and names its movement, in a totally self-reflexive verbal duration:

> What self, for example, did he contain that had not yet been loosed,
> Snarling in him for discovery as his attentions spread,
> As if all his hereditary lights were suddenly increased

By an access of color, a new and unobserved, slight dithering,
The smallest lamp, which added its puissant flick, to which he gave
A name and privilege over the ordinary of his commonplace—

A flick which added to what was real and its vocabulary,
The way some first thing coming into Northern trees
Adds to them the whole vocabulary of the South,
The way the earliest single light in the evening sky, in spring,
Creates a fresh universe out of nothingness by adding itself,
The way a look or a touch reveals its unexpected magnitudes.

The poem is a "prologue," but its act is endless, a kind of "late plural" (CP, 382) and thus at once abstract (the structure of the act) and changing (the act itself). The poem ends by marrying all the opposites of Stevens' world: real and unreal, interior and exterior, dark and light, self and other, language and silence. It moves from exterior to interior and out again—but the point is, it moves within the form it creates. It celebrates the "point of central arrival" as a necessity and a threat, an "instant moment" that is the central of the self and nothingness. "Prologues" locates the imagination in man's "need," as did "The Sail of Ulysses," his need for the poem. Thus it locates the self as center and point of departure, as in these lines from another poem:

The center that he sought was a state of mind,
Nothing more, like weather after it has cleared—
Well, more than that, like weather when it has cleared
And the two poles continue to maintain it. . . . [OP, 112]

For Stevens the center he seeks is always between two poles, between beginning and end and thus the present unreal on which beginning and end depend. It is a "state of mind" which defines itself between "two poles." But it exists in its motion between its coordinates, a silence between sounds. It is, finally, where one is at, the starting point without which there is no future and no past. The imagination is our need, but it is also its own necessity. It is both the "origin" of the "word" and the "subject of the poem."

NOTES

1. If one were seeking a strict philosophical analogue to Stevens' earliest reflections on the nature of mind and imagination, it would

probably be Santayana's epiphenomenalism. Yet this is simply to say that Stevens' reflections on the imagination took place in a post-Romantic, post-Transcendentalist world and depended very largely on the Romantic-idealist terminology. But the new contexts of that terminology preclude the idealization of spirit-mind implicit in the terminology. While the separation of mind and world were for Stevens experientially crucial, the interdependence of mind and world were a given: thus "Adam/ In Eden was the father of Descartes" (CP, 383). He begins, as Hillis Miller says, with the condition of Romantic dualism, but cannot assume a reconciliation of it in either a Romantic transcendence or a Romantic immanence.

It will not do to conclude with Frank Lentricchia, in *The Gaiety of Language, An Essay on the Radical Poetics of W. B. Yeats and Wallace Stevens* (Berkeley, 1968), that if Stevens rejected the idealistic or transcendental imagination and opted for one depending on reality, then his imagination must be called "naturalistic," the imagination as "secretary" to rather than author of the "world." Lentricchia's rather reductive history of ideas results in an either/or poetics which diminishes Stevens'. Stevens ultimately rejected both polarities (imagination and reality) as possible in themselves, and came to see them as nominal polarities between which the act of life moved. One can, if he wishes, relate Stevens' thoughts on imagination at any one particular time to almost every post-Cartesian theory of mind. But ultimately, only a phenomenology of the mind's *act of being* explains very much about Stevens' poetics; for in a very real sense, Stevens' theory of imagination is his search for a theory of imagination.

2. Georges Poulet, in *The Metamorphosis of the Circle*, trans. Carley Dawson and Elliott Coleman (Baltimore, 1966), speaks of the Romantic self as follows: "The romantic is a being who discovers himself to be a centering point. What matters more is not that the world of objects is out of reach, it is that at bottom there is in the romantic something which, as he knows, is inassimilable to an object and which is the subjective and most authentic part of his self. . . ." (p. 93); and "For the Romantic, man is first of all a self-generative force. He is a living point destined to become a circle." For Stevens the self as centering point can only realize itself by assimilating itself to the object, or by manifesting itself objectively. Otherwise the point remains nothing. Thus Stevens' self-generating imagination, as opposed to Whitman's self-generating center, does not expand toward an infinite horizon. For the modern poet, the very meaning of the self-generating center changes.

3. The quotations from Stevens' poems are made with the generous permission of Alfred A. Knopf, Inc., and Holly Stevens. They are from the following volumes, hereafter cited in the text:

(NA): *The Necessary Angel* (New York: Vintage Books, 1951)
(CP): *The Collected Poems of Wallace Stevens* (New York: Alfred A. Knopf, 1954)
(OP): *Opus Posthumous*, ed. with introduction by Samuel French Morse (New York: Alfred A. Knopf, 1967)
(L): *The Letters of Wallace Stevens*, ed. Holly Stevens (New York: Alfred A. Knopf, 1966)

4. J. Hillis Miller, *Poets of Reality* (Cambridge, Mass., 1965), pp. 218ff.

5. Stevens' "world of words" is fictional, a recognizable "as if" world. And "as if" is one of his dominant verbal positionings. As Hans Vaihinger has made evident in *The Philosophy of 'As If,'* trans. C. K. Ogden (New York, 1924), fictions are "mental structures" that could not have existed without the mind's experiencing the other, and thus are essential to our "struggle for existence." But "It must be remembered that the object of the world of ideas as a whole is not the portrayal of reality . . . but rather to provide us with an *instrument for finding our way about more easily in this world.* Subjective processes of thought inhere in the entire structure of cosmic phenomena" (p. 15). Vaihinger is more concerned with the reality of intellectual "fictions" than with the "fictions" of art or poetry or a seemingly concrete language. But as he makes clear, in an analysis which precedes somewhat the more discreet phenomenological analyses of language and forms, even a representational art and a concrete language must be treated as "fictions." Stevens' fictional world is "unreal" at the center, and could not be objectified without forms of a "real" world. But naturalistic determinism, implying that if the real precedes the unreal it becomes ultimately the centering force and determinant of the unreal's shape, is hardly relevant to Stevens' poetics. Vaihinger's book, incidentally, is an important document in the history of ideas which were current in the twenties, and along with Whitehead's notional philosophy, Santayana's epiphenomenalism, and Ramon Fernandez's "philosophical criticism" offers valuable perspectives (I did not say influences) on Stevens' evolving poetics, as existential phenomenology provides an essential perspective on the later poetics. Like Sartre in his early writing on imagination, Stevens recognizes the essential "unreality" of the imaginary or fictional as its own kind of reality, the aesthetic reality that is "pleasure," disinterested enjoyment that spares us from the absurd and contingent, from leaping into the "heart of existence." The "pleasures of merely circulating" or "merely going round" are experiences of the physical world elevated into the space of imagination, which mitigates the contingent while seeming to allow its reality.

6. Stevens' modern self begins where Milton's Adam and Eve end, or leave Paradise to begin. The space which Stevens' self inherits is a fully "subjected plain" (*Paradise Lost*, Book XII, 1. 640), both subjective and subjected, or spatially reduced. But Stevens' space is not reduced below the dominant eye of the divine Center. It is emptied, like those intimate homes Gaston Bachelard speaks of in *The Poetics of Space*, trans. Maria Jolas (New York, 1964). We recall those homes in the distances of our memory as places away from which we are moving (see "The Rock"), as absence, yet know them as places which we must reconstitute with our present self, as one might seek to reconstitute the original security and wholeness of the family. Bachelard's bourgeois nostalgia becomes Stevens' existential necessity. Stevens' modern self is left an orphan in an empty house, a poetic space which when refurnished will constitute his self as center.

7. "Life is an affair of people not of places. But for me life is an affair of places and that is the trouble" (OP, 158).

8. While I was in the process of writing this essay, Edward W. Said published "Beginnings" in *Salmagundi*, II (Fall, 1968), 36–55, a "meditation" which takes up the significance of "beginning" in post-Cartesian and especially existential thought. Said's reflections offer an invaluable confirmation of the emphasis I put on "beginnings" in Stevens' poetics. "Writing," he says, "is the unknown, or the beginning from which reading imagines and from which it departs in what Sartre calls a method of guided invention. But that is the reader's transitive point of view which is forced to imagine a prior unknown that the reader calls writing. From the point of view of the writer, however, his writing—as he does it—is perpetually at the beginning. Like Rilke's Malte he is a beginner in his own consciousness" (p. 50).

9. Georges Poulet, *Le Point de départ* (Paris, 1964).

10. This is precisely Jean Wahl's view in *Poésie, pensée, perception* (Paris, 1948), a book that mentions Stevens briefly. Wahl and Stevens were friends while Wahl was teaching in the U.S. during World War II, and corresponded thereafter. Stevens' later theorizing on poetics reveals some of the cast of Wahl's existential aesthetics.

11. See Miller, *Poets of Reality*, pp. 282–84.

12. Stevens joins William Carlos Williams here in stressing the essential destructive act that initiates the modern imagination's renewals. The decreation of old forms is implicit in the re-creation of the self, or in the renewal of language, a kind of "discovery" of radiance in the pitchblend of accumulated dross or meaning. For Williams, the act was essential to escape the tyranny of history; for Stevens it was as inevitable as it was for Bergson, the continuing creation of any moment implying the unmaking of the self the moment before. This particularly pre-existential dimension of Bergson's thought is articulated by Poulet

in his introduction to *Studies in Human Time*, trans. Elliott Coleman (Baltimore, 1956), pp. 34–37: "If . . . the mind wishes to apprehend itself as creator, it must recognize in its act of creation an act of annihilation; it must create its very nothingness in order to give itself being" (p. 36).

13. See James Baird, *The Dome and the Rock, Structure in the Poetry of Wallace Stevens* (Baltimore, 1968), pp. 231ff., for the "structure" of Stevens' use of place, and especially of the relation between North and South in his poetry.

14. "Beginnings," p. 42.

From Language to the Art of Language: Cassirer's Aesthetic

WALTER F. EGGERS, JR.
UNIVERSITY OF WYOMING

ERNST CASSIRER'S INTEREST IN THE SYMBOLIC FORM called language arises directly out of his allegiance to the long tradition of idealist philosophy. The history of attitudes toward language which comprises the introductory chapter of his *Phenomenology of Linguistic Form* (the first volume of *The Philosophy of Symbolic Forms*) reaches from Plato to Croce,[1] and whatever impedes the gradual revelation of Kantian epistemology in the realm of language analysis gets short shrift. For example, he dismisses the dull mechanics of modern descriptive linguistics as an evasion of that same, fundamental problem of language which empiricism in all its historical shapes could never solve. A psychology of simple associations, whether strictly rationalist or "psycho-physical," offers no explanation for language in its creative aspect. For this we need an image of man which frees him to create, a philosophy which grounds a "universal principle of form" in the originality of human action.[2] Such has been the basic tenet of idealism throughout its history:

> This desire and capacity for giving form to experience is what Herder and Humboldt show to be the essence of language, what Schiller points to as the essential nature of play and art, and what Kant shows us to be true of the structure of theoretical knowledge. For them, all of this would not be possible as outgrowth, as sheer product, if unique modes of formal construction [spheres of possibility] did not underlie [the working out of] these creations. The very fact that man is capable of this type of productivity is precisely what stands out as the unique and distinguishing characteristic of human nature.[3]

That the actions of man are essentially problematic, that the modes themselves through which he perceives his world are finally irreducible, *sui generis*—it is here that Plato, Kant, and Croce all begin.[4]

To Croce goes the credit for turning the tide against linguistic positivism by equating language with spiritual expression and viewing the analysis of language as ultimately a problem in applied aesthetics. But Crocean "expression" is too reductive a concept for a systematic philosophy of the scope which Cassirer proposes. Aesthetics has its place within the full range of symbolic forms; but each of these forms, each of the "sciences of expression,"[5] must be kept in place if only for methodological reasons. Unless first we recognize their independence one from another, we cannot go on to describe the generic humanity which underlies them all: "Despite any systematic *combination* into which [language] may enter with logic and aesthetics, we must assign to it a *specific* and autonomous position within the whole."[6] It is true that there is "no break in the life of the spirit"[7] between the various symbolic forms; they are functionally identical as modes of symbolization, and the symbol-systems they produce lie on a continuum.[8] Indeed, it is this argument which ties the three volumes of *The Philosophy of Symbolic Forms* together. But this is the argument to be proved, and we can proceed only analytically. In fact what Cassirer discovers when he surveys the full range of languages and possible languages is that although the impulse which lies behind the perpetual re-creation of language is spiritually free, its evolution seems inevitably to be away from the metaphorical and the concrete toward "the expression of pure relation."[9] His demonstration is a complex one, and we will return to this point later in this essay.

Cassirer attacks Croce's notion of expression on more strictly aesthetic grounds as well. For Croce, all of the human domain is divided into two parts, the artistic and the scientific, the intuitive and the logical:

> Knowledge has two forms: it is either *intuitive* knowledge or *logical* knowledge; knowledge obtained through the *imagination* or knowledge obtained through the *intellect*; knowledge of the *individual* or knowledge of the *universal;* of *individual things* or of the *relations* between them; it is, in fact, productive either of *images* or *concepts.*[10]

Not only are these two realms independent of each other, they are fundamentally antagonistic—the artistic image is "pure intuition,"[11] simple and singular in its expression, revealing no trace of the abstract, the logical, the universal. Moreover, expression itself is bound immediately to intuition—to isolate the phenomenon of expression is only to view the process of intuition the other way around, from object to subject, from image to artist.[12] It is on this basis that Croce is able to condemn as "the greatest triumph of the intellectualist error" the concept of "genre," the "theory of artistic and literary kinds."[13] We cannot, he argues, apply a canon of normative values to a work of art which, by the nature of its inception in the imagination of the artist, posits its own rules. The logical mind is unable to penetrate artistic intuition: it can with its abstract schemes manipulate the art-object, but it cannot apprehend the object of expression because the object manifests a unity of its own.

Cassirer too is suspicious of normative aesthetics. What he disputes is Croce's apparent disregard of artistic medium. In Crocean terms, the distinctions between material modes of artistic construction are simply accidental; intuition will out in one form or another, and the very individuality of the expression becomes an argument against considering material form: "one painting is as different from another as it is from a poem; and painting and poetry have value, not because of the sounds filling the air or the color refractions in the light, but because of what they are able . . . to convey to the mind."[14] Cassirer's complaint is that to regard distinctions in material form as "mere 'physical' differences in means of presentation"[15] is to destroy that same unity of intuition and expression which Croce insists upon:

> As I see it, such a view does not do justice to the artistic process; for it would break the work of art into two halves, which would then stand in no necessary relation to each other. In actuality, however, the particular manner in which the work of art is expressed belongs not only to the *technique* of the construction of the work but also to its very *conception.* Beethoven's intuition is musical, Phidias' intuition is plastic, Milton's intuition is epic, Goethe's intuition is lyric. In each case this fact involves not only the surface but the very heart of their creative work. It is only with this reflection that we strike the bedrock, the true meaning and profound justification for the classification of the arts into various "species."[16]

What may here appear to be little more than an assertion on Cassirer's part takes on the weight of argument when we regard it as an integral element of his complex system: significantly it is by generalizing on this subject of genre that he concludes his *Logic of the Humanities.* The chapter from which it is drawn, "The 'Tragedy of Culture,'" is perhaps Cassirer's most expansive and most eloquent statement of his broad humanistic concerns. Like Croce with whom he takes issue, he uses the art-construct as a paradigm of human freedom. Their vocabularies here are identical: "By elaborating his impressions, man *frees* himself from them. By objectifying them, he removes them from him and makes himself their superior."[17] In all, there could be no better summation of Cassirer's own humanistic thrust than these words of Croce.

But we have concluded before we have begun. One specific purpose of this essay is to elucidate the concept of "genre" in Cassirer's terms, to provide in some detail the defense which he only hinted at for an aesthetics of artistic kinds. For this purpose we must keep Cassirer's dispute with Croce clearly in mind. Yet even in reviewing Cassirer's own terminology we are susceptible to two extremes. On one hand, in order to remain faithful to the spirit of the man, we cannot avoid generalizing as in the paragraph above on some of the broader issues involved. On the other—because this too is a part of Cassirer's philosophic spirit—we must proceed step by step, utilizing the scattered bits of aesthetic theory throughout Cassirer's works for what they reveal. Still, Cassirer does provide a general methodological framework for an investigation of this sort in the three volumes of *The Philosophy of Symbolic Forms.* The attempt in this essay will be to extend his analysis of language as a symbolic form in Volume I to the particular problem of poetic language, language turned to the special purposes of the symbolic form called art. We should expect of the *art* of language what we find in each of the symbolic forms, a "specific structural principle," a "modality" which is "specific to it and in a sense lends a common tonality to all its individual structures."[18]

Of all the theorists of language who have had the courage to deal with the problem of its evolution historically and logically, Cassirer is indebted primarily to two—to Herder for his concept of "reflection" and to Wilhelm von Humboldt for solving the objective-subjective crux of communication by incorporating the concept of "subjective universality" in the domain of language analysis. Together these two philosophers provide a firm foundation for an idealist's approach to language, and thus it is here that we should begin.

> Even if all language is rooted in feeling and its immediate instinctive manifestations, even if it originates not in the need for

> communication but in cries, tones, and wild, articulated sounds—even so, such an aggregate of sounds can never constitute the specific "form" of language.[19]

Cassirer's insistence upon the radical distinction between man and beast, his identification of the symbolic forms as specifically and exclusively human—this is the axiom upon which his entire systematic philosophy rests,[20] and it is this which accounts for his scientific preoccupation with "threshold experiences," with so-called animal languages,[21] with aphasia and amusia,[22] with Helen Keller and Laura Bridgman,[23] and with as many primitive languages as were available to him.[24] But if the materials he draws upon for demonstration most often take on an historical shape, and if his emphasis falls continually on the rudimentary or the primitive, still, the importance of his historical speculations lies in the models or patterns they offer for the philosophic analysis of linguistic conceptualization. So it is that he is willing to accept a metaphorical explanation where an historical illustration cannot be found.

On "reflection," which he designates as the specifically "human function" in the process of language formation, he quotes Herder at length:

> Man demonstrates reflection when the force of his soul works so freely that in the ocean of sensations that flows into it from all the senses, he can, in a manner of speaking, isolate and stop One wave, and direct his attention toward this wave, conscious that he is doing so. He demonstrates reflection when, emerging from the nebulous dream of images flitting past his senses, he can concentrate upon a point of wakefulness, dwell voluntarily on One image, observe it calmly and lucidly, and distinguish characteristics proving that this and no other is the object. He demonstrates reflection when he not only knows all attributes vividly and clearly, but can *recognize* one or more distinguishing attributes: the first act of this recognition yields a clear concept; it is the soul's First judgment—and what made this recognition possible? A characteristic which he had to isolate and which came to him clearly as a characteristic of reflection. Forward! Let us cry *eureka*! The first characteristic of reflection was the word of the soul. With it human speech was invented![25]

The general Kantian orientation is apparent here, but the discovery which accounts for Herder's enthusiasm lies beyond the strict domain of Kantian epistemology, beyond the simple mechanics of cognition. An application of the Kantian "organic form"—the form which a voluntarist epistemology recognizes as the unfilled content of perception—to the cultural phenomenon of language is an extension of the Kantian model of perception to the domain of the *understanding.* It makes legitimate an analysis of *culture* in terms of the "new science" and thus is the necessary first step in the establishment of that "morphology of the human spirit"[26] which Cassirer took as his own life's work.

More specifically, Herder's concept of reflection affirms as irreducible the unit-elements of the understanding. Such an assertion is, as we have already noted, characteristic of the whole tradition of idealist philosophy. But what is more important in terms strictly of language analysis is that it offers a new perspective on that tendency toward the general (or abstract, or universal) which seems inherent in the very process of language formation. Locke saw in the mechanics of language a model example of the sensation combined and separated: the universal is abstracted from the independent particles of empirical data. But with Herder no longer do we have "an artificial system of signs" hung onto our perceptions, the natural stuff of our experience; rather, "here perception itself, by virtue of its spiritual character, contains a specific factor of form which, when fully developed, is represented in the form of words and language."[27] The essence of language could now no longer be sought in "abstraction from differentiation" but only in the "totality of differentiations,"[28] since it was this totality which for Herder determined the formal nature of abstraction in language.

The thrust of Herder's argument was of course directed against empiricist skepticism: having forsworn the rationalist faith in a pre-existent harmony between the ideal and the real, the universal and the particular, Berkeley for one could only conclude that if language is a mirror, the mirror of language falsifies and distorts. Humboldt followed Herder in attempting to affirm the truth value of language in general and poetic language in particular. But before we proceed to consider Humboldt's contribution to the idealist philosophy of language, we need to examine further the implications of "reflection" for Cassirer's own system in the *Language* volume.

Cassirer devotes an entire chapter to the problem of "concept and class formation in language" and opens it with his own attack on the nominalist view of abstraction. Language, it is argued, provides not only the perfect paradigm for concept formation in general; in fact, says the nominalist, language is the functional basis for conceptualization. And the means through which the concept arises is linguistic abstraction: common characteristics are abstracted from similar things, and these characteristics are identified by *names*. But the question is, how do we get the concepts by which we judge "common characteristics"? The nominalist argument on this point is simply circular: "any attempt to form a concept by abstraction is tantamount to looking for the spectacles which are on your nose, with the help of these same spectacles."[29]

To solve this problem, Cassirer attempts to discover the conditions of that first intuition or "primary formation"[30] effected in language which provides the foundation for later complex syntheses. The "secret of predication" is discoverable in the factors of synthesis and analysis which determine the formation of individual words, and as he builds his examination of the verbal concept from rudimentary to the complex, Cassirer explicates the term "reflection" more precisely.

The first step in concept formation is not to raise our perceptions to a higher degree of universality but rather to make them more determinate. In order for contents of perception to be classed according to similarities, they first must be identified *as* contents, they must be objectified. The content is recognized as objectively real—and yet this reality is not independent of the content. Rather, the content is determined *for* knowledge, "identical with itself and recurrent amid the flux of impressions."[31] This act of "objectivization" (reflexive in the sense that it posits its own phenomenal reality) is designated a "naming": a "whatness" is conferred upon specific content as it is individuated, and this "whatness" is its form.[32] Thus the formal nature of the primary intuition is irreducible; but as we shall see, what logically are secondary elaborations of this process of objectivization, complex "namings," retain this same quality of irreducibleness.

The next step in the formation of the concept is the articulation of various relationships between "named" contents. The relationships are not arbitrary since they themselves disclose objective forms; yet neither can they be abstracted from their contents and considered apart from them. Now for there to exist objective and yet not substantial relationships between perceptual contents, we must conclude that the giving of a name, the logically original formation, has been a qualifying formation—the thing is named on the basis of some particular property:

> The work of the spirit does not consist in the subordinating the content to another content, but in distinguishing it as a concrete, undifferentiated whole by stressing a specific, characteristic factor in it and focusing attention on this factor. The possibility of "giving a name" rests on this concentration of the mind's eye: the new im-

> print of thinking upon the content is the necessary condition for its designation in language.[33]

All of this is rather difficult, but we need to follow the intricacies of Cassirer's argument on this one point in order to appreciate fully the impact of the general argument which lies behind it. And we are here at the heart of the one issue which will most concern us throughout this essay. Once again, the process of linguistic conceptualization is functionally identical with "objectivization" in any and each of the symbolic forms. When we turn to the specific problem of artistic genre —the designation in artistic symbols of relationships between contents of perception—there too will we see that the complex "naming" is irreducible, that the relationships are objective and yet not substantial, and that the intuition of relationships may be viewed as simultaneous with the "naming" of simple contents since this "naming" itself is a qualifying formation. For now, what we need to recognize about the nature of reflection in each of the symbolic forms is that as an intuitive transformation of impressions into representations and representations into concepts it does not abstract but *particularize* and that in its particularity it determines the whole before the part. By now it should be clear that for Cassirer reflection designates man's symbol-making function itself: the paradox of a concept which in its particularity expresses the whole is the familiar paradox of the symbol.

The final elaboration or complication of concept formation in language manifests itself in that whole which is an entire language. And here we return to Humboldt, for it is at this point that Cassirer introduces Humboldt's concept of "inner form":

> That each particular language has specific inner form meant for [Humboldt] primarily that in the choice of its designations it never simply expressed the objects perceived in themselves, but that this choice was eminently determined by a whole spiritual attitude, by the orientation of man's subjective view of objects.[34]

It is this general orientation which man brings to the formation of his language—to the very process of naming—which is determinate. The example Cassirer draws here he repeats later in the *Essay on Man*: that the moon in Greek is named "the measurer" and in Latin "the glittering" indicates that words in different languages cannot be fully synonymous, for here the same sensory impression is "assigned to very different notions of meaning and made determinate by them."[35] And the inner form of a language determines its larger structural features, not simply its vocabulary. With the help of Humboldt, Cassirer has extended the scope of the reflective process to include among the undifferentiated and irreducible unities of expression languages themselves. But here two difficulties arise. If we cannot grasp the special subjectiveness of various languages, how do we attain the objectivity in language which makes communication possible? And how can we rise from the perspectives of various languages to the perspective of language itself, since it is with language as a unique symbolic form that we are primarily concerned? These questions are, of course, directly related, and it is Humboldt again who provides the basis for an answer to them both.

With Humboldt, the subjective-objective dualism of language is almost completely resolved. Each individual language is an individual world view, and objectivity is attainable only within the community of world views:

> . . . language is subjective in relation to the knowable, and objective in relation to man as an empirical-psychological subject. Each language is a note in the harmony of man's universal nature: "once again, the subjectivity of *all* mankind becomes intrinsically objective."[36]

We are not far at this point from the Kantian subjective universality in epistemology, but what is more important here is the idea that objectivity is not a given only to be described but "a goal which must be *achieved* by a process of spiritual formation."[37] Language-making is a function of man's characteristically purposive activity. That objectivization which is an integration of individual world views into the languages by which we communicate constitutes the project of language as symbolic form. Such we should expect is the relationship too between individual artistic intuition and the articulate whole which is art.

We have so far left out of our consideration the second and third chapters of the *Language* volume, and before we can proceed to draw our own conclusions from Cassirer's systematic investigation of this primary symbolic form we need to recognize the distinction he draws between "sensuous" and "intuitive" expression. The plan of the volume as a whole is progressive—Cassirer builds from the simple to the complex, from the mechanics of naming to the "expression of pure relation"—and thus to rearrange its chapters is to violate the essential unity of his argument. Yet the sense we now have of the argument as a whole should help enforce the point of these central chapters and carry us from language to the art of language. For in Cassirer's terms it is with the radical distinction between sensuous and intuitive expression that we find the moment of the symbolic form called art.

To this point we have reviewed Cassirer's logical demonstration that the genesis of the linguistic concept is unique. In chapters two and three he substantiates his understanding of the genesis of language on other than logical—on anthropological—grounds. At the center of the anthropologist's view of language is the element of "dynamism"—expression viewed as the movement of will and action directed toward one single point—and this concept is sanctioned even by the psychologists. Dynamism as willed action argues against the very basis of sensationalist psychology, however; and its workings are apparent even in the simple gestures of sign languages. The sensationalist would regard the pointing gesture of the human as an attenuation of the grasping or clutching movement of the animal. But this is false anthropology. Rather, Cassirer insists, the very disparity between animal *movement* and human *action* underscores the uniqueness of the human animal: "It is one of the first steps by which the perceiving and desiring I removes a perceived and desired content from himself and so forms it into an 'object,' an 'objective content.'"[38] Since for Cassirer conceptual learning means surpassing "sensory immediacy," the human gesture of indication is a threshold experience in man; it reveals a process of objectivization as dynamic activity.

But besides the deictic or indicative gesture there is the mimetic or imitative, and this second fundamental class seems by its nature to deny that very freedom from the constraint of sensation which we regard as characteristically human: the more accurate the imitation, the more bound the "I" is to outward impression, the less spontaneous. But imitation may be understood in a broader, distinctly Aristotelian sense as something more than mere reproduction. The difference between the inarticulate imitation of animal sounds which express mere sensation and the articulate mimesis of human speech is that mimetic "reproduction never consists in retracing, line for line, a specific content of reality; but in selecting a pregnant motif in that content and so producing a characteristic 'outline' of its form."[39] This is to say that the simplest human mimetic act is implicitly symbolic. With the spoken word, the symbolic possibilities of mimetic gestures are manifest, since the single word not only expresses immediate duration and location in the moment of its utterance but it carries with it as well reference to a systematic whole of which it is the definitive part: "the element exists only insofar as it is constantly regenerated: its content is gathered up into the act of its production."[40] Language is vital precisely in that it is self-perfecting strictly according to its own laws. Cassirer devotes the remainder of his second chapter to this new perspective on the evolution of language through its mimetic, its analogical, and finally its fully "symbolic" phases.

Yet once again what appear to be later and more complex phases of development in the process of language formation prove instead to be aspects of the intuitive whole which is language itself, aspects separated one from another strictly for purposes of explanation. It is difficult here as throughout the *Language* volume to decide upon the logical or chronological priorities involved. Where a phonetic representation breaks the tie with a single sensuous object or sense impression to express *relation*, we have an instance of *analogical* signification. The linguistic phenomenon of reduplication is a good example. At first reduplication seems to be governed by the principle of imitation since phonetic repetition resembles repetition in the sensuous reality or impression. But there is a curious inconsistency which argues against such an interpretation. Reduplication can be an intensifier or an attenuator, and in temporal sequences it can designate past, present, or future: "This is the clearest indication that it is not so much a reproduction of a fixed and limited perceptual content as the expression of a specific *approach*, one might say a certain perceptual movement."[41] Cassirer wants to view the linguistic phenomenon of reduplication as an implicit trope, itself an "unfilled content" which becomes functional in language according to the purpose it takes on. He has reduced what might seem a secondary and mechanical complication of the principle of imitation to a simple and primary intuition in itself. It is the semblance of purpose which this phenomenon reveals—its "content as the expression of a specific approach"—and not its relational character which Cassirer stresses. What he discovers is that in fact his tripartite division of linguistic functions breaks down; for however we wish to describe the character of the individual linguistic phenomenon in its capacity to *designate* (whether the relationship between sign and referent is imitative or analogical), in its capacity to *signify* the individual element of language partakes of the symbolic function of language as an intuitive and undifferentiated whole:

> All these phenomena, to which we might easily add others of like nature, make it evident that even where language starts as purely

> imitative or "analogical" expression, it constantly strives to extend and finally to surpass its limits. It makes a virtue of necessity, that is, of the ambiguity inevitable in the linguistic sign. For this very ambiguity will not permit the sign to remain a mere individual sign; it compels the spirit to take the decisive step from the concrete function of "designation" to the universal and universally valid function of "signification." In this function language casts off, as it were, the sensuous covering in which it has hitherto appeared; mimetic or analogical expression gives way to purely symbolic expression which, precisely in and by virtue of its otherness, becomes the vehicle of a new and deeper spiritual content.[42]

In this passage too, Cassirer seems to establish a sequence of development in language from designation to signification. But we misapprehend the very basis of his argument if we fail to recognize that language as symbolic action presupposes a fundamental identity between the objective and subjective spheres of intuition, an identity which renders designation and signification simultaneous aspects of a single process. This point should become clearer as we move on to Cassirer's third chapter.

Cassirer's primary concern in this chapter is with the interpenetration of sensuous and spiritual experience in language, and for this purpose he describes the dependence of linguistic conceptualization upon the Kantian intuitions of space, time, and number. For the substance of his argument he draws a full array of illustrations from anthropology and child psychology. But more pertinent to our investigation is the new conclusion he reaches about the relationship between designation and signification. It is true that a part of what language does is to give us new specifications for what we regard as the world of objects; this function (we might call it the "nominal" function of language, the "naming" or "noun-making" function) is expressive in that the objective and subjective spheres are correlative (to confer a name is to objectify the self). But language has another independent means of giving form to subjective existence, for the terms which disclose the reality of the self are not drawn exclusively from those of the external world. The pronoun does not "stand for" a noun: its priority is a necessary inference from the nature of the speaking situation.[43] This new function of language (in the broadest sense "pronominal") is perhaps best exemplified by the modal distinctions in verbs, another implicit trope or system of tropes by which the "I" expresses any of various attitudes toward or relationships with the sphere of objective reality.

And yet, as Cassirer goes on to point out, this subjective "I" continually seeks objective form: the worlds inside and outside must, when language first incorporates the "I," be differentiated on objective grounds. Thus the first personal pronouns are possessive pronouns.[44] Nonetheless, such objectivization is spiritual expression, and once more we discover that any attempt to break down the spiritual unity of expression into its component phases finally must fail:

> . . . the power demonstrated by language . . . lies not in regarding the opposition between subjective and objective as a rigid, abstract opposition between two mutually exclusive spheres, but in conceiving it as dynamically mediated in the most diverse ways. Language does not represent the two spheres in themselves but reveals their reciprocal determination—it creates as it were a middle realm in which the forms of substance and the forms of action are referred to one another and fused into a spiritual unity of expression.[45]

The model here for the relationship between subject and object obtains with reference to all symbolic activity; the concept of symbolic form as mediation is important for Cassirer's aesthetics.

He begins the last chapter of the *Language* volume with another of Humboldt's fundamental insights, that the true and original element in all language formation is not the simple word but the sentence.[46] It was Humboldt who described the conceptualization of the single word as expressive of "inner form," and up to this point it has been with the single word in its formation that Cassirer has dealt almost exclusively. And yet his procedure here is identical with his procedure throughout: what might seem a secondary complication is revealed as logically or chronologically prior. Now Cassirer is able to adopt the principle of "organism" and make it his own. Aristotelian "organism" postulates the whole as prior to its parts, and language proves itself organic in nature as we see "inner form" specifically expressed in the relationship between linguistic elements.

> Here again that relation between "essence" and "form" which is expressed in the old scholastic dictum *forma dat esse rei*, is confirmed also for language. Epistemology cannot analyze the substance and form of knowledge into independent contents which are only outwardly connected with one another; the two factors can only be thought and defined in relation to one another; and likewise in language, pure, naked substance is a mere abstraction—a meth-

> odological concept to which no immediate "reality," no empirical fact corresponds.[47]

Thus the "progression" toward the "expression of pure relation" which characterizes the development of language culminates in the expression of pure relation, the *copula* itself, the "is." And thus the culmination of linguistic development is at the same time the threshold of judgment, the expression without which no judgment is possible.[48] Yet even here there is no breakdown in the unity of subject and object, of the spiritual and material, in expression. For even the abstract form of pure relation cannot cast off its materiality or there can be no expression; rather,

> Here again, the spiritual form of relational expression can be represented only in a certain material cloak, which, however, comes ultimately to be so permeated with the relational meaning that it no longer appears as a mere barrier, but as the sensuous vehicle of a purely ideal signification.[49]

In the chapter on art in *An Essay on Man*, his most extended treatment of the subject, Cassirer focuses on two problems: first, he attempts to demonstrate the specifically symbolic character of artistic form, and second—because the danger arises immediately of our granting the domain of symbolic expression *exclusively* to art—he argues that artistic form is only one of the various symbolic realms of expression. It is here then that we should find the distinction Cassirer draws between language and the art of language. And it should be possible to elaborate Cassirer's aesthetics on the basis of our review of the *Language* volume. In particular, his discussion of genre in this chapter is only cursory. Perhaps on the basis of this chapter and the systematic philosophy of symbolic forms we can organize what are scattered arguments in defense of genre into a coherent exposition.

That same "basic division in the interpretation of reality" between objective and subjective which we found in the philosophy of language is apparent in the history of aesthetics.[50] Only, surprisingly, philosophers of art are even more susceptible than philosophers of language of falling to one or the other of the extremes of interpretation and of failing, in either case, to recognize the specifically symbolic function of the artistic form. The chief danger in the realm of language is to regard symbol as sign, to deny linguistic form its special autonomy and its expressive power. We tend not to see the trope in the syntactical element or the word. Although of course we never deny language its practical value as a vehicle of communication, its expressive value is seldom recognized. Aesthetic theorists, on the other hand, especially sensitive to the problem of communication, either defensively assert or radically deny the continuity of art with the rest of man's activities.[51] But there is another alternative. We can dismiss the criterion of communication as inadequate to explain either the motivation or the function of the art symbol and look instead to its expressive value. Beauty, according to Schiller, is "living form";[52] it is an active, "spontaneous" intuition of the forms of things. And the symbolic function of the articulate whole which is art resolves the possible antinomy between truth and beauty:

> To be sure, it is not the same thing to live in the realm of forms as to live in that of things, of the empirical objects of our surroundings. The forms of art, on the other hand, are not empty forms. They perform a definite task in the construction and organization of human experience. To live in the realm of forms does not signify an evasion of the issues of life; it represents, on the contrary, the realization of one of the highest energies of life itself. We cannot speak of art as "extrahuman" or "superhuman" without overlooking one of its fundamental features, its constructive power in the framing of our human universe.[53]

But the spontaneous, constructive power of art (as of language) may be called into question by another misconception of its truth-function, the *imitation* theory.

In art as in language there is a sense in which the mimetic impulse is primary: "Language originates in an imitation of sounds, art is an imitation of outward things. Imitation is a fundamental instinct, an irreducible fact of human nature."[54] But in the sense that imitation is constraint, in the sense that it is understood as a mere mechanical reproduction either of external *things* or internal *emotions*,[55] in that sense the symbolic form of art would be denied the very quality of spontaneity which distinguishes it as symbolic. Art is not the shadow of reality but reality itself expressed in a unique mode of symbolization.

The artist does not find creative freedom simply by turning his attention from the external to the internal, from the sensual to the emotional life. It was Croce's mistake to think that freedom is attained for artistic intuition simply by its becoming inner-directed, that it gains its creative strength by withholding itself for the moment of art from sensuous medium. Croce's emphasis upon the spiritual is a healthy one, but as a solution to the problem of freedom in art it is simply inadequate. By denying the function of sensuous medium in the process of artistic intuition, Croce has fallen back upon an essentially imitative concept of art; he has failed to recognize that as a symbolic form art unifies the spiritual and the sensual and only thereby attains freedom:

> Like all the other symbolic forms art is not the mere reproduction of a ready-made, given reality. It is one of the ways leading to an objective view of things and of human life. It is not an imitation but a discovery of reality.[56]

The purposive activity of art as symbolic form is the same process of "objectivization" which characterized "discovery" in language.

But the Crocean construct of the imagination is inadequate on other grounds as well. At this point we need to explore further the way in which such objectivization works in the symbolic domains of language and art. Once again, the "motive for metaphor,"[57] the impulse toward the symbolic *use* of language is a private one; it does not rise out of any need to communicate. To Goethe's despair over the way that language seems finally to be a barrier and not a bridge between men, Cassirer answers:

> If the function of language and art were only that of building bridges between the inner worlds of different subjects, the objection that this task is utopian would be justified. . . . [But] language is *not merely* an *externalization* of ourselves; like art and any of the other symbolic forms, it is a *pathway to* [the realization of] ourselves. It is productive in that consciousness and knowledge of ourselves is first achieved by means of it.[58]

The artist discovers himself in the art which he creates in that, simply, the artist expresses himself in substantial form. For such an internal dialogue there is no direct need for an audience. If art is to be understood as communication, it is communication, as Susanne Langer says, "not anxious to be understood." On this point there would seem to be no disagreement with Croce, for what Cassirer is reminding us of is that the objectivity which we attribute to our surroundings is a quality which we have given them, that when the artist identifies what is inside with what is outside he does so not to get along with the external world but to satisfy an order within. But Cassirer qualifies his argument with his concept of symbolic form as *mediation* within that community of "artists" which *as* a community represents the possibility for objective value in art:

> . . . the "I" does not exist as an original and given reality which related itself to other realities . . . thus entering into communion with them.[Rather,] *separation* between "I" and "you," and likewise that between "I" and "world," constitutes the *goal* and not the starting point of the spiritual life.[59]

We can see more clearly the tradition in which Cassirer stands by comparing his concept of symbol as mediation with what Schiller has to say about the freedom which art affords in the *Letters on the Aesthetic Education of Man.* Schiller's starting point too is language, but the myth of the origin of language which he draws has broader implications:

> Whilst man, in his first physical condition, is only passively affected by the world of sense, he is still entirely identified with it; and for this reason the external world, as yet, has no objective existence for him. When he begins in his aesthetic state of mind to regard the world objectively, then only is his personality severed from it, and the world appears to him an objective reality, for the simple reason that he has ceased to form an identical portion of it.[60]

What art instructs us in is the capacity for reflective contemplation:

> Whereas desire seizes at once its object, reflection removes it to a distance and renders it inalienably her own by saving it from the greed of passion. The necessity of sense which [man] obeyed during the period of mere sensations, lessens during the period of reflection; the senses are for the time in abeyance; even ever-fleeting time stands still whilst the scattered rays of consciousness are gathering and shape themselves; an image of the infinite is reflected upon perishable ground. . . . Nature, which previously ruled him as a power, now expands before him as an object. What is objective to him can have no power over him, for in order to become objective it has to experience his own power.[61]

What Schiller describes as the objectivizing power of the artistic symbol Cassirer would extend to all of man's symbolic forms, which is to say from one point of view that all of man's symbols are artistic and from another that art holds no unique sway over the powers of the imagination. This is a point to which we will return immediately, for in it lies the crux of Cassirer's dispute with Croce. But about Schiller we should notice first that he makes no distinction here between artist and audience but rather speaks of man in his *aesthetic state of mind* and second, and in this connection, that the criterion of communication between artist and audience plays no part in the power the symbol has in freeing the human spirit through objectivization.

The ideal audience, that audience the writer writes for, is his projection of himself in the realm of freedom; the reader who approximates this ideal realizes that freedom which for Cassirer separates man from beast. What we learn from our experience of art is that the artist creates in a state of freedom; what we do then, because we too would be free, is to become artists ourselves, to recognize the manifold symbolic forms which constitute culture as human creations and strive to make them beautiful. To return to Schiller:

> Does . . . a state of beauty in appearance exist, and where? It must be in every finely harmonized soul; but as a fact it is only in select circles, like the pure ideal of the Church and state—in circles where manners are not formed by empty imitations of the foreign, but by the very beauty of nature; where man passes through all sorts of complications in all simplicity and innocence, neither forced to trench on another's freedom to preserve his own, nor to show grace at the cost of dignity.[62]

Cassirer and Croce both subscribe to the idea that culture as a purposive activity is a possible realm of expressive freedom.

But Croce would subsume all of man's cultural activities under the broad heading of aesthetics. Cassirer spends a good portion of his chapter on art in the *Essay on Man* marking the bounds of the aesthetic domain, marking it off from others of the symbolic forms:

> Language and science are abbreviations of reality; art is an intensification of reality. Language and science depend upon one and the same process of abstraction; art may be described as a continuous process of concretion. . . . [Art] does not inquire into the qualities or causes of things; it gives us the intuition of the form of things.[63]

> What we call "*aesthetic* semblance" is not the same phenomenon that we experience in games of illusion. Play gives us illusive images; art gives us a new kind of truth—a truth not of empirical things but of pure forms.[64]

> Science gives us order in thoughts; morality gives us order in actions, art gives us order in the apprehension of visible, tangible, and audible appearances. . . . Art may be defined as symbolic

> language. But this leaves us only with the common genus, not with the specific difference. In modern aesthetics the interest in the common genus seems to prevail to such a degree as almost to eclipse and obliterate the specific difference. Croce insists that there is not only a close relation but a complete identity between language and art. . . . There is, however, an unmistakable difference between the symbols of art and the linguistic terms of ordinary speech or writing. These two activities agree neither in character nor purpose; they do not employ the same means, nor do they tend toward the same ends. Neither language nor art gives us mere imitation of things or actions; both are representations. But a representation in the medium of sensuous forms differs widely from a verbal or conceptual representation.[65]

Taken together, these remarks scattered throughout the chapter all point in one direction. The specific difference between art and language is a difference of medium, and so Croce, who would leave out of aesthetics any consideration of material form, misapprehends the very process of artistic creation.

It is precisely this consideration of material form which demands that as critics of art we recognize the function of artistic genre. The principle of Aristotelian "organism" which is evident in language in the priority of the sentence over individual syntactical elements and individual words—a phenomenon in language which Humboldt designates "inner form"—has its parallel application within the realm of art. Artistic intuition is unique and undifferentiated in its logically and temporally primary phase: it is an intuition of the whole which only subsequently (or consequently) becomes differentiated into its parts. Thus Cassirer may speak of the various idioms of art and the architectonic process by which intuition finds material expression.[66]

Such a statement carries its own qualification, for the intuition does not *seek out* the medium of its expression; rather, characteristically of symbolic activity in general, the medium itself is a part of that intuition:

> The context of a poem cannot be separated from its form—from the verse, the melody, the rhythm. These formal elements are not merely external or technical means to reproduce a given intuition; they are part and parcel of the artistic intuition itself.[67]

Croce argues that to remove from the individual poem a single one of its constituents is to destroy its essential unity, that "the poem is born with [its] words, rhythms, and meters."[68] "From this," says Cassirer,

> it also follows that the aesthetic intuition is born at the same time —i.e., as musical, plastic, lyric, or dramatic—and that these distinctions are, therefore, not mere verbal labels or notations which we fix on works of art, and finally, that true differences of style, divergent directions of artistic intention, correspond to these differences.[69]

The term "epic" as it applies to an epic poem works in two ways. On one hand it *designates* a certain complex of characteristics which seem derived, seem to be secondary elaborations of individual words or lines or images when those elements of the poem are taken as its simplest constituents—when, that is, we read the poem word by word, line by line, image by image. An epic poem is a complex poem. At the same time, though, the simplest constituent element of an epic poem is that single, comprehensive intuition (or "direction of intention") which is its epicness. And this is what the term epic *signifies.* When does that epic form come into being? Not, of course, until the complex of the poem which it designates is complete. And yet that comprehensive intuition which "epic" signifies exists prior to the individual words, lines, images, etc., which embody it since it determines their relationship one to another. In more simple terms, the form is fulfilled over the course of the poem—fulfilled and discovered simultaneously. In more practical terms, the reader comes to an epic poem with a certain expectation of its major form, and that expectation is satisfied or frustrated.

But our "practical" conclusion begs several very practical questions. Is genre in fact an intuition born of the artistic medium and not a mechanical and academic deduction on the artist's part from a tradition of historical precedents? Can the intuition which is genre ever be perfectly expressed? Is its expression invariable? What specifically is the relationship between one epic poem and another? Cassirer answers questions like these in a convincingly practical way by examining the function of tradition in the history of culture at the conclusion of his *Logic of the Humanities.*

Clearly the kind of coherence, the unique "rationality of form,"[70] which the successful poem or statue or piece of music exhibits is a sufficient guarantee and the only guarantee of its truth, for such coherence is the only criterion for symbolic expression. Yet the symbolic form called art, like the other symbolic forms, is a comprehensive and articulate whole with its own specific modality (representation in the medium of sensual forms) and its own history. Two opposing factors are continually at work in the historical evaluation of art and the arts, the factor of "constancy of form" and the factor of "modifiability of form."[71] But this evolution, this process, can only be carried on by individual artists. The tradition remains in one sense autonomous, and the individual retains his freedom within that tradition:

> The creative process must always satisfy two different conditions: on the one side, it must tie itself to something existing and enduring, and, on the other, it must be receptive to new use and application. Only in this way does one succeed in doing justice to both the objective and the subjective demands [implicit in the creative act]. . . . The tie to tradition is most readily evident in what we call technique in the various arts. It is subject to rules as fixed as in any other use of tools; for it is dependent upon the nature of the materials in which the artist works. Art and craft, imaginative activity and skill, have disengaged themselves only very slowly; and it is precisely when artistic achievement is highest that we are likely to find a particularly intimate union between these two factors. No artist can really speak his language if he has not previously learned it through the relentless experience of give and take with its materials. And this is by no means restricted merely to the material-technical side of the problem. It also has its exact parallel in the sphere of form as such. For, once created, even the artistic forms become part of the fixed tradition handed down from one generation to another. . . . The language of forms assumes such fixity that specific themes, with their determinate modes of expression, seem so firmly grown together that we encounter them again and again in the same or only slightly modified forms.[72]

Indeed Cassirer observes of lyric form that "there are, after all, only a few great and fundamental themes to which lyric poetry may apply itself."[73] The reason for this phenomenon lies not so much in the limitations of human experience, of course, as in the restricted nature of *that* experience which lyric intuition discloses. For Croce, such "restriction" seems a constraint, but only because he persists in regarding form and matter as antagonistic forces in the process of creation. With Cassirer, the opposition of form and matter is resolved in their reciprocal determination:

> From the standpoint of phenomenological inquiry there is no more a "matter in itself" than a "form in itself"; there are only total experiences which can be compared from the standpoint of matter and form and determined and ordered according to this standpoint.[74]

The concept of genre is a meaningful one precisely in that the degree of determination which it identifies is the measure of freedom achieved. Such, as Harry Slochower describes it, is the thrust of Cassirer's insistence upon art as mediation.[75]

But there can be no perfect lyric, no perfectly lyrical poem. Nor is the expression of lyric intuition invariable. We can erect critical paradigms for genres in art—in fact as critics responsive to generic unity within individual works of art we are obliged to—but we will find no single example which perfectly conforms to the paradigms we erect. Does this invalidate the concept of genre as a critical tool? Here we can appropriate Cassirer's defense of Burkhardt's generic "Renaissance man":

> Shall we regard it, in the logical sense, as a null class—as a class containing no single member? That would be necessary only if we were concerned here with one of those generic concepts arrived at through empirical comparison of particular cases, through what we commonly call "induction."[76]

But neither the historian nor the critic of art works quite this way. What Burkhardt discovered about men of the Renaissance was no common characteristic or set of characteristics but rather a "specific ideal connection," a "unity of *direction*, not a unity of *actualization*," a "common task," the manifestation of a specific "will."[77]

The historian's apprehension of epochal characterization, because it is a "logico-intellectual activity which is *sui generis*,"[78] is not functionally different from the aesthetic critic's apprehension of genre. The relationship between one epic poem and another is, likewise, an ideal relationship: epic poets cooperate in the task of disclosing epic experience, and the critic who is able conceptually to identify such unity of direction has penetrated into that articulate whole which is the symbolic form of art as it evolves in time. The process of that evolution, the dynamics of innovation in the arts, is, as we should expect, much like that in language itself. To speak of genre as static form with fixed characteristics would be to deny the vitality of culture as an achievement:

> In this process the hardened forms are also ever and again melted down, so that they cannot "clothe themselves in rigid armor"; but on the other hand, only in this process do even the momentary impulse, the creation of the moment, receive their continuity and stability. This creation would, like a bubble, have to dissolve be-

> fore every breath of air if it did not, in the midst of its originating and becoming, encounter earlier structures—forms already originated and in existence—to which it may cling and hold fast. Thus even this which has already come into being is for language not merely material, against which foreign and ever stranger material is ever pressing; but is the product and attestation of the same formative powers to which even language itself owes it existence. . . . And the same fundamental relationship exhibited here in the realm of language holds true of every genuine "symbolic form."[79]

We can return in this connection to Schiller's description of the relationship between artist and audience. The critic's activity is finally not much different from that of the artist himself, for in his apprehension of genre the critic engages in the process of objectivization inherent in all symbolic activity. Artist and critic alike are liberated for participation in that culture which is their common task.

NOTES

1. *The Philosophy of Symbolic Forms*, 3 vols., trans. Ralph Manheim (New Haven: Yale University Press, 1953), I, 117–73. The three volumes will be designated *Language*, *Mythical Thought*, and *The Phenomenology of Knowledge* respectively throughout this essay.
2. Cassirer, *Language*, p. 80.
3. Cassirer, *The Logic of the Humanities*, trans. Clarence Smith Howe (New Haven: Yale University Press, 1960), p. 22.
4. The only Plato that would approve this wording is what Cassirer calls the "Kantian Plato" (*An Essay on Man: An Introduction to a Philosophy of Culture* [New Haven: Yale University Press, 1944], p. 180), whose formulation of the problem of knowledge Kant recognized as implicitly his own (see *Critique of Pure Reason*, trans. Norman Kemp Smith [London, 1929], p. 310). As for Croce, although, as we shall see, his reservations about the Kantian epistemology are crucial to his aesthetic theory, by defining "intuition" as "the undifferentiated unity of the perception of the real and of the simple image of the possible" (*Aesthetic as Science of Expression and General Linguistic*, trans. Douglas Ainslie [London, 1922], p. 4), he affirms as unassailable the unit-factor of perception.
5. Cassirer, *Language*, p. 175.
6. Ibid., p. 176; see also p. 71.
7. Cassirer, *The Phenomenology of Knowledge*, p. 340.

8. Ibid., p. 108. See Katharine Gilbert, "Cassirer's Placement of Art," *The Philosophy of Ernst Cassirer*, ed. P. A. Schilpp (Evanston, Ill., 1949), pp. 607–30.

9. Cassirer, *Language*, p. 313.

10. Croce, *Aesthetic*, p. 1.

11. Ibid., p. 17.

12. "Intuitive activity *possesses intuitions to the extent that it expresses them*. . . . It is impossible to distinguish intuition from expression in this cognitive process. The one appears with the other at the same instant, because they are not two, but one" (Croce, *Aesthetic*, p. 8).

13. Ibid., p. 35.

14. Croce, *Grundiss der Aesthetik* [German version] (Leipzig, 1913), p. 36, quoted by Cassirer in *The Logic of the Humanities*, p. 207. See *The Essence of Aesthetic*, trans. Douglas Ainslie (London, 1921), p. 43.

15. Cassirer, *Logic of the Humanities*, p. 208.

16. Ibid., p. 206. See also *Essay on Man*, pp. 141–42.

17. Croce, *Aesthetic*, p. 21.

18. Cassirer, *The Phenomenology of Knowledge*, p. 13.

19. Cassirer, *Language*, p. 152.

20. Cassirer's "anthropological philosophy" is most clearly outlined in his *Essay on Man*; his concept of "animal symbolicum" as a key to man's creative activity has been accepted as axiomatic by such diverse thinkers as Susanne Langer (see *Mind: An Essay on Human Feeling*, [Baltimore, 1967], I, 60ff.) and Kenneth Burke (see *Language as Symbolic Action* [Berkeley, 1967]).

21. Cassirer, *Language*, pp. 189–90; see also *Essay on Man*, pp. 28–33 and 116ff., and *Logic of the Humanities*, pp. 68–77.

22. See *Essay on Man*, p. 57ff., and *The Phenomenology of Knowledge*, pp. 205–32, 263–71.

23. See *Essay on Man*, pp. 33–37 and 131ff., and *The Phenomenology of Knowledge*, p. 112.

24. For an index, see *Language*, pp. 321–23.

25. Cassirer (*Language*, pp. 152–53) quotes Herder, "*Über den Ursprung der Sprache*" (1772), *Werke*, ed. B. Suphan (Berlin, 1877–90), V, 34.

26. Cassirer, *Language*, p. 69.

27. Ibid., p. 153.

28. Ibid., p. 155.

29. Cassirer (*Language*, p. 279) quotes C. V. Sigwart, *Logik* [German version], I, 320ff.; see trans. Helen Dendy (London, 1895), I, 248–49.

30. Cassirer, *Language*, p. 281.

31. Ibid., p. 280.

32. Ibid., pp. 281–82.
33. Ibid., pp. 283–84.
34. Ibid., p. 284. See also Hendrik J. Pos, "The Philosophical Significance of Comparative Semantics," trans. Sheila A. Kerr, *Philosophy and History: Essays Presented to Ernst Cassirer*, ed. Raymond Klibansky and H. J. Paton (New York, 1963), pp. 269–70 and 276.
35. Ibid., p. 285; see also *Essay on Man*, p. 134.
36. Cassirer (*Language*, p. 159) quotes Humboldt, *"Über das vergleichende Sprachstudium," Werke*, ed. Albert Leitzmann (Berlin, 1903–08), IV, 21ff.
37. Cassirer, *Language*, p. 159; see also Pos, pp. 270–71.
38. Ibid., p. 181. This quality of "dynamism" is nowhere more apparent than in mythic "possession": "the spark jumps somehow across, the tension finds release, as the subjective excitement becomes objectified and confronts the mind as a god or a daemon" (*Language and Myth*, trans. Susanne Langer [New York, 1946], p. 33).
39. Cassirer, *Language*, p. 183.
40. Ibid., p. 185.
41. Ibid., p. 196.
42. Ibid., p. 197.
43. Ibid., pp. 249–51.
44. Ibid., p. 260.
45. Ibid., p. 259.
46. Ibid., pp. 303-4.
47. Ibid., p. 306.
48. Cassirer (*Language*, p. 314) quotes Kant: "I find that a judgment is nothing other than the mode of bringing given cognitions under the *objective* unity of apperception. This is plain from our use of the term of relation *is* in judgments, in order to distinguish the objective unity of given representations from the subjective unity" (*Kritik der reinen Vernunft*, 2nd edition, p. 142).
49. Cassirer, *Language*, p. 318. Wilbur M. Urban ("Cassirer's Philosophy of Language," *The Philosophy of Ernst Cassirer*, ed. Schilpp, p. 420) regards the crux in the dual tendency toward pure signification on the one hand and realization in the medium of language on the other as not satisfactorily resolved.
50. Cassirer, *Essay on Man*, p. 138.
51. See above, pp. 166–67.
52. See "Letter XV," *Letters on the Aesthetical Education of Man, The Works of Friedrich Schiller*, ed. Nathan Haskell Dole (New York, 1902), p. 53.
53. Cassirer, *Essay on Man*, p. 167.
54. Ibid., p. 138.
55. Ibid., p. 141.

56. Ibid., p. 143.

57. This phrase is Northrop Frye's, whose understanding of the essentially private impulse toward poetic creation is identical with Cassirer's. See *The Educated Imagination* (Bloomington, Ind., 1964), pp. 13–33. See also the last chapter in *Language and Myth* ("The Power of Metaphor," pp. 83–99) in which Cassirer discriminates between language, myth, and art in terms of the motive and function of metaphor within each symbolic domain.

58. Cassirer, *Logic of the Humanities*, pp. 112–14.

59. Ibid., p. 189.

60. Schiller, "Letter XXV," p. 91.

61. Ibid., pp. 91–92; see *Essay on Man*, p. 166.

62. Schiller, "Letter XXVII," p. 110.

63. Cassirer, *Essay on Man*, p. 143.

64. Ibid., p. 164.

65. Ibid., p. 168.

66. Ibid., p. 154. See Slochower's description of "art as the dialectic of concrete totality," pp. 642–45.

67. Cassirer, *Essay on Man*, p. 155.

68. Croce, *Essence of Aesthetic*, p. 44; see *Logic of the Humanities*, p. 208. Katharine Gilbert (p. 618) calls attention to other passages in which Croce seems to recognize artistic medium.

69. Cassirer, *Logic of the Humanities*, p. 209.

70. Cassirer, *Essay on Man*, p. 167.

71. Cassirer, *Logic of the Humanities*, p. 209. Such are the two main "laws of the spirit" manifest in all cultural growth; see Robert S. Hartman, "Cassirer's Philosophy of Symbolic Forms," *The Philosophy of Ernst Cassirer*, ed. Schilpp, pp. 297–99.

72. Cassirer, *Logic of the Humanities*, pp. 200–202.

73. Ibid., p. 209.

74. Cassirer, *The Phenomenology of Language*, p. 199; see Hartman, p. 321.

75. Slochower, pp. 645–47.

76. Cassirer, *Logic of the Humanities*, p. 138.

77. Ibid., pp. 139–40.

78. Ibid., p. 140.

79. Cassirer, " 'Spirit' and 'Life' in Contemporary Philosophy," *The Philosophy of Ernst Cassirer*, ed. Schilpp, pp. 879–80.

Susanne Langer: Unity and Diversity Among the Arts

REID HUNTLEY
OHIO UNIVERSITY

SUSANNE LANGER entitles her three-volume magnum opus, of which the first volume has recently been published, *Mind: An Essay on Human Feeling*. In making the human mind, and especially the artistic imagination, her major concern, she has focused on one of the main problems of twentieth-century philosophy: how we know and what we know, how we feel and what we feel. This interest in the mind and in the imagination has also been a dominant theme in twentieth-century aesthetic literary criticism.

To trace Mrs. Langer's contribution to our understanding of the imagination, we need to consider the general development of this concept through her major publications, then return to one particular book, *Feeling and Form*, the most comprehensive expression of her aesthetic theory, and finally raise several questions concerning this theory. The conclusion that emerges from an examination of Mrs. Langer's writings is that, starting with the distinction between the "two entirely different modes of thought," discursive logic and creative imagination,[1] she has demonstrated the unity among the arts by the fact that they have their common origin and expression in the creative imagination. She has also suggested that the various art forms differ according to which mode of sensibility within the creative imagination they primarily express. This analysis of the diversity among the arts is her most important contribution to aesthetic theory.

Mrs. Langer defines the three major stages in her intellectual development when she describes the origins of the work now in progress: "This essay has arisen out of a previous book, *Feeling and Form*, which in turn arose from a predecessor, *Philosophy in a New Key*."[2] Her intellectual life has not been one of sharply demarked stages which necessitated a denial or reversal of earlier positions. Rather, each subsequent work has been a further ramification of certain major ideas which she expressed in embryo in an earlier work. As she says in the preface to the second edition of *Philosophy in a New Key*, "A book is like a life: all that is in it is really of a piece."

In her first book, *The Practice of Philosophy* (1930), she gave her view of the dead end which philosophy had reached. She saw an end to the Cartesian Age and predicted a new direction in philosophy based on Kant's idealism and Einstein's relativity. In this first publication she showed her philosophical, aesthetic sensibility. She also demonstrated her iconoclasm as well as her unwillingness to lose questions of meaning and wisdom in the midst of a study of facts and ideas. She held out both for the logic of the scientist and the intuition of the artist. She made her important distinction between "sign," which denotes some actuality, and "symbol," which connotes some realm of virtual life. She pointed to the higher importance of symbols in expressing the complex meaning of life: "The fundamental problem of meaning is not so much the interpretation of individual signs as of symbolic forms."[3] The Prefatory Note added by her teacher, Alfred N. Whitehead, reveals his presence as a major influence upon her at this time. In her second work, *An Introduction to Symbolic Logic* (1937, rev. 1953), her lifetime interests in system, generalization, abstraction, and "forms" predominate.

Philosophy in a New Key: A Study of the Symbolism of Reason, Rite, and Art (1942), Mrs. Langer's first major work, carried her interest in symbolization to a crucial distinction—that between science and art. In the Preface to the Second Edition of this book she asserts that knowledge, i.e., scientific knowledge, is not synonymous with human mentality because there is more to human mentality than knowledge. She distinguished between discursive forms (logical and scientific) and presentational forms (non-discursive and symbolic). The symbolizing of life, she said, led to such phenomena as rituals, myth, and art. As an example of the symbolic life expressed in art, she used the specific art of music. Here also was the germ of thought which led to her next important book, *Feeling and Form*. Already she was moving toward some differentiation among the arts. As she said, "[I] hesitate to say categorically, as many philosophers and critics have said, that the import of all the arts is the same, and only the medium depends on the peculiar psychological or sensory make-up of the artist, so that one man may fashion in clay what another renders in harmonies or in colors, etc."[4]

This book shows the influence of two men already mentioned, Whitehead, to whom it is dedicated, and Immanuel Kant. About the latter influence she acknowledges, "practically all serious and penetrating philosophy of art is related somehow to the idealistic tradition . . . launched by Immanuel Kant."[5] She goes on to say that the idealists were the first to show the essentially transformational nature of human understanding, to recognize the function of symbolic transformation as a natural activity characteristic only of man among the animals, and to give us an "illuminating literature of non-discursive symbolisms—myth, ritual, and art."[6] Yet she claimed that her own ideas sprang from different interests than those of Kant, that is from "logical rather than from ethical or metaphysical interests."[7] Besides Whitehead and Kant, there is the influence of a third philosopher in Mrs. Langer's work—Ernst Cassirer. Shortly after completing *Philosophy in a New Key* she translated Cassirer's *Language and Myth* (1946) and in the Translator's Preface to that work, summarized the cornerstone of her philosophy, which she had taken from Cassirer. This is the notion that language reflects man's mythmaking tendency even more than it does his rationalizing tendency. Language, therefore, exhibits "two entirely different modes of thought. Yet in both modes the mind is powerful and creative. It expresses itself in different forms, *one of which is discursive logic, the other creative imagination.*"[8] Such is the human mind: it has both a primitive, prelogical expression in symbols and an expression in logic and discursive reason, which was only achieved late in the history of man.

In *Feeling and From* (1953), her second major book, Mrs. Langer further refined her notion of the "creative imagination." She points out that all arts have in common their origin, expression, and comprehension in the symbolizing imagination. Each art genre differs according to which mode of sensibility within the imagination it can primarily express. Throughout this book, Mrs. Langer asserts a structure of correlations between two things—the genres of art and the "primary illusion" which is embodied in each of these art forms: virtual space in the plastic arts, virtual duration in music, virtual powers in dance, virtual memory in literature, and virtual destiny in drama. Put in other terms, she sees a structure of interrelationships between each artistic *form*, e.g., sculpture, and its artistically symbolized *feeling*, e.g., the feeling of an organism in space. Hence, the title of her work. We shall return to this book as the focus of this essay; for the moment, let us continue to trace her intellectual development on to the present.

In *Problems of Art: Ten Philosophical Lectures* (1957) she adapted her earlier ideas for lectures to particular audiences—dancers, music students, college students, and learned societies. These lectures add nothing new, but only offer a rewriting of her previous ideas. In 1958 she edited *Reflections on Art: A Source Book of Writings by Artists, Critics, and Philosophers*. These twenty-six articles are contributions toward the formation of a modern philosophy of art. What gives the collection unity is that all the essays "either expound or tacitly assume two basic concepts: the concept of expressiveness, as [she] treated it in *Feeling and Form*; and the concept of 'semblance' (Schiller's *Schein*), which defined the work of art as a wholly created appearance, the Art Symbol."[9] She claims that she herself tried to build a philosophy of art on these same fundamental ideas.[10] Therefore, in her Introduction to this work she presents what she conceives as the foundation of her aesthetics. *Philosophical Sketches* was published in 1962 as a series of in-progress "studies toward a single much larger work, a philosophy of mind. . . ."[11] These short pieces were an interim report on her forthcoming magnum opus.

The larger work toward which these aimed was *Mind: An Essay on Human Feeling*. The first of three volumes appeared in 1967, and it promises to be her most important work. Actually it assumes *Feeling and Form* as an earlier volume in the same series in order to avoid repeating her aesthetic theory which she still maintains as formulated in that earlier work. Here she traces the roots of science and of art to a common ground in the special nature of human feeling. The new concept of feeling which she expounds in this book derives from extensive reading in biology, biochemistry, psychology, and other technical disciplines, as well as in philosophy and aesthetics. She begins with the observation that the characteristically human element in cognition, that which makes human mentality very different from animal mentality, is man's symbolizing of his feelings. But when and how did this happen? To answer that question required extensive study of actual living form as biologists find it, and of actual phenomena of feeling, to which—she says—we have at present no scientific access. The search for an answer led her to a theory of the mind: "The central problem of the present essay is the nature and origin [the biological evolution] of the veritable gulf that divides human from animal mentality, in a perfectly continuous course of development of life on earth that has no break."[12] Her thesis in this book is that man's "departure from the normal pattern of animal mentality is a vast and special evolution of feeling in the hominid stock." This evolution of feeling "sets human nature apart from the rest of the animal kingdom as a mode of being that is typified by language, culture, morality, and consciousness of life and death."[13] Because this last work has more to do with biological evolution than with aesthetics, we shall now return to *Feeling and Form*, drawing upon *Mind* as upon her other works, when they are helpful in clarifying specifically her aesthetic theory.

The easiest approach to Mrs. Langer's "Theory of Art," the subtitle of *Feeling and Form*, is through the definitions which she offers for her most important words. From these definitions there emerges a theory quite radical in its implications, a theory which is sufficiently schematic to be presented in a diagram. Presenting a sense of the unique, sometimes difficult, meanings Mrs. Langer assigns to her key words will introduce most of her aesthetic theory. As Herbert Read has said, she is primarily a philosopher, and consequently much concerned with definition.[14]

"Art" is defined by Mrs. Langer as "the creation of forms symbolic of human feeling."[15] By "creation" she means more than producing or recording; she means using the imagination to form something entirely new and different from the actual. That which is symbolized in an artistic form is a feeling, and a particular kind of feeling: "what art expresses is not actual feelings, but ideas of feeling" (p. 59). This distinction between the actual feeling and the symbolic feeling—or the virtual feeling—lies at the base of her aesthetics. What she opposes is the spontaneous "expression" of an artist's own personal feelings. What she advocates is the "expression" of the concept of a feeling by means of appropriate symbols.

The word "feeling" is a crucial one for her. Herbert Read points out in *The Tenth Muse* that she distinguishes art from other symbolic activities by the nature of the material which it symbolizes;[16] since the material of art is feeling, one might expect that she would offer a definition of feeling. Curiously, she does not define it except to contrast the feeling in art with actual human emotions. The very notion of "an idea of a feeling" may seem an oxymoron. At best she associates feeling with such undefined words as "affects" and "sentience." In *Problems of Art*, her next book after *Feeling and Form*, she does offer a definition: "The word 'feeling' must be taken here in its broadest sense, meaning *every-*

thing that can be felt, from physical sensation, pain and comfort, excitement and repose, to the most complex emotions, intellectual tensions, or the steady feeling-tones of a conscious human life."[17] In her latest, most important book, *Mind: An Essay in Human Feeling*, she treats the subject of "Feeling" in the first chapter. There the word emerges with a very comprehensive definition. First she says that there is no such thing as "a feeling."[18] The basic misconception is, according to her, "the assumption of feelings (sensations, emotions, etc.) as items or entities of *any* kind . . . ."[19] Instead she claims that all mental phenomena are modes of feeling—all that the human brain does. And all the most impressive forms of mentation are feeling, including "symbolic expression, imagination, propositional thought, religious conception, mathematical abstraction, moral insight."[20]

Mrs. Langer creates another important set of terms in distinguishing between "sign" and "symbol." A "sign" points to an actual feeling, whereas a "symbol" expresses a virtual feeling. She later revises her terminology, using "signal" to refer to what she previously meant by "sign" and reserving the word "sign" as a generic term for both "signal" and "symbol." Art, as she says, expresses virtual feelings through symbols, not actual feelings through signs. Therefore art does not depict such a thing as clock time (a signal) but psychological time (a symbol fraught with complexity and virtuality). The word "symbol" relates to her original definition of art, "the creation of forms symbolic of human feelings," for a symbol is "from first to last, something created" (p. 67). She then attributes to "symbol" a very inclusive definition: "any device whereby we are enabled to make an abstraction" (p. xi).

By an "abstraction" she means a "semblance" of actual life. For example, an actor on the stage should express, not his own fear, but the feeling of fear in general. Such a semblance embodies a "significant form" of actual life, not actual life itself. Therefore a semblance is not a copy or an imitation of actual life—she has little traffic with mimetic realists or those who say that art should imitate life. She is even more harsh with naturalists, whom she calls "an epidemic" from which she hopes we are now fairly well recovered (p. 317). Further, a semblance is not a delusion, but an "illusion." These several words, "significant form," "semblance," "abstraction," "symbol," and "illusion," all refer to the same thing—the product of the symbolizing imagination. She links her notion of virtual life, of semblance, with Schiller's *Schein* (appearance). But her "virtual life" is divided and categorized into five major "semblances," something which Schiller's initial insight of art as appearance did not give him. The importance of this concept of appearance in art is, she says, that "it liberates perception—and with it, the power of conception—from all practical purposes, and lets the mind dwell on the sheer appearance of things" (p. 49). In Kant's terms this would free an aesthetic judgment (or an aesthetic creation) from any practical reason (moral purpose) or pure reason (scientific law). All arts are thus alike in their common expression of an appearance, of some virtual feeling.

But the arts are differentiated according to which virtual feeling they express. Mrs. Langer's major original contribution in this book is her assertion that each art form or genre has its own "primary illusion." That is to say, each art form has one main abstraction from actual life which it embodies; for example, dancing embodies the feeling of a virtual realm of powers. This feeling of virtual powers—human, daemonic, or magical—is expressed through the gestures of a dancer. Mrs. Langer is insistent that a work of art "can exist in only one primary illusion, which every element must serve to create, support, and develop. That is what happened to Wagner's operas in spite of himself: they are music. . . ." (p. 164) and not that which he attempted, a work combining all arts, a *Gesamtkunstwerk.*

Mrs. Langer does allow for "secondary illusions" within each work of art, however. For example, although dance embodies a semblance of actual life, primarily the semblance of powers, it can also have secondary semblances, such as time and space. As she says, "Powers become apparent in a framework of space and time" (p. 197). But she insists that there is only one primary illusion in any art form and that any other illusions are secondary and only support the primary illusion. The relation between illusions "is always kinship and not identity, so that two radically distinct orders never merge; a work never belongs to more than one realm, and it always establishes that one completely and immediately, as its very substance" (p. 205).

To explain what happens when an artist attempts to combine what she claims are discrete, mutually exclusive art forms, she uses the metaphor of "assimilation." If several arts are combined such as music and poetry, one art will predominate and "swallow" the others (pp. 154, 157). Of Wagner she says again:

> [His] theatrical inspiration is not expert stagecraft; the libretto is never great poetry; the scenery he demanded is no more great painting than any other, for scenery is not pictorial art at all; in short, his music drama is not the *Gesamtkunstwerk*, the work-of-all-

> arts, which he had projected in theory, but a work of music, like all the 'reprehensible' operas that went before it. [p. 161]

By this notion of secondary illusions, she escapes the dogmatism of asserting that each art form stands absolutely separate and apart from all other arts.

We are now in a position to relate her original theory of primary illusions to her specific understanding of the role of the imagination. The "imagination," a crucial word for her, is that which allows man to conceive, accept, and operate with virtual feelings in addition to actual feelings. It is because of the imagination that the human mentality is able to accept such things as the conventions of "fiction," that the time being portrayed on the stage need not be an actual three hours of real time, but can, for example, embody three decades in a man's life. Incidentally, it is because the neo-classic writers of the eighteenth century failed to understand these powers of the imagination and to apply them even to the most uneducated man, that they wrongly insisted on the literal unities of time and place. In Mrs. Langer's conceptualization, the imagination is that which correlates each virtual feeling with its appropriate art genre. The human imagination, for example, perceives and expresses virtual power in the dance form, virtual space in the plastic arts, virtual destiny in the dramatic form, etc. Our modes of sensibility (in the imagination) channel our modes of experience (our virtual feelings). Her system of feelings is correlated with the system of art genres.

If the imagination is a central concept for Mrs. Langer's aesthetics, we still need to understand a little more how it operates. For her an "intuition" in the imagination enables the artist to conceive of objects and forms of art which are as yet unexperienced and uncreated. For example, an architect can conceive of a virtual building, he can have a vision of how it will look when completed, without having first actually experienced or seen such a building. She says, in "handling his own creation . . . he learns from the perceptible reality before him possibilities of subjective experience he has not known in his personal life" (p. 390). It was the origin of such intuitions and imaginings that Locke's sense experience and associationism could not explain. It was left to Locke's critics, primarily Kant, to assert that the imagination is an active creative mechanism and not a passive receptor of mere sense impressions. In Mrs. Langer's words, the "imagination always creates; it never records" (p. 296).

For the significance or importance of a feeling which has been objectively embodied in a work of art, Mrs. Langer uses the word "import." She prefers this word to "meaning" because "meaning" contains too many connotations of how a work of art affects or impresses an audience. She is as little concerned with the audience's personal feelings as she is with the artist's actual feelings. Throughout this book she insists that her interest is with the work of art itself, with its import, its symbolized feeling, its significant form. She is, therefore, not interested in psychological criticism, historical criticism, or criticism based on audience response. Because of her focus on the art work itself, to the exclusion of any concern with the author's life, with his age or environment, or with his audience, she is very close to the "New Critics," such as Brooks, Warren, and Tate.

Mrs. Langer's theory of the expression of virtual feelings leads to a specific kind of art criticism. For the same reason that they all express actual feelings rather than feelings "transformed" into symbols, she scorns the following practitioners of art: Isadora Duncan in dance, literary naturalists like Zola, and musicians who use natural raindrops and tape-recorded hoofbeats for music. In contrast to these, she could be expected to praise Balanchine's choreography which is called "too abstract" by many, the literary symbolists like Melville who went unappreciated in an age of realism and pragmatism, and "abstract" painters like Picasso or Kandinsky.

The fact that Mrs. Langer rules out personal emotion in art has other implications. In music, for example, this would free the composer from concern with his own feelings and give him freedom fully to express the virtual feeling of time embodied in any particular musical piece. She says that if a performer is inspired entirely by the commanding form of the work, he does not have to restrain anything, but gives all he has (p. 140). The major problem for the performer of music is, according to Mrs. Langer, his ability to imagine the feeling being called for in the music. For that reason, a neophyte conductor would do poorly to attempt to conduct something as difficult as Beethoven's Ninth Symphony. According to her theory a musician also needs great training in the craft of his art; therefore a beginning violinist should not attempt to play Tchaikovsky's Violin Concerto. As performing requires a talent, so does listening require a special intelligence of the ear developed by exercise. Mrs. Langer slips over into the perspective of the audience when she says that listening requires an ability to experience the primary illusion of music, to feel the consistent movement of virtual time, of duration. For this reason she criticizes those people who listen to—no, who hear—a radio while studying something else, who are "learning not to listen," who cultivate passive hearing—which is the very opposite of listening (p. 147). Here she expresses her sophisticated aesthetic prejudice, her aristocratic and justifiable claim that talent, training, and concentration are all necessary to appreciate "good music."

So far regarding *Feeling and Form* I have tried to show that Susanne Langer's approach to the arts is through the art symbols themselves, and that she establishes her perspective as an art critic at a distance from nature, from the maker, and from the spectator. I have also tried to show that she conceives of the unity of all the arts on the basis of their common symbolization of human feelings, and that she differentiates among them according to which feeling is primarily symbolized in each art genre. This unites her with those critics who use the imagination to explain the difference between art and science. It separates her from other modern critics like Croce, who in his *Aesthetic* attacks the theory of distinguishable genres.

In Aristotle's *Poetics* the various arts are differentiated by the materials they use; that is, music is constructed from rhythms and harmonies, literature from language alone. But Aristotle allows these materials to be combined in drama, which he says uses all three materials: rhythm, harmony, and language. It is easier to conceive the merger of several arts on the basis of their materials than their differentiation on the basis of what Mrs. Langer calls their "primary illusions." It should be noted that Mrs. Langer's categorization of the five major art forms may have as its source the first chapter of Aristotle's *Poetics*, where Aristotle distinguishes these same five arts on the basis of their materials, objects of imitation, and manner of imitation.

Mrs. Langer's conceptual system of the arts may now be briefly summarized. The five major art forms are, according to her, distinguished from each other by the primary illusion which each embodies. The plastic arts, one genre, consist of three species: painting, sculpture, and architecture. They have in common the fact that each embodies some form of virtual space as its illusion. They differ according to what specific kind of virtual space each embodies. For Mrs. Langer painting expresses the feeling of the space in a scene, sculpture the feeling of the space of an organism, architecture the space of a place. Music, the second major genre, embodies primarily a feeling of virtual time, of duration in time. Dancing, the third major genre, expresses through gestures primarily the feeling of a virtual realm of powers—either human, daemonic, or magical.

Literature, according to Mrs. Langer, is a fourth major form of art, in which there are four species: lyric poetry, narrative poetry, prose fiction, and the combination of all of these in the epic form. All species of literature have in common their expression of a feeling of virtual memory. Whereas literature deals with past events, in finished realities, drama, the fifth major art form, deals with future acts, that is, with immediate visible responses of human beings which point toward the future. Through its virtual future acts drama expresses the feeling, not of virtual memory, but of virtual destiny. For Mrs. Langer there are two species of virtual destiny, Fortune embodied in comedy and Fate embodied in tragedy. By the distinction between fortune and fate Mrs. Langer offers her interpretation of the basic difference between the two major forms of drama, comedy and tragedy.

In an appendix she includes her preliminary supposition that the cinema is a different art form, important enough and different enough to be a sixth major art genre. She hypothesizes that the cinema has as its primary illusion the feeling of a virtual dream, which is expressed by the present acts shown on the screen. Her schematization of the art forms with their respective primary illusions may be shown in the diagram on the next page.

The diagram illustrates the separateness and distinctness of the five arts. It also shows the basis on which Mrs. Langer justifies considering cinema a unique art form. Her mention of the relatively new "art" of the cinema makes one wonder what she would do with another relatively new form of expression, single-picture photography, especially the symbolic photographs produced by artificial lights, telescopic and wide-angle lenses, and various color and refractory filters. Is photography a species of painting, or the cinema, or is it yet another art form?

Several theoretical questions and objections may be raised regarding Mrs. Langer's aesthetic theory. For example, when she talks about literature and drama, one might question some of her nice distinctions which seem too rigid. Comedy treats virtual destiny, specifically Fortune, in its optimistic, protective connotations; tragedy, on the other hand, treats virtual destiny, but more particularly Fate, with its pessimistic, deterministic connotations. This seems an illuminating distinction. However, less clear is her argument that literature should be distinguished from drama because literature deals with past events (finished realities); whereas drama deals with future acts (immediate visible responses of human beings which point toward the future) (p. 306). She implies that there is a neat and obvious difference between litera-

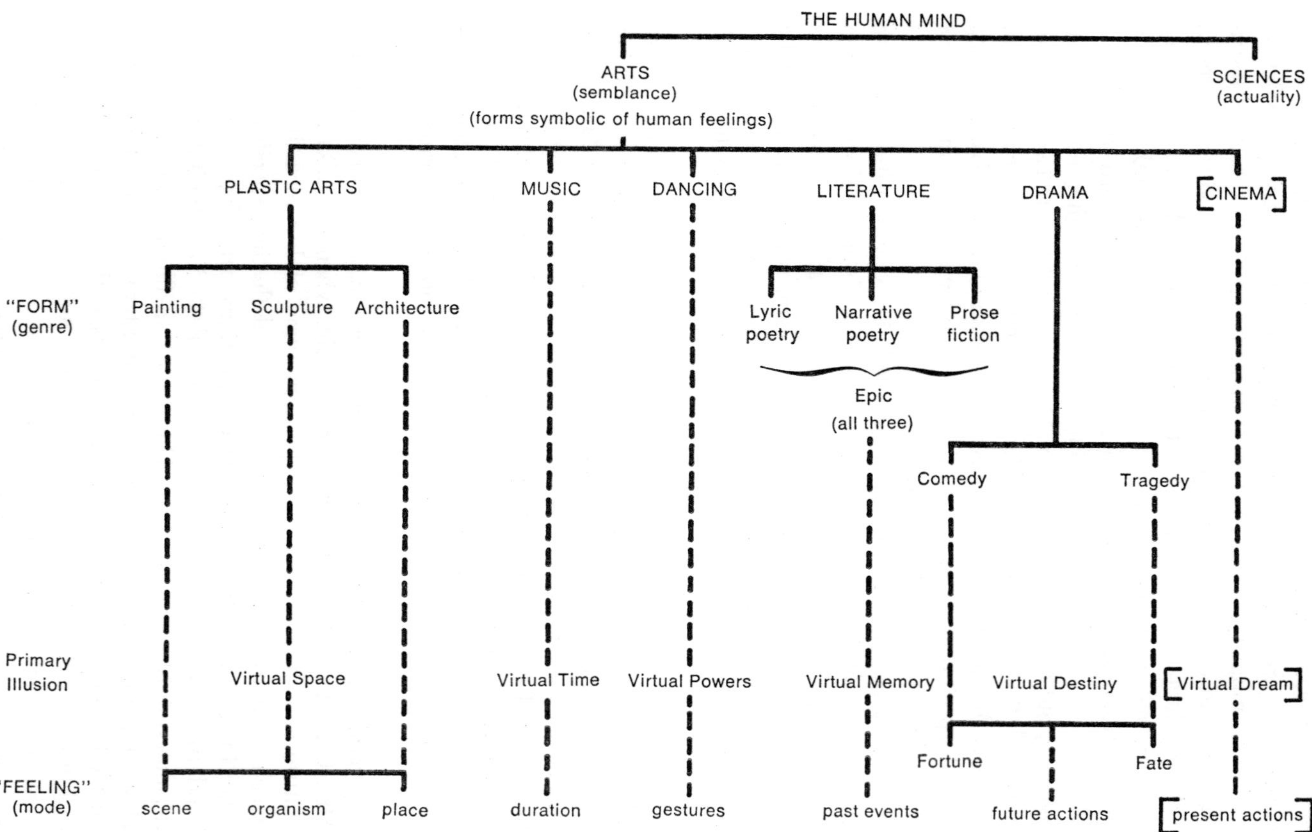
THE HUMAN MIND
ARTS
(semblance)
(forms symbolic of human feelings)
SCIENCES
(actuality)
PLASTIC ARTS
MUSIC
DANCING
LITERATURE
DRAMA
[CINEMA]
"FORM"
(genre)
Painting
Sculpture
Architecture
Lyric poetry
Narrative poetry
Prose fiction
Epic
(all three)
Comedy
Tragedy
Primary
Illusion
Virtual Space
Virtual Time
Virtual Powers
Virtual Memory
Virtual Destiny
[Virtual Dream]
Fortune
Fate
"FEELING"
(mode)
scene
organism
place
duration
gestures
past events
future actions
[present actions]

ture and drama, but is it not impossible to distinguish between a literary plot and a dramatic plot? Her assertion that events and acts are the primary illusions of literature and drama, respectively, does agree with Aristotle's claim that the heart of tragedy is the plot (the events or the action in the story). Aristotle, too, distinguishes between the literary mode of Homer and the dramatic mode of Aristophanes, but on different grounds. In Chapter Three of the *Poetics* Aristotle says that drama is expressed exclusively in a dramatic manner (by acting), whereas literature is expressed in a mixture of dramatic and narrative manners.

Another limitation in Mrs. Langer's treatment of drama is her relegation of virtual memory of past events to a "secondary illusion" in drama. In this she seems to be denying the role of history in drama, which would apparently exclude Shakespeare's history plays from the category of drama. Perhaps she would answer this objection by saying that his history as taken from his sources belongs to the actual past, whereas in the art world, the realm of the virtual, we are involved with the story on the stage in the virtual present at each moment as it looks toward, is pregnant with, the future.

One can also question her definition of art by asking if the actual must, or can, be so absolutely distinguished from the virtual. Is it not possible that an artist expresses his own personal experiential emotion, but when embodied in an art form—say in painting—it becomes both an expression of the personal emotion and also an objective correlative, that is, a virtual feeling? For example, in painting one of his self-portraits Rembrandt represents himself as a perceptive and weary artist. The abstract, virtual feeling of a weary man is therefore in and involved with the particular man Rembrandt's concrete actual feeling of weariness. By a reverse process, the viewer grasps the universal feeling embodied in a painting, in this instance, weariness; but then as this impresses itself upon him, he correlates the universal feeling with his own subjective experience of this feeling, and so the painting recalls for him his own actual feeling. Take another example. We see Rubens' work exhibited in the Louvre. In it we observe the universal fleshiness of women; but we assent to this as a universal feeling because in our own personal and subjective experience we know this same kind of fleshiness. In other words, it is difficult to accept the idea that virtual feelings can be neatly separated from actual feelings, or even for that matter, that the Platonic realm of ideas can be separated from the concrete world of particulars. They interpenetrate. Each is known by the other; actual lust is enhanced by dwelling on the concept of imagined lust; the concept of lust is enhanced by an actual experience of lust. Blake would say, we "see a World *in* a Grain of Sand."[21] He does not say that an idea of the world (a virtual feeling) is totally divorced from a particular grain of sand. Mrs. Langer herself recognizes that the origins of the ideas for much art are personal experiences and cites Wordsworth as an example (p. 254). But this perception does not lead her to qualify her radical distinction between actual feeling and virtual feeling: "As surely as some experiences of real life must inspire art, it must be entirely transformed in the work itself. Even the personality called 'I' in an autobiography must be a creature of the story and not the model himself" (p. 254).

Another question concerns subject matter. Can the various arts be so clearly differentiated according to the primary illusions which they symbolize? For example, in Mrs. Langer's basic conceptualization, the categories of time and space are entirely disjoined. Does a play not take place equally in time and space? Can one limit such an important illusion as space to one artistic form, even though one may allow it to appear as a secondary illusion in other genres of art? Some paintings, such as Delacroix's *Liberty Leading the People,* express virtual feelings of a whole age and time, that of the French Revolution. Mrs. Langer would seem to exclude such an interpretation of this painting as being history or time. It seems she needs a distinction between virtuality as applied necessarily to the *medium* of an art form (a dance must consist of gestures which are virtual) but not necessarily as applied to the *subject matter* of an art form (e.g., a dance may express either virtual fear or actual fear as the dancer has worked herself into this state of mind by "method acting").

A further question is whether the arts must be completely pure; whether their primary illusions must necessarily swallow their secondary illusions. Is singing (music) unequivocally distinguished from lyric poetry (literature) in, for example, Beethoven's adaptation of Schiller's "Ode to Joy" in his Ninth Symphony? Cannot a poem be sung so that both virtual duration and virtual memory are equally conveyed? Or to take another example, is *Porgy and Bess* primarily music or drama? Again, is the dancing in *West Side Story* really assimilated by the music? Is not ballet *dancing* always combined with instrumental *music,* so that both a dancer's performance and the musical orchestration of *Swan Lake* can be perfectly fused? In short, Mrs. Langer seems overzealous "to discover *one* fundamental 'primary illusion' or 'basic abstraction' in each art."[22]

By corollary, the parallelism of the five categories of illusion (virtual space, time, powers, memory, and destiny) with the five categories of art (plastic arts, music, dancing, literature, and drama) seems overly schematic. Although these five art forms may be clearly separable species under the one genus, artistic expression, the five primary illusions do not seem to be discrete, equal species of the same genus, semblance or virtuality. For example, virtual memory expressive of past events (literature) and virtual destiny expressive of future actions (drama) seem themselves to be subspecies of virtual time, which Mrs. Langer restricts to the primary illusion of music. Again, making the category of virtual powers parallel to the categories of time and space is a little like classifying rocks with rabbits—that is, equating species that do not belong together.

Whatever one's reservations, it remains true that Mrs. Langer has made several unique contributions to modern criticism. Her radical distinction between the different modes of human thought, discursive logic and creative imagination, is both important and fruitful. Her attempt to order the creative imagination into particular modes of sensibility, and her suggestion that each of the major genres of art expresses primarily one of these modes of sensibility marks perhaps the major advance in twentieth-century aesthetics over nineteenth-century organicism and is certainly her most distinctive contribution to aesthetic theory. While fraught with problems and uncertainties, it remains the chief modern effort to bring order out of the chaos in which other forms of aesthetic criticism have threatened to leave the arts.

NOTES

1. Langer, Translator's Preface to Ernst Cassirer, *Language and Myth* (New York: Dover Books, 1946), p. ix.
2. Langer, *Mind: An Essay on Human Feeling*, I (Baltimore: Johns Hopkins University Press, 1967), xv.
3. Susanne Langer, *The Practice of Philosophy* (New York, 1930), p. 128.
4. Susanne Langer, *Philosophy in a New Key* (New York: Mentor Books, 1951), p. 218.
5. Ibid., p. vii.
6. Ibid., p. viii.
7. Ibid.
8. Translator's Preface to *Language and Myth*, p. ix.

9. Susanne Langer, *Reflections on Art* (Baltimore: Johns Hopkins University Press, 1959), p. xi.

10. Ibid., p. xii.

11. Susanne Langer, *Philosophical Sketches* (Baltimore: Johns Hopkins University Press, 1962), p. vii. (Also available in paperback.)

12. *Mind,* I, xvi.

13. Ibid., I, xvii.

14. Herbert Read, *The Tenth Muse: Essays in Criticism* (New York, 1957), p. 246.

15. Langer, *Feeling and Form* (New York: Scribner, 1953), p. 40. All references to this book are to the Scribner's paperback edition and hereafter will be cited within the body of the essay.

16. Read, *The Tenth Muse,* p. 246.

17. Langer, *Problems of Art* (New York: Scribner, 1957), p. 15.

18. *Mind,* I, 21.

19. Ibid., I, 19.

20. Ibid., I, 32.

21. Blake, "Auguries of Innocence."

22. Bernard C. Heyl, *New Mexico Quarterly,* XXIV (1954), 467.

Jacques Maritain's Aesthetics: To Distinguish, To Unite

D. NEWTON SMITH
WESTERN CAROLINA UNIVERSITY

IT IS UNFORTUNATE that the English translation of *Distinguer pour unir ou les degrés du savoir* is titled only *The Degrees of Knowledge*, for more than any other phrase "distinguish to unite" characterizes the thought and method of Jacques Maritain.[1] His works cover a wide range of topics, yet in almost everything he has written he gives the impression that the topic at hand is being analyzed only to show its relation to a larger unity. His method is analytical, but while he is distinguishing he is uniting the parts of his subject to a whole and the whole to a greater one. In the end his system is one of the most ambitious yet proposed by a twentieth-century aesthetician.

By taking his profession as a philosopher very personally Maritain achieves an otherwise impossible unity over the range of his works. He regularly prefaces his non-philosophic works with the remark that he is not an expert, only a philosopher interested in the subject at hand. Typically, he then fits the topic into a larger metaphysical system and proceeds to analyze it in terms of this system. As a result, each of his works is related directly or indirectly to the whole corpus of his thought.

Throughout his career, Maritain has assumed the stance of a metaphysician addressing himself to the whole of reality in the study of being qua being and utilizing all the tools of analysis of modern philosophy —from phenomenology to mathematical logic. More precisely he is a neo-Thomist, but he is by no means a medieval resisting the twentieth century. Although he accepts Thomism as an essentially sound system, he continually renovates it by adapting the advances of contemporary thought. He has felt the influence of almost all the modern trends in philosophy, especially phenomenology and existentialism. But he is essentially a metaphysician, and as such he differs from Kant, the phenomenologists, and idealists on one side, and the materialists, the neopositivists, and existentialists on the other, for he stresses being in its totality, not merely phenomena, essence, matter, or existence. In short, his works are an encounter and a dialogue with the foremost issues of the present.

When Maritain entered the Sorbonne to study biology, the basic assumptions his contemporaries accepted were a belief in progress through science and technology and a confidence that science alone offered positive knowledge. The scientific explanation of everything, from art to sociology, seemed to declare that there was no such thing as truth; there were only facts.

While still a student at the Sorbonne, Maritain crossed the street to the College de France to listen to Henri Bergson. Bergson was at that time one of the very few who spoke in opposition to the established materialism and determinism of the day. Bergson insisted that it was possible to penetrate to the real essences of things, but by means of the intuition rather than the intellect. The intellect, he asserted, could grasp the unity and the workings of the mind itself, which science had failed to do. Bergson reaffirmed the belief in free will and posited his optimistic creative evolution. In short, he shattered the rigid structure of positivism and opened the way for Maritain's later thought.

There were portions of Bergsonian philosophy that disturbed Maritain but for which he found no solution until he and his wife, Raissa, read Leon Bloy's work, *La Femme pauvre*. This led to a friendship with Bloy and their conversion to Roman Catholicism. With his conversion Maritain began his study of Thomism. He has since spent much of his life renovating classic Thomism, which he feels possesses a still valid methodology and set of principles, providing it with an aesthetic, rehabilitating its secular theories, adequating it to contemporary problems of epistemology, giving new life to its metaphysics, and exploring the problem of mysticism.

When he published *Art et scholastique* in 1920, Maritain surprised both the art world and his fellow philosophers.[2] The book owes much of its inspiration to Maritain's friendship with the painter Rouault. Maritain's home was frequently a salon where artists such as Rouault and Chagall, writers such as Cocteau, musicians such as Satie, mystics, explorers, and missionaries gathered. In 1926, because of the papal ruling on the Action Française movement, Maritain found he had to engage in a social and political contest. In spite of the fact that he had contributed frequently to the magazines of the movement, Maritain spoke against it in support of the Church. With this dispute he began his long career of social and political inquiry in which, with a broad tolerance, he carefully distinguished the things which were Caesar's from those that were not.

The most important development in Maritain's social thought and the one on which all his secular thinking rests is the distinction between person and individual. He suggests that when we speak of an individual, we mean that he is a distinct and unique part of a species. But as a singular example of the species, he is, therefore, expendable. A person, on the other hand, is more a whole than a part. It is the person who possesses dignity of action. Since a human being is neither pure person nor pure individual, there are some things which a human being as an individual owes the species just as there are times when the demands of the species must give way to the person. Maritain suggests on the basis of this theory that medieval humanism is preferable to Renaissance humanism since the latter in fact stressed the individual. It developed through rationalism to present-day scientism and presently ministers to the needs of the individual (that is, the needs of the species), rather than to the needs of the person. Medieval humanism, on the other hand, gave man the dignity of having an existence beyond that of his species, thereby elevating him and giving him a freedom because of his allegiance to another realm beside that of the quotidian.

Maritain's political, social, and educational theories are all based on the distinction between person and individual. His writing has caused him to be termed a humanist and to be associated with the personalism of Gabriel Marcel. His educational theories, while not radical in any way, are remarkable for the respect they grant the student.

In 1914, at the beginning of his career, Maritain published *La Philosophie bergsonienne.*[3] In it he acknowledged his many debts to his former teacher, particularly to Bergson's theory of duration. Bergson had arrived at this theory intuitively, and because reason had contributed nothing to his theory he discredited it, saying it had no access to truth. At this point Maritain began his opposition. In denying the intellect access to truth Bergson had taken the stance of an anti-intellectual. He had refused to grant intuitive power to the intellect. To Maritain this was dividing rather than distinguishing. From this view no unity was possible.

In order to demonstrate Bergson's error Maritain presents his version of the history of Western thought that anticipated Bergson. It is the first of such histories that Maritain outlined and is interesting for that reason. He begins with the perennial scapegoat, Descartes, who maintained that thought was immanent to itself, which is to say, thought finds its object in itself. Kant had attempted to rectify this passive theory by postulating the active nature of cognition. However, Kant had continued to maintain the Cartesian notion

> that thought attains immediately its own representatives, and that if there is anything supra-sensible in it and known to it [the mind] cannot have received and taken it from things. Anything that is supra-sensible in the knowing mind is exclusively its own structure, or in other words, its *a priori* forms.[4]

In other words anything in the mind that went beyond the senses was a product of the mind and its a priori categories and derived in no way from the object. Bergson had seen that even with this the mind was constrained to know only itself.

When Bergson had attempted to get directly to the thing in itself he repeated Kant's error. He pointed out that the a priori forms were nothing but mental habits of materiality and that those habits enclose us in a world of mechanistic illusions. To Bergson the only way to avoid these illusions and reach the real is by means of an intuition, which, he says, transcends the intellect and gets to the concrete object itself. The inference from Bergson's propositions is that the intellect is a self-enclosed vacuum containing nothing but itself and that the concept can assert no claim to truth.

Such a position Maritain quite naturally opposes. He says that there may be two kinds of intuition, sensual and intellectual. To deny truth to one merely because of its methods of operation is nonsense. It is the same activity in the mind that engenders a concept and perceives a phenomenon. An object remains what it is throughout the manipulations of the mind or the imagination. That is, the object continues to be itself. The manipulations and divisions of the object within the mind concern only the manner and not the truth of what we conceive. The ability to intuit represents, to Maritain, a remnant of our spirituality, while the necessity to divide is a product of our materiality. The two are inextricably intertwined; any separation is to repeat the Cartesian split.

The core of Maritain's argument here is that the intuition is not the end step; it is only the beginning. An intuition may take either of two directions: it may lead to an action, either in a doing or a making; or it may lead to a concept. The first course may result in a moral action or an artistic creation. The second course results in some kind of knowledge. Nonetheless, the process leading to knowledge begins with an intuition. The first concept it produces is the concept of being. From this concept first principles are arrived at, e.g., all that *is* cannot at the same time *not be*, or, everything that begins or is contingent has a cause. Even these principles are one step removed from intuition. They are products of intelligence *and* intuition. Were one to stop at this first stage one would know that a man *is* and that he exists in some way differently from all other things. The intuition would have provided very little information. To know that man is mortal, free, and rational, requires discursive and intellectual labor.

An intuition is not knowledge. Knowledge is a product of the intellect and the intuition. An intuition is a whole, a unit, entirely integrated. The intellect distinguishes segments of this whole from one another arbitrarily. Knowledge comes as a result of this distinguishing and contrasting. The intellect, distinguishing for the sake of its operation with the spirit of a supposition, does not destroy the integrity or the unity of the intuition. This distinguishing, or intellectual abstraction, is a process of stripping away material obscuring the intelligibility of the object. Since the mind's state is an immaterial state and therefore cannot know materiality unless it be rendered in some way immaterial, this paring away of matter is a requisite action for knowledge.

Before continuing with Maritain's epistemology a look at a few of his definitions is in order. He defines intuition as

> a very simple sight, superior to any discursive reasoning or demonstration. . . . [It is a] living, penetrating, illuminating contact with a reality which [the soul] touches and which takes hold of it.[5]

The reality he speaks of is called "being" elsewhere. Being he defines as "what is primarily known and in which every object of thought is resolved for the intellect."[6] Being is also the unchanging and changeless substance that underlies an object's visible qualities and appearances and which endures through durational time. Perhaps an illustration similar to the ones Thomists use will make things a bit clearer. While I am walking home, I see something approaching me. Before I know *what* it is I know *that* it is—that it exists. If it exists it must have being. Being, then, must be posited before thought is possible. Being saturates all things. It is what Maritain calls a "transcendental object of thought."[7] Modern philosophers do not usually make the distinction Maritain is making here. To them being is *in* a thing, which suggests that being is limited and bound by that thing. Maritain maintains that being is not included in things but includes them.

Essence is the common intelligibility between thing-as-thing and thing-as-object, if thing-as-thing is understood as what continues after the process of its manufacture ceases and thing-as-object is considered as that which in the mind continues to accrue predicates. Essence is what continues to *be* in the thing-as-thing and what continues to attract predicates in the thing-as-object.

Concerning existence Maritain says things have two different forms: (1) their rightful existence by which they act and hold themselves apart from nothingness, and (2) the existence which they take on in the apprehension of the soul in order to be known.[8] In discovering our own existence we become aware that we can have existence without being existence, that we only participate in existence without totally occupying it, and that other things participate in existence as well.

Maritain summarizes the intuition of being in *Raison et raisons*:

> Precisely speaking, this prime intuition of being is both the intuition of *my* existence and of the existence of *things*, but first and foremost of things. When it takes place I suddenly realize that a given entity, man, mountain, or tree, exists and exercises that sovereign activity *to be* in its own way, in an independence from *me* which is total, totally self-assertive, and totally implacable. And at the same time I realize that I also exist, but as thrown back into my loneliness and frailty by such an affirmation of existence in which I have positively no part.[9]

Thus in the same intuitive experience there are three intellectual leaps: (1) to an actual existence assertively independent from the subject, (2) to the threatened existence that opens to the subject the concept of nothingness and death, and (3) to the concept of an existence that is free from nothingness and death and that seems to be suggested by the presence of being in any other thing whatsoever. In other words, one sees in a wordless intuition that his being is liable to extinction, that it depends on the totality of nature or on the whole whose part he is, and that his being-with-the-possibility-of-nothingness implies, in order to have come into existence, a being-without-nothingness. For Maritain, then, the apprehension of being implies the existence of the Being of God.

The knower cannot violate his own existence, and this existence as knower is immaterial or spiritual. The object to be known, however, is material and bound up in matter. This matter, purely as such, is unknowable. It becomes knowable only insofar as it is actualized by form. In order to know an object the knower must be identified with it. But he cannot cease to be his natural self. Therefore it is necessary to admit of another form of existence in which the knower can be the object and the object can be in him without either violating their natural beings. This other form of existence is entirely tendential and immaterial and disengages the thing from its limits. This form of being is called "intentional being." It is intentional being that permits the knower to identify with the intelligible being of the thing. The mind abstracts from the material thing the immaterial form that holds the thing separate from nothingness. The mind, then, grasps the essence by stripping away the thing's singularity and matter.

The notion of intentionality is crucial to Maritain's theory of knowledge:

> I use the word "intentional" in the Thomistic sense, . . . which refers to the purely tendential existence through which a thing—for instance, the object known—is present, in an immaterial or suprasubjective manner, in an "instrument"—an idea for instance, which, in so far as it determines the act of knowing, is a mere immaterial tendency or *intentio* toward the object.[10]

This concept serves as a bond of kinship between Maritain and the phenomenologists. Husserl discovered intentionality in reviewing Thomism and used it as a keystone of his philosophy. He had been trying to arrive at a knowledge of the real which circumvented the Kantian assertion that the *Ding an sich* is unknowable. The discovery of intentionality provided the solution. In the state of intentional being the self, while remaining intact, steps outward to meet the object. It enters the realm of being and there discovers the being of the object. By uniting itself with the essence of the other, the self knows the being of the other and returns to its natural state with a knowledge of the reality of the object. Though Husserl and Maritain differ on the origin of being, they are in agreement on the principle of intentional being. Like Husserl, Maritain ascribes form to the thing rather than restricting it to a priori categories. Through the agency of intentional being the mind can know an exterior thing.

Maritain, insisting as he does on unity, could not accept the division between the objective and the subjective world resulting from Kantian epistemology. He continually insists on the existence of the external world and that that existent is knowable. He points out that even though the sensory act begins and ends in the mind of the perceiver, both the perceiver and the object of the perception are oriented toward and completed in something that is already complete before sense perception begins. The mind can know truth but by no means all truth. Since to know is, in a certain sense, to become another thing than oneself, a true thought consists in its conformity with that thing. It follows that there is only one nature whose essence we can grasp in full—our own.

Maritain, in contrast to Kant and most of his successors, proceeds directly from epistemology to metaphysics. Intuition, as indicated earlier, is only the starting point. From the intuition there are two directions thought can take: speculative reasoning or practical reasoning. Speculative reasoning seeks knowledge for its own sake; practical reasoning seeks knowledge as a guide to action. The completion of speculation is in a concept, but the completion of practical reasoning is either a right action or a right work. In this sense the speculative realm finds its end in truth while the practical is completed in the good.

The process of speculative reasoning is abstraction. The implication is that perfect knowledge can only be of the universal and the necessary. The knowledge of the particular, since it is not completely abstracted, can only be contingent. Thus Maritain establishes his hierarchy of knowledge.

The first degree of abstraction is knowledge of a sensory nature. At this level the general cannot be conceived without matter. Maritain divides this degree into two parts, and this innovation of traditional Thomism is one of his most significant contributions to that system. He divides it into the empirical sciences and the philosophy of nature. The sciences describe and measure the operations of the universe while the philosophy of nature has the task of explaining and accounting for them. The sciences deal with the sensible and the philosophy of nature deals with the substantial that underlies phenomena. To the sciences change consists of motion and sensible objects. To the philosophy of nature change is mutability and substance.

The second degree, previously ignored by Thomists, is diagrammatically off center, for it does not concern itself with real being. It is called Mathematica, and it operates best when detached from all sensible qualities. It considers quantity, number, and extension—"objects of thought which cannot *exist* without sensible matter, but which can be conceived without it."[11]

The third degree of abstraction is called Metaphysica. In it the mind

> considers abstract objects from which matter has been entirely eliminated, where nothing remains of things but the being with which they are saturated, being as such and its laws; objects of thought which cannot only be conceived without matter but which can even *exist* without it, which may never have existed in material form at all, such as God and pure spirits, or which may equally exist in material and immaterial things, such as substance, quality, act, potency, beauty, goodness, etc.[12]

Beyond metaphysics Maritain places the wisdom of theology which begins with God and proceeds upward. Beyond theology there is the knowledge of God lived, as with the mystics and the saints.

In his approach to art Maritain might be classed either in the aesthetic tradition or in the humanist tradition. His aesthetic proper usually agrees with those of current aesthetic criticism; however, many of his comments and much of his practical criticism, with its moral concern, resemble that of the humanist tradition of Matthew Arnold. But in Maritain's case it is probably wisest to avoid such classification and to consider him in a separate class altogether or, more probably, as an example of an attempt to unite the two strains. Whatever we make of these two strains of criticism, it is obvious in his writings that the foundation for his theories is Thomism and the method is that of a philosopher—rigorously systematic.

For a philosopher, the number of his publications on aesthetics or criticism is remarkable. He knew and has written about a large number of writers, painters, and composers. His familiarity with the contemporary scene and his analysis of it has had a perceptible effect on the development of his aesthetic. In his early work, *Art et scholastique*, Maritain structured his aesthetic on the Thomist notions of the practical intellect and the practical arts. From a definition of art as the "creative or producing, work-making activity of the human mind," he proceeded to analyze both the pure and practical arts, particularly as they relate to beauty.[13] This analysis, though it contributed much to the field of aesthetics because it emphasized the actual production of art at a time when this aspect of art was receiving almost no attention, is somewhat deficient. It is deficient because it cannot adequately account for the intuition of the artist and because it has almost nothing to say about poetic knowledge. Becoming aware of the profound difference between classical French writers and Mallarmé, Rimbaud, the Surrealists and others, Maritain began to use the term "poetry" in 1935 in *Frontières de la poésie et autres essais.*[14] From that time to the publication of *Creative Intuition in Art and Poetry* he has pursued the implications of poetry, which he defines as

> that intercommunication between the inner being of things and the inner being of the human Self which is a kind of divination. . . . Poetry, in this sense, is the secret life of each and all of the arts.[15]

Nonetheless, he has continued to stress the practical aspect of creation, maintaining art and poetry are inseparable even though we distinguish between them. Maritain used these terms, art and poetry, usually in their generic sense as defined above, though at times they may be used to refer to the literary arts or the plastic arts.

Maritain began his work in aesthetics by concentrating on art. To get a proper understanding of this foundation and to sense his progress, one must also begin with art. Art is the "undeviating determination of works to be made."[16] As such it belongs to the realm of the practical intellect. The end of art is to impress an idea on matter, and thus it remains entirely within the mind of the artist and is a quality of that mind. Now the intellect, whether practical or speculative, is affected by appetite and stands in relation to truth. The appetite in the practical intellect permeates the intellect with a movement toward the action to be brought about. Truth establishes a "straight tendential dynamism" toward the thing to be created or done.[17] Art requires an *habitus*, or a persistent usage of all the faculties of the subject. This *habitus* is analogous to the training life of an athlete; it is an inner quality or disposition and is as necessary to art as it is to morality. An *habitus*, then, is a virtue, and because it is a virtue the art arising from it has an infallibility in *direction* regardless of the result of the execution. The *habitus* makes art a virtue of the practical intellect, for art is concerned with the good of a work.

Art is divided into the practical arts and the fine arts. Both aim at the production of a beautiful object. The general end of the practical arts is the use to which the object shall be put. The general end of the fine arts is toward beauty:

> Art in general tends to make a work. But certain arts tend to make a beautiful work, and in this they differ essentially from all the

> others. The work to which all other arts tend is itself ordered to the service of man, and is therefore a simple means; and it is entirely enclosed in a determined material genus. The work to which the fine arts tend is ordered to beauty; as beautiful, it is an end, an absolute, it suffices of itself; and if, as work-to-be-made, it is material and enclosed in a genus, as beautiful it belongs to the kingdom of the spirit and plunges deep into the transcendence and the infinity of being.[18]

Art cannot, however, create beauty, because beauty is a transcendent and cannot be captured in a work.

Maritain defines beauty as "that which, being seen, pleases."[19] Beauty "delights the intellect through the senses."[20] There are three conditions of beauty: (1) integrity which is fullness of being, (2) proportion which is order and unity, and (3) radiance or clarity. Radiance is the most important. It is "the splendor of the form on the proportional parts of matter. . . . It is the fleshing of intelligence on a matter intelligibly arranged."[21] In other words, beauty is a transcendent and as such cannot be fully enclosed in a material genus; there will always be an excess. Beauty, however, is always seized in and through the sensible. Beauty is the radiance of all the transcendentals united, and aesthetic beauty is beauty that confronts the senses imbued with intelligence. The fine arts, then, are most immediately moved to produce a *good* work rather than a beautiful work, because to seek beauty as an object is to attempt to produce a transcendent. The artist instead engenders in beauty.

Having located art in the realm of the practical intellect, which is directed toward the good, Maritain was put into the position of saying that beauty is a form of the good. However, given the definition, a thing is beautiful if it pleases when seen, he was constrained to add that beauty has a relation to truth as well, since beauty is a knowledge by assimilation of the senses. His solution was to say that beauty adds a cognitive faculty to the good, but that it is related more to the good than the true because it is more a delight than a knowledge. Considered as truth he must say that beauty is a formal cause in spite of the fact that he at other places calls beauty the end beyond the end of art.

Basically the problem is that there is poetic knowledge, and any attempt to explain art without employing this concept is incomplete. Because art is related to knowledge, it refuses to stop at pure forms, colors, sounds, or words as things. Art uses these elements to make known something beyond them:

> The more the object of art is laden with signification (but with spontaneous and intuitively grasped signification, not with hieroglyphic signification), the greater and richer and higher will be the possibility of delight and beauty.[22]

The delight of a beautiful work lies in its truth as a manifestation of a certain form or a "radiance of being in matter."[23] However, this truth is neither discursive nor conceptual; it "suggests without properly making known and . . . it expresses that which our ideas cannot signify."[24] The aim of art, then, is to make an object beautiful by exhibiting a form by means of sensible signs. To that end each work has its own rules, but the rules are not rigid patterns. The artist is not held by the rules; "it is he who *holds*, through them, matter and reality."[25]

Apparently Maritain sensed the weakness of his early position, for once he had completed his first work that treated poetry and poetic knowledge—*Frontières de la poésie et autres essais*—he added it as a supplement to *Art et scholastique.* It is a fortunate combination, for the two halves of the book present the two directions of Maritain's aesthetic. As his analysis of artistic creation continued, he arrived at the definition of poetry we noted above: "that intercommunication between the inner being of things and the inner being of the human Self which is a kind of divination."[26] From this it can be seen that poetry is not directed toward an object-to-be-made specifically, but is rather a sort of knowledge which tends to engender. Poetry in its tendency goes toward that which delights the intellect, or beauty. But in another definition of poetry, Maritain indicates that poetry is activity of the free creativity of the spirit and therefore has no object. By this he means that poetry is coequal or connatural with beauty, and is attached to beauty in a relationship like that of lovers. Thus, in speaking of the fine arts we cannot say that they aim to produce beauty, for beauty cannot be contained in a genus. Rather, the fine arts aim to produce beautiful things. The attempt to produce beauty leads to academism, which, as the perversion of the arts, serves only to diminish beauty.

The word poetry, as Maritain uses it, has subsumed to it poetic knowledge and poetic intuition. The general nature of the activity of intelligence is to produce within itself its mental words which are its means of knowing. These words, still below the level of consciousness, are formed by the free creativity of the spirit which transfers to the words a superabundance which in turn tends to express and manifest outside itself, to superabound in a work or concept. In cognitive reasoning the mind produces its word which produces in consciousness the concept. In an analogous way poetic knowledge produces its word, the poetic intuition, which superabounds and tends to produce a work. Since poetic knowledge is an intellection which has for its exterior concept not the object of knowledge but the work itself that is to be made, it follows that poetic knowledge is fully completed only when the work is finished.

Maritain has defined poetic knowledge as a "knowledge by *affective* connaturality with reality."[27] It is a nonconceptualizable knowledge because it awakens in the subject his own creative depths:

> The primary requirement of poetry, which is the obscure knowing, by the poet, of his own subjectivity, is inseparable from . . . another requirement—the grasping, by the poet, of the objective reality of the outer and inner world: not by means of concepts and conceptual knowledge, but by means of an obscure knowledge . . . through affective union.[28]

In other words, all that the poet knows or discerns and divines from things, he knows not as other than himself, as would be the case in speculative knowledge, but as inseparable from himself.

The interior word or the poetic intuition shares this same quality. This word (unutterable) contains both the self of the poet and a flash of reality with unforgettable individuality and with infinite meaning and capacity. Poetic intuition is directed toward concrete existence as connatural to the soul penetrated by emotion. It does not separate the essence from the existence of the object as does speculative reasoning: it cannot, because the subjectivity of the poet and the being of the object are united. The intuition is still in a state of spirituality; it still is activated by the free creativity of the spirit. Therefore, the intuiton tends to engender; it is turned from the start toward the operative, toward making. At the same time because it has no conceptualized object, the intuition tends and extends toward the infinite, toward all reality or all the reality surrounding any singular existing thing.

So it is seen that the intuition is both creative and cognitive. Considered as cognitive the question arises, what is the thing grasped by the poetic intuition? To Maritain, the thing grasped is "the singular existent which resounds in the subjectivity of the poet, together with all the other realities which echo in this existent, and which it conveys in the manner of a sign."[29] Another cognitive function of the intuition is to reveal obscurely the subjectivity of the poet. The thing grasped and the subjectivity are known together in the same experience, and the thing grasped is grasped only through its affective resonance in and its union with the subjectivity. According to Maritain the experience of the things of the world is the most immediate, but the most important is the experience of the self, since it is this experience that gives intentionality to poetic knowledge. In any study of the fine arts it becomes evident that there is a double invasion of man into nature and nature into man and that no matter how "realistic" or "objective" the work may be, the personality of the creator is present. This double invasion may be compared to the experience of primitive man or to what the magician evoked—a divination, an awareness of the Other, giving man the feeling that things are full of spirit, the same spirit that is at the center of his own being.

When poetic intuition is considered as creative, one must first remember the free creativity of the spirit. In science and philosophy the intellect has an object—being—which it must conquer and make its own. In art there is also an object—the work to be made. The creativity of the intellect is subordinated to this object. But poetry has no object; there is nothing by which the creativity of the spirit is formed or constrained, nothing acts as a determinant to it. Poetry, then, is free. Poetry has only that attribute of the spiritual which causes it to abound in the mental word, the poetic intuition, and which causes that intuition to superabound. "In poetry, there is only the urge to give expression to that knowledge which is poetic intuition, and in which both the subjectivity of the poet and the realities of the world awake obscurely in a single awakening."[30] In other words, the poetic intuition is filled with excess energy that is tending toward expression. Since the intuition is still a dynamic union of subjectivity and reality, any work it effects will in turn superabound—expanding to infinities and suggesting all the realities surrounding the matter of that work.

Even though poetry has no object, being a transcendent it tends toward that which gives the intellect pleasure—beauty. But beauty is also a transcendent, and for this reason it cannot be the object of poetry. For poetry there is no specifying end, but beauty is the "necessary *correlative* and *end beyond any end* of poetry."[31]

Since in poetry the creativity of the spirit has no object, poetry must, therefore, create an object for itself. Thus it is that poetry is engaged in the same activity as art; the expression it yearns to give to poetic intuition will necessarily have to pass out of the pre-conscious into the conscious, something made.

Poetic intuition, then, even though it is spiritual must operate in the world of the flesh. It is natural that there will be a conflict between the two orders. But like religious activity, to retain the full degree of its spirituality the poetic intuition must obey first the rule of the spirit, and then the rule of the world. Creative intuition, then, is the poet's first and foremost rule. The poet must remove all that is not necessary to manifesting in matter the spiritual form of his intuition. Because poetic intuition is born of the spiritual, and because it tends toward its correlative, beauty, there are an infinitude of ways of producing a beautiful poem that follows the rule of creative intuition.

A question might arise concerning the practical arts and beauty. The practical arts aim at the production of a good work, but in the act of creation the intelligence steps beyond itself toward an object-to-be-made, and in this act of intentional being, the intellect encounters being which transcends all genera including the work-to-be-made. It is this element of the transcendent which is brought into the work in a sensual form that gives beauty to the work.

Between the poetic intuition and the work lies the domain of art. Art works, however, often fail:

> Yet the fact remains that from the very start poetic intuition virtually contains and encompasses the poem as a whole, and demands to pass through as a whole; when it does not succeed in appearing save in a fragmentary way, it is because it has been betrayed by the art of the poet.[32]

This brings up the problem of Maritain's practical criticism. He has a tendency, no doubt annoying to professional critics, especially those schooled in New Criticism, to quote extracts of poems that probably should be quoted in full. In his own words, "Poetic intuition may happen to appear with striking radiance even in a poem lacking in integrity."[33] This reasoning is philosophically suspect; however, experience suggests that the general reader (and the critic when off his guard) reads a poem with an ear attentive to that "striking radiance" even before he is aware of the structural integrity of the work. The only problem is that in Maritain's case one suspects, perhaps unjustly, that he selects only those passages of a poem which suit a subjective alignment of his own. Further, he rarely deals directly with the work at hand; rather he too often drifts toward what must be called impressionistic criticism. But, as Maritain himself frequently points out in the prefaces to his books, he is not a critic. He is a philosopher who wants to talk about art, and as a philosopher his responsibility is to develop a system by which we can investigate art. It is not his system that fails him, for it is a sound basis for close reading; rather, his training as a philosopher failed to prepare him fully for the business of criticism.

If his philosophical background puts him at a disadvantage in the close analysis of literature, it is an advantage in a general analysis of art's historical and intellectual development. As he indicates, the fine arts in the western world have become increasingly self-conscious. Poetry since Romanticism has become increasingly aware of its spirituality, while poets have, at the same time, become more aware of their subjectivity. The result, in fortunate works, has been an increasingly revealed poetic intuition. Perhaps the most appealing development of modern poetry is the appearance of what Maritain calls the "*immediately illuminating image*," which he opposes to the conventional "*purposive comparison*."[34] Essentially the purposive comparison is the bringing together of two things that have a similarity already present in nature, e.g., youth is like spring—both are already united by the concept of rising vitality. The immediately illuminating image is the bringing together of things, without comparison, uniting them by the intuition, revealing an intelligible meaning, though not a conceptual meaning. These images spring directly into life out of the impetus given by the free creativity of the spirit; they do not have to go through concepts, as was the case in classical poetry. Two things are not compared, but reveal one another. Maritain points out that though the immediately illuminating image is a primary characteristic of modern poetry, it does not occur exclusively there. Such an image occurs, for example, in *King Lear*:

> But I am bound
> Upon a wheel of fire, that my own tears
> Do scald like molten lead. [IV, 7, 46–48]

Poetic intuition, it will be remembered, is both cognitive and creative. As the fine arts have developed they have nurtured these two aspects to the point that Maritain feels they have become dangers. At the same time modern art has discovered its freedom from everything that is not its own essential law. The problem arises when a contemporary artist tries to attain either pure creativity or pure knowledge. The attempt to attain pure creativity can be seen most clearly in the plastic arts. Jealous of everything that was not born of itself, modern painting attempted to divorce itself from things as they exist in the world. The artists resorted to the nonrepresentational, geometrical style that for some time has dominated the art world. A similar thing occurred in the Symbolist movement in French poetry. Just as the line, form, and color became the only elements the painter allowed himself to use, so the rhythms of sonorous words, detached from external meaning, became the tools of the poet. Maritain points out that though the intuition does demonstrate to the subjectivity its creative nature, the subjectivity itself becomes informed and takes its shape through contact with things. If the artist deprives himself of things, he deprives himself in the end of his poetic intuition. Nonetheless, Maritain does not question the merits of this development in painting or poetry as an experiment. He only cautions against the dangers, suggesting that abstract expressionism can become a new form of academism.

When the arts strive after pure knowledge, there is a different sort of danger. Poetic knowledge is obscure, contains more experience than knowledge, and is neither rational nor abstractive. It has no intelligible boundaries and expands to the infinite. The temptation is to concentrate on pure spiritual experience, leaving all else aside including beauty. Maritain suggests that the Dadaists such as Henri Michaux are attempting this. Another temptation is to develop the aspect of poetic knowledge that is a sort of divination of the inner side of things to the point that poetry becomes a craving and a search for magical knowledge. Finally poetic knowledge can be exploited to become the means of examining subjectivity. To understand the dangers of this use of poetry that yearns only to know all and not to produce, one need only remember Rimbaud.

The purpose of poetry is not to communicate ideas but to keep contact with the poetic intuition. Concentrating once again on the poetic intuition, Maritain formulates a suggestive structure by which he demonstrates the roles of radiance, integrity, and proportion; explains the activity and the progression of poetic sense, action, and theme, and number; and positions the three genres—poetry, drama, and the novel. The most basic intentional value of a poem is its poetic sense or inner melody. This is the closest to the creative source and signifies the inhabited subjectivity of the poet. Poetic sense is the radiance of the creative intuition shining through the work. Poetry, though it superabounds into the following categories, most naturally resides closest to the poetic sense.

The second intentional value is action—either action as it exercises itself on the reader, such as purgation or pity, or an immanent action, which is what the poem *does*. The theme is the significance of the action, though still irreducible to a logical statement. Theme is the most objective of the three values. It is theme that can be translated into a logical statement even though doing so deprives it of existence in the poem. It is action and theme that rise out of the integrity of the poetic intuition. The integrity of a work is manifested in the immanent action of it and its employment of theme. This is the domain of drama.

The third intentional value is number or harmonic expansion. This refers to the poetic space in which the parts of a poem always expand so that the poem is full. It refers also to the relation of the parts in this space. Each poem has its own peculiar space in which the parts are arranged and proportioned. Harmonic expansion best demonstrates the proportion of the poetic intuition. This realm, the furthest removed from intuition, is the most discursive—it tends to create its own world. It is the realm of the novel.

One of the major achievements of Maritain's analysis of art and aesthetics is his distinction between art and morality. Quite naturally this investigation grows from his Thomistic background. Both art and morality belong to the realm of the practical intellect. Maritain distinguishes between them: morality is concerned with the good of man—his right action; art is concerned with the good of the work-to-be-made—the right work. Each claims everything to be under its dominion, and conflict between the two is continual. To illustrate the conflict (and the unity on some points) Maritain tells the story of the talented painter who felt he drew under a satanic inspiration. He could not change his style, for that would have violated his artistic conscience. To have betrayed his artistic conscience would have violated his moral conscience as well. Because the direction of his art violated his moral conscience and because he could not change his style in any way because of the dictates of his artistic conscience, the artist gave up painting. Maritain insists that in the case when an artist's work is morally bad but artistically good the solution involves changing the *man*, not the *art*. If the art work contains something morally bad, the fault lies not with art, but with the man. To effect any change that does not desecrate the art, one must purify the source, that is, purify the man. Maritain admits that the result of this purification unfortunately does not necessarily improve the art. It might weaken it, particularly in a minor artist.

"Morality has nothing to say when it comes to the good of the work, or to beauty. Art has nothing to say when it comes to the good of human life. Yet human life is in need of that very Beauty and intellectual creativity, where art has the last word."[35] The two are autonomous realms that cannot ignore one another. But Maritain points out that the artist is both a man and an artist. As a man he is responsible to himself, his state, and his God. As a man he necessarily must order his actions to his own moral good. Since his art is one of his actions, it too falls in the domain of moral action. The struggle of an artist to maintain integrity and, at the same time, the health of his soul demands a heroic effort. To accomplish this task requires nothing short of a Fra Angelico in a contemporary world.

This is precisely what Maritain would have the artist be. In Maritain's design the artist would have a most honored place. Art is one of the virtues of the practical intellect and poetry is a transcendent activity. It is no wonder Maritain would say:

> No one can live without delectation. . . . Art teaches men the delectation of the spirit, and because it is itself sensible and adapted for their nature, it can lead them to what is nobler than itself. . . . It prepares the human race for contemplation (the contemplation of the saints).[36]

NOTES

1. Jacques Maritain, *Distinguer pour unir ou les degrés du savior* (Paris: Desclée, de Brouwer et cie., 1932). *The Degrees of Knowledge* (New York, 1938). References hereafter will be designated *Degrees.*
2. Jacques Maritain, *Art et scholastique* (Paris: Louis Rouart et fils, 1920); with the supplement: *Frontières de la poésie* (1935). There are two translations in English: *Art and Scholasticism,* translated by J. F. Scanlan (New York, 1930), and *Art and Scholasticism and The Frontiers of Poetry,* translated by Joseph Evans (New York, 1962) (also available in paperback). All quotations come from the latter, which shall hereafter be referred to as *A. S.*
3. Jacques Maritain, *La Philosophie bergsonienne. Etudes critiques* (Paris: M. Rivière, 1914). *Bergsonian Philosophy and Thomism* (New York, 1954).
4. *Bergsonian Philosophy and Thomism,* p. 26.
5. Jacques Maritain, *Sept Leçons sur l'être et les premiers principes de la raison speculative* (Paris: P. Téqui, 1934). *A Preface to Metaphysics: Seven Lectures on Being* (New York, 1948), p. 46.
6. Maritain, *Degrees,* p. 59.
7. Ibid., p. 258.

8. Ibid., p. 104.

9. Jacques Maritain, *Raison et raisons* (Paris: Egloff, 1947). *The Range of Reason* (New York, 1952), pp. 88–89. (Also available in paperback.)

10. Maritain, *Degrees*, p. 120.

11. Ibid., pp. 45–46.

12. Ibid., p. 46.

13. Jacques Maritain, *Creative Intuition in Art and Poetry*, The A. W. Mellon Lectures in the Fine Arts, National Gallery of Art, Washington (Princeton, 1953), XXXV–I Bollingen Series, p. 3. (Also available in paperback.) Quotations will refer to the Princeton edition and will be cited *C. I.*

14. Jacques Maritain, *Frontières de la poésie et autres essais*. This work is included in *Art and Scholasticism and The Frontiers of Poetry*.

15. *C. I.*, p. 3.

16. *A. S.*, p. 9.

17. *C. I.*, p. 47.

18. *A. S.*, p. 33.

19. *A. S.*, p. 23.

20. *A. S.*, p. 24.

21. *A. S.*, p. 25.

22. *A. S.*, p. 55.

23. *A. S.*, p. 57.

24. *A. S.*, p. 58.

25. *A. S.*, p. 39.

26. *C. I.*, p. 34.

27. Jacques Maritain and Raissa Maritain, *Situation de la poésie* (Paris: Desclée, de Brouwer et cie., 1938). *The Situation of Poetry* (New York, 1955), p. 66.

28. *C. I.*, pp. 114–15.

29. *C. I.*, p. 126.

30. *C. I.*, p. 170.

31. *C. I.*, p. 170.

32. *C. I.*, p. 135.

33. *C. I.*, p. 135.

34. *C. I.*, pp. 327–33.

35. Jacques Maritain, *The Responsibility of the Artist* (New York, 1960), p. 41.

36. A. S., p. 75.

The Quest for Pure Consciousness in Husserl and Mallarmé

NEAL OXENHANDLER
DARTMOUTH COLLEGE

THE INTERACTION OF PHENOMENOLOGY AND LITERATURE begins with Plato and includes, in a sense, that vast compass of our literature in which the text is seen as given by—or to—a human consciousness. The very vastness of the topic allows me to set arbitrary limits. I shall not deal with the major theoretical statements about literature that have been made since Husserl, since these works are large in scope for the most part and stand or fall on the accuracy of their analysis of specific literary problems. Again, in order to set reasonable limits, I have neglected those critics who have been directly or indirectly inspired by Husserlian phenomenology.

Thus I am setting aside Roman Ingarden's seminal work, *Das Literarische Kunstwerk*; the various writings of Jean-Paul Sartre that deal with literature; Merleau-Ponty's *Phénoménologie de la perception* and his *Signes*. An excellent analysis and evaluation of Sartre and Merleau-Ponty is available in Eugene F. Kaelin's *An Existentialist Aesthetic*. I am also "bracketing," as it were, Mikel Dufrenne's *Phénoménologie de l'expérience esthéthique*, as well as essays by Schutz, Natanson, and others which present literature in the light of phenomenology. Although in the course of the following pages I shall refer often to one contemporary critic, Jean-Pierre Richard, I have not attempted to summarize or evaluate the writings of other major critics in the phenomenological tradition such as Maurice Blanchot, Gaston Bachelard, Georges Poulet, or Roland Barthes. Each rethinks the nature of literature from his own vantage point, each renews perennial problems in a radically new and personal language. It would have been beyond the scope of this essay to attempt a synthesis or reinterpretation of these critical positions that would draw them together in respect to their shared heritage of Husserlian phenomenology.

What I have done instead is to return to the source, to Husserl himself, and to ask the question: How can Husserlian phenomenology help us to understand poetic consciousness? I have done this, not by drawing general precepts from Husserl which might then be applied with more or less exactness to writers at large; instead, I have focused on the work of one writer, Stéphane Mallarmé, whose poetic quest seems in a profound way to parallel the spiritual discipline of Husserl's own effort to move from the "natural attitude" to transcendental subjectivity. My aim is not, of course, to show any direct connection between the two, but rather the startling similarity of intent and method of each working within the formal limits of his own discipline.

The work of one illuminates the other; both clarify, from an unexpected perspective, the quest for transcendental subjectivity, the difficulties and limits of that quest, and the obscurities of a personal language whose aim is to open for inspection a domain that lies beyond language itself.

What philosophy seeks, literature takes as given. And what philosophy takes as given, literature seeks. Within the densely articulated texture of poetic language a universe of objects, emotions, persons, and events reveals itself in an essential relationship to consciousness, that relationship which philosophy seeks so laboriously and so precariously to establish. Yet the status of transcendental consciousness, which philosophy takes as its fundamental and unchallenged basis, appears in poetry only by starts and flashes, seems grasped in acts of metaphoric juncture only to dissolve and slip back into the flux of mental phenomena as if it were nothing but a fantasy or figment of imagination. Poetic consciousness, never once and for all attained, never decisively at rest, manifests itself always as tragic, while its permanent subject is its own failure. Philosophical consciousness, calmly contemplative, happily triumphant, becomes tragic only when it realizes that it has lost the world and that the intricate net of its logical constructions cannot capture once and for all the elusive data of man's quotidian existence.

Poetry serves philosophy by offering living proof of the possibility of synthesis or fusion between mind and world; and philosophy, by rendering thematic what poetry takes for granted, helps the poet resign himself to the tragedy of his enterprise. Each discipline complements the other and together they provide evidence for the partial attainment of what Maurice Merleau-Ponty saw as the goal of modern thought—to draw the irrational within the purview of reason. Together the two disciplines describe the trajectory of modern thought, an arc which moves toward an as yet invisible horizon. No doubt that horizon, which would be full expressiveness and intelligibility, will never be reached, either because of the countervailing forces of nihilism and the irrational or because the very nature of the enterprise forbids it. There can be no ultimate escape from the polar opposites of human existence, no Book like that which Stéphane Mallarmé dreamed of which could give once and for all "the orphic explanation of the world." The great poetic synthesis of Mallarmé and the great philosophical synthesis of Edmund Husserl appear as mere fragments borne on the maelstrom of contemporary experience. Both men saw their work as fragmentary and incomplete; yet the two together, serving as mirrors one for the other, are more than a debris or fragment. Each serves to complete the other by revealing a dimension that the other could not attain.

In the following pages I have attempted to examine the poetics of Mallarmé within the context of Husserlian phenomenology. I am aware of the difficulties that arise in the transposition back and forth between the two modes. Indeed, the attempt may seem quixotic, even futile. Poetry eschews the language of abstract thought for the language of images. Its shaping concern is the communication of poetic *exstasis* rather than the attainment of apodictic truth. It seeks less to be descriptively exhaustive than emotionally compelling, and it is guided by formal conventions rather than logical or evidential canons. Nonetheless, there is a close bond between Husserl and Mallarmé. Both are trackers of the absolute, both eschew the psychological for the transcendental, both seek to evade the Scylla of idealism and the Charybdis of realism. Though they work in different formal modes, they are persistently concerned with the theme of man's presence to the world. Finally, both resolve that theme in a way whose very inconclusiveness is its answer. For more specific parallels, we must turn to the works themselves.

Poetry and phenomenology begin with an "ontological proof" which establishes the priority of consciousness over and against the world. From the side of phenomenology this takes the form of the statement "The world is not only 'for me' but draws all its being status from me."[1] Whatever exists in the mind must have its correlative in the world. We do not turn to sense experience to check or control our ideas; rather, these ideas determine whatever we are to know or experience in the world. Only through a careful inspection of consciousness, one that follows procedures which will eliminate from experience all that is accidental or contingent, all that is based on unexamined presuppositions —only thus can we return to experience with confident assurance that we are seeing things in their utter and authentic simplicity. As Husserl says:

> I, the transcendental phenomenologist, have *objects* (singly or in universal complexes) as a theme for my universal descriptions: *solely as the intentional correlates of modes of consciousness of them.*[2]

Objects can be apprehended only as correlates of intentional consciousness, and so while their existence does not depend on consciousness, their intelligibility and their philosophic givenness do. The famous imperative "back to the things themselves" means precisely this, and not some form of naive realism, as is sometimes understood. Phenomenology goes in search of things, but this search is conducted within the field of a carefully purified consciousness where things are made available as noematic essences, i.e., purified data for intentional consciousness.

In poetry, on the other hand, the ontological proof operates implicitly though with no less rigor. This proof takes the form of the statement "Whatever exists in *language* must have its correlative in the world."

Taking Mallarmé as paradigmatic, we see the poet turned inward in an intense act of reflexive concentration. Listening to language, which may have its roots in past literature or in daily speech or in dream, he summons via that language the life-world which it implies and which resides within it as a vast array of hidden virtualities. Because the poet speaks, the world exists:

> I say: a flower! and, from out of that oblivion to which my voice relegates any contour, insofar as it differs from the calices as known, musically arises, idea selfsame and suave, the one that is absent from all bouquets.[3]

Language does not merely prove it *summons* or creates the world to live within itself. The power of language (and of the creative consciousness which lies behind it) is Mallarmé's fundamental premise and the source of his poetic power.

Mallarmé's first attempt to formulate the relation of mind to world was through Baudelaire's doctrine of "correspondences," a symbolist doctrine which assumes the constancy hypothesis (the equivalency of external stimulus to internal response) and founders on the reef of philosophical realism. In his early period he believed in the existence of a real transcendental dimension external to man, symbolized by the blue sky (*l'azur*) of his early poems. With the collapse of his religious beliefs and greater mastery of the complexities of the epistemological question, he moved toward the Hegelianism which henceforth dominated his intellectual life. In his 1865 crisis, he discovers himself a victim of "negation," "nothingness," "sterility"; yet Hegel teaches him the power of this negation: destruction can become creative, victory can rise from failure. He begins to absorb the forms of Absolute Spirit. He writes: "I have just passed a terrifying year; my Thought thought itself, and achieved a pure Concept."[4] His thought extends itself until it occupies the entire universe; it incorporates history and mankind—this intellectual drama is related in his obscure *Igitur*. Richard notes that the influence of Baudelaire and Poe leads Mallarmé to identify Absolute Spirit with lucidity and creative thought: " . . . at the end of the world's history stands for Mallarmé not the philosopher but the poet, and he is characterized by reflection, by the consciousness of an entire past reflected in himself, and to which he brings light."[5] Nonetheless, Mallarmé is not Hegelian in his understanding of the nature of consciousness; it is not Absolute Spirit that he seeks in his poems but rather the pure or transcendental subjectivity of Husserlian phenomenology.

Mallarmé does remain a Hegelian, however, in at least one important respect: the dialectical character of his poetry. Each of his poems affirms a negative proposition and then contests it, negating the negation, moving toward at least a problematical synthesis; for, as Richard reminds us, "The idea, for him, is always menaced by chance and entropy; even its upspringing remains subject to risk."[6]

The poems of Mallarmé are nuclei which generate a dialectic of images and an infra-language of antithetical themes. The dominant negative images may be: space, ice, snow, the tomb, the blue sky, water, the mirror, the dice-toss, shipwreck, virginity, etc. His implied themes are: solitude, sterility, death, chance, entropy. The contestation or negation of the negation occurs as the severed head of John the Baptist glances toward the sky; or the icy virginity of Herodias is melted by thawing sunlight; or the blackness of Night in "Ses purs ongles" is overwhelmed by the heavenly Constellation. The rhythmic, logical, perceptual, and linguistic complexities of this exchange are what constitute the poem and can be understood in full only after the most minute analysis. (We are indebted to Robert Greer Cohn who in his two studies of Mallarmé has given us an invaluable exigesis which shows the hardwon and problematical nature of this contestation.)

Herodias' struggle to escape her sterile virginity; the poet's struggle against the misinterpretation of his work; the swan's vain efforts to dislodge itself from the ice of a lake; the faun's pursuit of elusive nymphs who may be his own dream—from such dramatic nuclei the poems move toward at least a momentary transcendence, a momentary "expansion" into some "third dimension" which is implied by images such as whiteness, light, the poem, the Constellation, the creative act. This third dimension is not necessarily coextensive with the pure consciousness of Husserlian phenomenology, yet it may and often does coincide with that inward dimension or region which is the goal of Husserl's dialectic.

The following definition of the spiritual dimension as a "*jaillissement*" or "spurting forth" shows one of the forms pure consciousness may take in Mallarmé: "For a long time—indeed how long—I believed—that my idea was exempt from any accident even true; preferring, to chance, to delve for, in its origin, the spurting forth."[7] The effort to free the "spurting forth" from all contingent elements ("any accident") takes place within what Husserl called the "life-world" and can never attain perfect autonomy since the self-revelation of consciousness must always be mediated by concrete perceptions. Each poem begins with an act of doubt both of self and world and rises to a brief revelation of pure consciousness only to end with the poet's recapture by the contingent.

Pure consciousness, in its various forms, remains within experience, within the life-world, always to some degree subject to the contingent. This consciousness is attained now as source (*jaillissement*), now as pure essence (*l'idée*), now as the reflexivity through which knowledge of the self is founded (*le regard*), now as nothingness (*le néant*), now as the ground or field of perceptual experience (*il faut penser de tout son corps*), now as dream (*Maint rêve vespéral*); it is not as a psychological state, that is, a modification of some particular emotion such as anguish, joy, or sexual desire that the Mallarmean poem attains consciousness, but rather as ontic reality, as spirit.

This transcendental dimension is *not* the Absolute Spirit of Hegel, but rather an inner dimension of spirit conquered by various poetic strategies. It "lives" within the poem just as pure consciousness "lives" within Husserl's various analyses of the content of mind. Exhibited in linear and dialectical sequences in the analyses of the philosopher, this same spiritual dimension is exhibited in the spatial metaphors of the poems:

> It is thus that Mallarmé himself conceives, as we know, the internal reality of the poem and the ideal architecture of the objects that the poem must re-arrange within itself: grotto, diamond, spiderweb, stained-glass window, kiosque, shell, in such images as these appears the aim of a total correlation of nature with itself, and a perfect harmonization of things. Spirit is then dreamt as the keystone of that architecture: absolute center through which all communicates, compensates, neutralizes itself . . .[8]

While Mallarmean consciousness appears as transient and threatened by the contingent and negative elements of experience, a first reading of Husserl seems to imply no such metaphysical pathos but rather a determined and victorious affirmation of the absolute priority of consciousness. This reading, however, is false.

Beginning as a resolute attempt to avoid the fallacy of idealism (I know only my own mental states) and the fallacy of realism (I somehow know things in themselves), Husserl attempts to construct for himself a position which can affirm the supremacy of consciousness over and against the world without draining from the world its factual reality. His approach is "to view the real world and its elements as pure intentional objects which have the foundation of their existence and identity in the depths of pure consciousness."[9] As Husserl himself said:

> Thus the being of the pure ego and his *cogitationes*, as a being that is prior in itself, is antecedent to the natural being of the world—the world of which I always speak, the one of which I *can* speak. Natural being is a realm whose existential status is secondary; it continually presupposes the realm of transcendental being.[10]

In what sense is consciousness prior to the natural world? Priority cannot refer to the genetic order, the order of creation; consciousness is not "created" temporally *before* any other dimension of reality. Nor can this priority refer to the order of experience, since the natural order, the world in which man lives, breathes, eats, sleeps, and deals with other men is taken as the starting point of phenomenological investigation. The priority of consciousness can only be one of *status*, that is to say, consciousness is neither created first nor considered first but rather taken as first since it is a pre-condition which makes possible the apprehension of the natural world. Husserl attacks the "naturalization" of consciousness which posits a continuity between nature and psyche and assumes that consciousness is in the world like any other part of nature and continuous with nature. For consciousness neither arises from nor is grounded in the natural order. It is given as the enabling reality within whose field any further reality is to be discovered.

This givenness is not in any sense readily apparent; transcendental subjectivity does not arise by the waving of a phenomenological wand nor does it appear by magic after a mere clearing of the perceptual underbrush. What we attain through the phenomenological procedure is a "new idea of the grounding of knowledge" which lays open to me "an infinite realm of being of a new kind."[11] The movement is in two directions, from objective world to transcendental ego and from transcendental ego to world. The objective world gives a "transcendental clue" which leads the phenomenologist back to his own ego and allows him to see the world in a new light:

> What are others, what is the world, for me?—Constituted phenomena, merely something produced within me. Never can I reach the point of ascribing being in the absolute sense to others, any more than to the physical things of Nature, which exist only as transcendentally produced affairs. . . . The world is a meaning, an accepted sense. When we go back to the ego, we can explicate the founding and founded strata with which that sense is built up, we can reach the absolute being and process in which the being of the world shows its ultimate truth and in which the ultimate problems of being reveal themselves—bringing into the thematic field all the disguises that unphilosophical naiveté cannot penetrate.[12]

Husserl's dream of a total philosophy is comparable to Mallarmé's dream of a single Book which would be "the orphic explanation of the world." Neither Husserl nor any of his followers attained the complete reconstitution of the world within transcendental subjectivity but rather returned over and over again to beginnings in the attempt to found the *possibility* of that subjectivity.

The internal time in Husserl's philosophical meditation is not continuous from one work to the next and does not establish a positive "duration" within which that meditation evolves; rather, it is like the "duration" of the poet's work, made up of a series of local movements, each with its beginning, its ascending and falling rhythm, and its end. Constantly renewing his effort from different entry points, constantly modifying his formulations in the attempt to solve new and unexpected problems, constantly breaking off when faced with the impossibility of his enterprise, Husserl appears less as the triumphant conqueror of the realm of pure consciousness than as the poet-seeker of Mallarmé's "Toast funèbre":

> Nothingness to this man who has ceased:
> 'Memories of horizons, what, I ask you, is the Earth?'
> Yells this dream, and voice whose clarity fades,
> Space gets for plaything the cry: 'I know not!'[13]

Nothingness asks the dead poet (Théophile Gautier) "What is the meaning of the world?" The question is posed from the point of view of the "natural attitude," i.e., from the aspect of *horizonal* knowing. We see only aspects, profiles, adumbrations of objects which are always limited by a specific horizon; and, empty space, the transcendent in its negative or unattained version, mockingly echoes the cry: "I know not!"

> Daily practical living is naive. It is immersion in the already-given world, whether it be experiencing, or thinking, or valuing, or acting. Meanwhile all those productive intentional functions of experiencing, because of which physical things are simply there, go on anonymously. The experiencer knows nothing about them, and likewise nothing about his productive thinking. The numbers, the predicative complexes of affairs, the goods, the ends, the works, present themselves because of the hidden performances; they are built up, member by member; they alone are regarded.[14]

So Husserl describes the starting point of phenomenology: it is simply ordinary daily life as lived by each one of us from day to day, from minute to minute. In one sense Husserl will never go further than this life-world since the full weight of the presuppositions which bind us inextricably to it remains implicit even at the most advanced stages of the phenomenological dialectic. Whatever doubts or "reductions" are practiced serve merely to focus our attention on the hidden core of meanings within experience, but they can never obliterate the mental and perceptual habits which constitute our learned situation within the life-world.

The act of "epoché" which Husserl performs is similar to Cartesian doubt. By this act the phenomenologist abstains "from every believing involved in or founded on sensuous experiencing":

> I, as reflecting philosophically, no longer keep in effect (no longer accept) the natural believing in existence involved in experiencing

> the world—though that believing too is still there and grasped by my noticing regard. The same is true of all the processes of meaning that . . . belong to my lifestream; the non-intuitive processes of meaning objects, the judgings, valuings, and decidings, the setting ends and willing means, and all the rest. . . .[15]

This does not deprive us of the world, it does not leave us "confronting nothing": "On the contrary we gain possession of something by it; and what we . . . acquire by it is my pure living, with all the pure subjective processes making this up, and everything meant in them, *purely as* meant in them: the universe of 'phenomena'. . . ."[16]

So begins the march "back to the things themselves," the return to objects in their immediate givenness to pure consciousness. The phrase from Mallarmé's poem now achieves a new emphasis, since the phenomenologist is indeed a man who replies to the question "What is the Earth?" What is the true meaning of things and their interrelatedness not as spatio-temporal entities but as presentations to consciousness?

In what sense does the poet, too, perform an epoché? In what sense does he suspend his believing in the spatio-temporal world in order to consider objects anew within the field of pure consciousness? The "suspension" involved in poetic statements is described in the following way by Roman Ingarden:

> The intentionally projected circumstances build up a world of their own. . . . The iridescence of this being-in-the-world and yet existing in a kind of suspension, without a foothold in reality, produces the peculiar magic of works of this sort.[17]

As Ingarden's quote indicates there is an act of epoché performed in *every* literary work, since it is a turning from the fact-world to a world projected or constituted within consciousness; the writer must "suspend" his attention to the fact-world or, in Hegelian terms, "negate" it in order to create his imaginary cosmos. The question then is not whether or not an epoché is performed but how exactly the imaginary world relates to the fact-world. In general, we can detect two tendencies: the first, which holds for any kind of literary "realism," presents the "intentionally projected circumstances" as if they were the retrieval of the fact-world within consciousness. The main business of such literature is to achieve, through specific strategies which we cannot discuss here, an "as if" status. We take it *as if* we were directly regarding the world of contingent, factual experience. The other tendency, which holds for Mallarmé, presents its cosmos in a direct and immediate relationship to pure consciousness. It insists on the fact that, in Husserl's term, objects and events in consciousness are "irrealities," that is, "pure fictive possibilities," exemplars or prototypes of actual events. The poet's task, then, becomes the clarification of these "irrealities" within a purified consciousness.

Mallarmé, again in "Toast funèbre," defines the poet's task as an "ideal duty" imposed upon him by the material or factual world ("the gardens of this star"):

> . . . I hope to see
> Him who, yesterday, vanished in the ideal
> Duty imposed by the gardens of this star,
> Survive for the honour of the calm disaster
> By a solemn agitation in the air of words . . .[18]

Poetic language "survives" as the matrix within which the fact-world is reinterpreted, not in its relationship to daily life but rather in its relationship to the "ideal," to pure consciousness. It is precisely the difficulty of this task which renders the poet's work so agonizingly imperfect, since the poet must struggle against the ordinary meanings of words, reshaping them to serve a new and higher purpose.

This poetic vocation is presented once again in what may be Mallarmé's most difficult poem, "Prose pour des Esseintes":

> Yes, in an island that the air weighs
> With sight and not with vision
> Each flower grew more open
> Without our commenting upon it.
>
> As such, immense, so that each
> Ordinarily bedecked itself
> With a lucid contour, a margin,
> Which kept it aloof from gardens.
>
> Glory of long desire, Ideas
> All within me exalted seeing
> The family of iridescent ones
> Surge forth to this new duty.[19]

The flower as poetic emblem does not emerge within a false otherworldly perspective ("vision") but within the field of purified perceptual experience ("sight"). The grandeur and formal perfection of these flowers make of them formal essences which are now "separated" from the "garden," i.e., the material or life-world. The isolation of the word "Ideas" singles it out and sets it apart. These "Ideas" are the flowers as purified essences (in the French text "*Idées*" is in apposition with the pronoun "*Telles*" which refers back to the flowers). The poet's task, then, appears to be the realization of these essences which now acquire the "surging" characteristic of pure consciousness.

Space does not permit us to examine each aspect of poetic epoché for possible parallels with the rigorous epoché of the phenomenologist. But if we limit ourselves to those forms of doubt by Husserl indicated on pp. 157–58, a number of parallels can be drawn.

Believing involved in or founded on sensuous experience. While certain poets may render sensuous experience directly, it is clear that for Mallarmé sensuous experience as such is always held at a remove from the actual images presented by the poems. It lies just over a horizon, that horizon from which Mallarmé always withdraws when he writes a poem.

The natural believing in existence involved in experiencing the world. The enabling act of poetry for Mallarmé is precisely the suspension of belief in the world and the quest for a new and more fundamental basis for experience.

The judgings, valuings, and decidings, the setting ends and willing means. Many activities are included here and obviously all are not excluded from Mallarmé's poetry. The judgment, as the basic modality of thought by which a predicate is attributed to a subject, still functions but *not as regards empirical objects.* The world of empirical objects in fact falls away, appearing as an indeterminate flux where judgments as to existence and the like are not possible. On the other hand, "valuing" plays an important role in the poetry of Mallarmé—in a sense, the function of each poem is to create a value. Still, these values obtain within the universe of the poem and not in the life-world. The last two activities may also be excluded from Mallarmé's poetry for the most part, since rarely are concrete situations demanding action of one kind or another presented. Hence, poet and phenomenologist have much in common at this first crucial phase of the movement from the life-world into transcendental subjectivity.

The next act (or group of acts) by which the phenomenologist further purifies the field of experience is known as the "eidetic reduction."

> It is concerned with a residuum presented in the phenomenological orientation; it is the status of the elements of the residuum which

> are now of interest. The eidetic reduction is a method by means of which the phenomenologist is able to attend to the character of the given, setting aside that which is contingent and secondary and noting that which shows itself as universal.[20]

In epoché the phenomenologist has already set aside causation, spatio-temporal relations, history, value, and belief in the world. Now his task is to obtain the "eidos" or essence, that is, to move from the singular of *my* experience to the structure of that experience as generalizable for all. He brackets the "I know" to remove from it the individual biographical elements and in order to establish the structural identity of that knowing. Within that knowing the essences (of whatever class of phenomena) are given as universal types purified from the various empirical determinations involved in the perspectival and sensate experience of the natural attitude.

It seems at first glance paradoxical to speak of an eidetic reduction in poetry, since the relation of poetic images to existential experience and their concreteness and particularity is generally assumed. We assume that the poem occurs in a present "now" and that it exhibits the life of consciousness in an immediate relation with persons and things.

Yet the "now" of the poem is identical neither with some unreproducible life-experience which may have been its generating impulse nor with the "now" of the poem's composition, which may stretch over many months or even, in the case of Mallarmé, many years. This "now" is rather a temporality created by the collaboration of reader and poetic speaker, a speaker not exchangeable with the poet himself, but rather an impersonal presence implied within the poem. Indeed, Mallarmé insists on the poem's impersonality and its disjunction with his own personal experience. The Book, in Mallarmé's term "impersonified," exists in a neutral space between poet and reader:

> The Book, wherein lives satisfied spirit, in case of misunderstanding, himself obligated by a certain purity of action to throw off the weight of the moment. Impersonified, the volume, insofar as one can separate oneself from it as author, claims no approach by the reader. As such, know then, that among human accessories, it occurs in isolation: made, being. The buried meaning moves and arranges itself, as a choir, among the pages.[21]

This impersonification is comparable to Husserl's "neutrality modification" which functions in every act of reduction to lift the phenomenon out of its fact-world. Husserl illustrates the neutrality modification by referring to Dürer's engraving, *The Knight, Death, and the Devil.* We see the engraving first as a "thing" composed of black ink lines on a sheet of paper. Then through the neutrality modification we move to the aesthetic perception of a portrayed scene in which recognizable shapes embody allegorical personages.

> This *depicting picture-object* stands before us *neither as being nor as non-being,* nor in any other positional modality; or rather, we are aware of it as having its being, though only a quasi-being, in the neutrality-modification of Being.[22]

The being of the eidos is not at issue; rather, it is its appearance as an essence or type, recognizable through the typifications of abstractive consciousness, which allow us to see in it the fullness of Dürer's intention.[23]

The fact that the poem is an eidos rather than an empirical construct may be shown by looking at several images from the poetry of Mallarmé.

> Victoriously fled is the beautiful suicide
> Brand of glory, blood in foam, gold, tempest![24]

The sonnet from which these lines are taken is built upon the opposition between the setting sun ("the beautiful suicide") and the golden ringlets of Mallarmé's mistress Méry Laurent. The dying sun does not merely destroy himself but, by extension, poses the theme of entropy and biological decay; yet by insisting on Méry's present and actual beauty, the poet is able to disarm the cosmic irony and, in the poem's finale, turn from it to the enjoyment of the present. If we isolate the image of the sun we see at once that it is not presented as the sun of any one unique perceptual act or as the sun of any specific moment of Mallarmé's existence. Rather the descent and destruction of this most magnificent of all symbols gives us the setting sun as the type of all decay and physical change; we might say that it rephrases the eternal Mallarmean question: "What is the meaning of the Earth?" Richard formulates the thought/object relationship in the following way:

> Sometimes, in fact, the Mallarmean object serves to incarnate a subjective project, which inheres in it and expresses itself through it. . . . Sometimes it serves as prop and partner for the operations of a thought which, seizing it first as external to itself, tries to resolve it and reintegrate it within itself; we see it then as the concrete

> point of departure for an entire alchemy, which aims to transform it into meaning. . . .[25]

The only correction that should be made here is to insist that the Mallarmean "object" is never a sensate perception, but rather an eidos or type which has already undergone the eidetic reduction.

Another poem, "Le Tombeau d'Edgar Poe," shows the same use of an eidos or essence, although here it is a person rather than an object that is portrayed:

> Such as to himself eternity's changed him,
> The Poet rouses with his naked sword
> His age terrified for not having known
> That death was triumphing in that strange voice![26]

The Poet here is not merely Poe (whose name is not mentioned till the eleventh line) but rather the Poet as type, the Poet *sub specie aeternitatis*; he is every dead poet, just as the sun of the preceding poem is the sun of every sunset. We are presented with the Poet as eternal type, just as in the preceding poem we are presented with the sun as eternal type of cosmological entropy; and, in both cases, the complex web of echoes and resonances built into the poem refers to the represented entity as type rather than individual.

Yet the eidos of Mallarmé is not an essence which can be stabilized or realized more or less fully, as would be the case for the essences attained by phenomenology, but is rather given in a brief flash of insight, generated through the dialectical movement of the poem and lost when the poem has ended. Still, we may regard the attainment of this eidos as the ultimate goal of poetry. It is this Mallarmé speaks of, in the following statement, when he refers to "the pure notion":

> To what end the marvel of transposing a fact in nature into its almost vibratory disappearance according to the play of language, however; if it is not to permit, without the hindrance of a near or concrete echo, the emanation of the pure notion.[27]

The purified "fact of nature," that is to say, the eidos, is spoken of in Mallarmé's Hegelian language as an "absence." It is the flower which is "absent from all bouquets," the Poet who is absent from his tomb, the poem which has not been written on the "white page." This eidos, which is often called by Mallarmé the "Idea," arises when the poet turns his purifying glance on the phenomenal world:

> Virginity, which solitarily, confronting a transparency of the adequate stare, is of itself as it were divided in its fragments of candour, the one and the other nuptial proofs of the Idea.[28]

The final act of bracketing, the act which gives transcendental subjectivity in its purest form, seeks to eliminate from the residuum all that which is given by others, all that derives from the "we" of experience. We inhabit a world given to us by others and our inspection of it is determined in large part by shared habits of perception and expressed in a shared language rife with hidden presuppositions. In the eidetic reduction, the phenomenologist moves from the "I" of individual experience to the "I" as underlying structure of any experience. In the transcendental reduction, through the elimination of presuppositions given by the communal or shared nature of experience, he at last attains that pure consciousness in which all experience is grounded.

This reduction, too, is operative in the poetry of Mallarmé, and in fact the attainment of pure transcendental subjectivity may be his greatest or at least his hardest won achievement as a poet. It may also explain the difficulty of his poetry, a poetry in which the "I" is never the poet as existential being and the "we" seems to have been eliminated, allowing pure subjectivity to appear in brief intuitive flashes.

While it is essential to ground our reading of Mallarmé in a knowledge of the specific scenes and dramas enacted by the poems, we can never understand these poems if we fail to read backwards, as it were, from transcendental subjectivity to the poem as specific event. The event, seen only in its own terms, exhibits that element of contingency and chance Mallarmé struggled so hard to extirpate. But when that event, those arbitrary congeries of symbols, those speech rhythms with their necessarily temporal and concrete character are seen in reference to what lies *behind* the poem—transcendental subjectivity itself—then it is clear that their contingent character provides no more than the field within which the poet will work toward the ultimate insight, that "third aspect" which arises from the juncture of poetic images: "Institute a relationship between exact images, so that a third aspect clear and soluble may present itself to our divination."[29] Paul Ricoeur describes reduction as "the first free act because it is one that liberates from mundane illusion. Through it I apparently lose the world that I truly gain."[30] This accurately describes the arc of Mallarmé's poetry—a turning from the world only to discover it, a penetration to ultimate consciousness in which both consciousness and world, as co-founders of human existence, are ultimately given and received.

This world, rediscovered in poetry, has the freshness of Eden and the strangeness of a domain we have known in a previous existence and then forgotten. The world, in its ultimate relation to human consciousness, is *the* world. Our attainment of it, as I suggested at the outset, may be doomed to brevity and tragic incompleteness. But to have attained it at all marks Edmund Husserl and Stéphane Mallarmé as adventurers of spirit who at once define the limits of our condition for us and choose as their destiny the pushing back of those limits toward the horizon.

NOTES

(All translations from Mallarmé and Richard are my own unless otherwise indicated.)

1. Paul Ricoeur, *Husserl: An Analysis of His Phenomenology*, trans. E. G. Ballard and L. E. Embree (Evanston, 1967), p. 10.
2. Edmund Husserl, *Cartesian Meditations: An Introduction to Phenomenology*, trans. Dorion Cairns (The Hague, 1960), p. 37.
3. Stéphane Mallarmé, *Oeuvres complètes* (Paris, La Bibliothèque de la Pléiäde, 1945), p. 368.
4. Stéphane Mallarmé, *Correspondance*, 1862–1871 (Paris, 1959), p. 240. Letter dated May 14, 1867.
5. Jean-Pierre Richard, *L'Univers imaginaire de Mallarmé* (Paris, 1961), p. 233.
6. Ibid.
7. Mallarmé, *Oeuvres complètes*, p. 355.
8. Richard, *L'Univers imaginaire*, p. 27.
9. Roman Ingarden, as quoted by V. M. Hamm in "Roman Ingarden's *Das Literarische Kunstwerk*," in *The Critical Matrix* (Washington, D. C., 1961), p. 172.
10. Husserl, *Cartesian Meditations*, p. 21.
11. Ibid., p. 27.
12. Ibid., p. 52.
13. Mallarmé, *Oeuvres complètes*, p. 55; translation by Roger Fry (New York, 1951), p. 95. References hereafter are to the Fry translation.
14. Husserl, *Cartesian Meditations*, pp. 152–53.
15. Ibid., p. 20.
16. Ibid., pp. 19–20.
17. Ingarden, in V. M. Hamm, *The Critical Matrix*, p. 184.
18. Mallarmé, *Oeuvres complètes*, p. 55.
19. Ibid., p. 56.

20. Maurice Natanson, "Phenomenology: A Viewing," *Methodos,* No. 40, vol. X (1958), p. 11.

21. Mallarmé, *Oeuvres complètes,* p. 372.

22. Husserl, *Ideas: General Introduction to Pure Phenomenology,* trans. W. R. Boyce Gibson (New York, 1962), p. 285.

23. Sartre uses the same example in his discussion of imaginary entities in *L'Imagination.* For a discussion of the issues raised by Sartre's analysis see Eugene Kaelin, "The Visibility of Things Seen," in *An Invitation to Phenomenology* (Chicago, 1965), pp. 37–38.

24. Mallarmé, *Oeuvres complètes,* p. 68.

25. Richard, *L'Univers imaginaire,* p. 403.

26. Mallarmé, *Oeuvres complètes,* p. 70. (Roger Fry, p. 109.)

27. Ibid., p. 368.

28. Ibid., p. 387.

29. Ibid., p. 365.

30. Ricoeur, *Husserl,* p. 20.

Jean-Paul Sartre: The Engaged Imagination

CHARLES ALTIERI
STATE UNIVERSITY OF NEW YORK AT BUFFALO

I

THE CORRESPONDENCE between William James and his brother Henry is an illuminating document for those interested in the history of modern literary criticism. Henry was the artist concerned with freeing art from practical relevance to life in order to broaden the subject matter it could treat and to make possible a greater concern for formal excellence. But William, in writing that *The Europeans* is "thin and empty," that Henry has sacrificed subject to form, takes an antithetical point of view. What appeared to him as an excessive aestheticism was the outgrowth of the efforts of nineteenth-century artists to free themselves from the restrictive moralism of the Philistines. He exemplifies the ever-recurrent tendency of socially oriented thinkers to criticize aestheticism as "escapist" and "narrow," and to demand that the artist devote himself to what they consider the central aspects of human experience.

This reaction against aesthetic formalism constitutes an important dimension in the work of several twentieth-century critics. Edmund Wilson, Irving Babbitt, and T. S. Eliot come immediately to mind. Even a "New Critic" such as I. A. Richards felt compelled to construct a psychology which would give poetry a more relevant position in human life than formalist claims to pleasure or even to transcendence could offer. Like William James, Richards takes what may be considered a syncretic position. Being sensitive to the logical basis and value of the aesthetic position, he does not wish to refute it so much as to combine it in some meaningful way with a system that asserts art's social relevance.

For Samuel Johnson, art reflects reality; form is a means of focusing and highlighting the essential truths man needs to be reminded of. A century later, as form became an end in itself, as artists experimented with the tone poem, with the poem as musical entity, and with Dada and the like, it became more difficult to claim that art can contribute to the fulfillment of our normal establishmentarian lives. Yet many critics have taken up the challenge of finding a relevance in art by concentrating on the crucial role imagination plays in human activity. In addition to Richards, we have the Neo-Kantians like Ernst Cassirer and Susanne Langer, who insist that art is a symbolic function of the imagination which captures and communicates feelings that are inexpressible in ordinary conceptual language. There are also theorists of the mythic imagination like Carl Jung and Northrop Frye, who see in the creative imagination a means of extending man's dominion by impressing human value on an indifferent world. Then there are the proponents of the phenomenological imagination—thinkers as diverse as Jacques Maritain, Mikel Dufrenne, and Gaston Bachelard—who are united in their agreement with Husserl's ideas of anti-reductionism and intentionality. Anti-reductionism opposes positivistic simplifications of the complexites of man's affective existence; and intentionality, the idea that human consciousness is in contact with the real world, insists that the artistic imagination is a means of perceiving and expressing essential intuitions into man's encounter with nature.

The position of Jean-Paul Sartre in this direction of twentieth-century thinking is difficult to ascertain. His earliest theoretical statements in *Psychology of the Imagination* (1940) follow the phenomenological lead. But Sartre uses phenomenology to deny the possibility of a synthesis between aesthetics and moral or social concerns. His study of the imagination proposes that the art object as image is necessarily unreal and can only be enjoyed if it is dissociated from the world of normal human experience. If his study of the imagination had ended at this point, we would have to concede that Sartre's aesthetic is a throwback to the nineteenth-century's radical divorce of art and life. However, Sartre, after the Second World War and after his promise of a positive ethics to mollify the critics of *Being and Nothingness*, sought in literary theory a means of reestablishing the essential connection between imagination and practical existence. This search for a humanistic imagination reached fruition for him in his theory of the novel as communication, a theory in which he applied a developing idea in his thinking—the idea that the imagination has a central place in the human engagement with reality. For this reason, the best way to approach Sartre's aesthetic is by studying his developing concept of the imagination, from *Psychology of the Imagination* (1940) to *What Is Literature?* (1948), with some attention to the essays in literary criticism in which his ideas are applied.

The development is a subtle one, because Sartre never completely renounces his position in *Psychology of the Imagination*; nevertheless, we cannot understand his later position unless we admit a change. Eugene Kaelin is in a sense correct when he claims that Sartre's idea of imagination remains constant. One can say, with Kaelin, "When imagination is conceived as 'the absentification of the present or the presentification of the absent,' as Sartre does conceive it, the value of the imagined object becomes the revelation of the world as it is,"[1] but some qualification is needed. For one must explain how in his earlier work on imagination Sartre can insist that desire is incompatible with beauty (*IM*, 180) and then in *What Is Literature?* demand that the literary object become an obsession for the reader (*WL*, 231).[2]

Only by realizing what Sartre does with the imagination in *What Is Literature?* can one see the coherence of his argument that "at the heart of the aesthetic imperative we discern the moral imperative" (WL, 56–57), the argument that is the central thesis of the book. Only by showing how the imagination of the reader is at one and the same time in touch with the real world and morally responsible for that world can Sartre make good his claim. This he does by changing the standpoint from which he had earlier viewed the imaginative object. Whereas the art object originally had been for Sartre purely a re-creation of the perceiver's imagination, in *What Is Literature?* the novel is seen as communication, that is, as an appeal to the whole person. The novel is not given to the imagination but to the whole consciousness of the person, one of whose properties is imagination. Imagination, then, is no longer an isolatable entity to be studied phenomenologically, but part of a human subject who can only be studied in relation to his entire human situation by existential analysis.[3]

II

At this point we must look more fully at Sartre's phenomenology of the imagination and the implications of this phenomenology for aesthetics. Imagination can function in itself or as an element in conscious awareness of the world. In either case "the image *as long as it is imagined* differs in nature from the type of existence of the object grasped as real" (*IM*, 261). The creation of an image is always accompanied by an awareness of the non-existence of the real referent of the image.

Thus, (to use Sartre's example in *Psychology of the Imagination*) when I have an image of Peter in my mind, I am aware that the Peter in my mind is not the Peter before me. When I look at a work of art, I am aware that the figure in my mind, say the figure of Charles VIII in a portrait, is unreal in that it is distinct from the lines and colors which constitute the object before me (*IM*, 274; 31–32). It is in this sense that Kaelin's description of imagination as "absentification of the present or presentification of the absent" is correct.

Although Sartre concludes his study of the imagination with an indication of the future direction his concept of it is to take, the ethical direction of "situation,"[4] his primary concern is with the imagination as it functions in the act of knowing and as it serves as an epistemological proof for human freedom. In the *Psychology of the Imagination*, Sartre arrives at the conclusion that the activity of the imagination or the unrealizing power of the mind is present in all acts of conscious determination. (By "determine" I understand Sartre to mean the act of bringing a perception into conscious awareness. I am not sure if imagination functions on the simple level of animal perception, but in order to know what one has seen, one must imagine.) As the scholastics insisted, "*omnis determinatio est negatio*"—"every definition is an exclusion." In the act of conscious determination, the imagination must unrealize the total world presented to the person before he can isolate any aspect of that world in consciousness. To define a tree, the person must be able to synthesize and negate a world which is not the tree so that the tree may stand out as not the world.

Sartre's proof that imagination is essential to consciousness then becomes for him the further proof that the human being is free. Freedom cannot be a property of the real because the real, being material, is subject to the laws of causality. But the real cannot negate the real, for negation can only be the result of non-being applied to being, while the real is characterized as pure being. Human consciousness, since it can negate the real, must not be pure being; there must be in its functioning power a non-being which, precisely because it is not being, is free. Sartre's proof here is rigorous and difficult to disprove, but Sartre came to see, in *Being and Nothingness*, that epistemological freedom, both in its imaginative power to deny reality altogether and in its conscious function of denying reality in order to know it, is too abstract. Epistemological freedom is not necessarily practical, ethical freedom. Even the staunchest determinist would agree that I am either free to ignore the determined life I lead or free to imagine I am free.

Sartre's aesthetic in *Psychology of the Imagination* is the direct result of his view that the product of the imagination is necessarily an unreality. Only if "we can at once formulate the law that the work of art is an unreality" (*IM*, 274), that beauty which is the end of art "is by its very nature out of the world" (*IM*, 275), can we understand Kant's theory that the work of art is an end in itself, to be enjoyed only in disinterested aesthetic experience (*IM*, 277). Because the real world is *de trop* and absurd, beauty, which implies purpose and form, must be a "negation of the world in its essential structure. . . . This is why it is stupid to confuse the moral [which demands action in the world] with the aesthetic" (*IM*, 281).

In drawing out the implications of Sartre's aesthetic of the imagination so that they may be compared with the implications of his later view of the engaged imagination in his analysis of the novel, it will be helpful to relate both theories to the four perspectives Meyer Abrams uses in *The Mirror and the Lamp* to classify aesthetic positions: the creator, the audience, the work, and the universe.

Sartre says very little about the creator in *Psychology of the Imagination* because one can analyze phenomenologically only the data of consciousness, and the creative act is outside anything which the normal consciousness can verify. One can, however, see Sartre's view of the role of the creator in the production of the purely imaginative object from his analyses of poetry and of aestheticism in *What Is Literature?*. The artist is not situated; his work is in no way obliged to reflect the real world because he is concerned with creating an unreal object and not a reflection of reality. In fact, the artist is "forbidden to engage himself" (*WL*, 13) because engagement might make the object impure. The artist serves to liberate man, but what he liberates "is neither desire, nor the human totality, but pure imagination" (*WL*, 191). The artist need not concern himself with the problem of truth, a problem which for Sartre demands the novel of "pure presentation." The artist is concerned only with beauty, with turning the world into an unreal object to be contemplated. The artist views the universe as "pure beholding from the point of view of God" (*WL*, 123). Because the artist divorces himself from reality, it is difficult if not impossible for him to justify his existence as necessary for the world. Thus he frequently seeks to deny the reality of the world and to establish his own work as the only reality.

Like the artist, the audience for a work of pure imagination is not situated. Its freedom in re-creating the work is not an existential freedom, but the freedom of a dream, the freedom of pure contemplation.

Indeed, the work of art often sets us against existence because the return from the freedom of the work can arouse "the nauseating disgust that characterizes the consciousness of reality" (*IM*, 281). The audience is free to deny the world, but it denies it in favor of an impossible world, a world in which Sartre was to see later there is no real freedom because there is nothing lacking and because there is no desire (*BN*, 482–83). The pleasure we receive in aesthetic contemplation is the pleasure we receive from objects which pose no task for us and consequently are not appeals to our freedom. Aesthetic pleasure is solipsistic because no communication takes place between creator and audience or among the members of the audience.

Sartre denies that in the object created for aesthetic contemplation there can be any relation between the image or content of the work and the universe, that is, the condition of man in the real world. For we can produce the image only by denying our existential situation. The pure aesthetic object is an "epoché," a bracketing or neutralizing of the world of existence (*WL*, 123). Aesthetic pleasure is possible only because the imagination grasps the object as an unreal whole, while completeness is impossible in reality where there is a plenitude of relationships (*IM*, 276). Thus the poet deals not with language as a sign, but language as an object (*WL*, 9–13) so that his work can exist independent of reality. And since the object exists as a whole it is not perceived as dated (that is, as an object in history) either with respect to its performance or to its date and circumstances of composition (*IM*, 281).

Sartre's aesthetics in *Psychology of the Imagination* has two important similarities with the aesthetic tradition as it originated with Kant and Coleridge. Like them, Sartre asserts the radical independence of imagination and in this goes counter to positivist attempts to explain it as aberrant and/or psychologically determined by other known physiological and psychological factors. Like Kant and Coleridge, he insists on the transcendent quality of the imagination, the quality by which the imagination surpasses or "unrealizes" known reality, as the basis for his philosophical proof of freedom.[5]

The second similarity is Sartre's partial agreement with Kant that "the imagination (as a productive quality of cognition) is very powerful in creating another nature, as it were, out of the material that actual nature gives it."[6] Indeed, one may say that the modern aesthetic tradition, with its stress on formal beauty, on the wholeness of the art object and the importance of the organic unity of its parts, and on the transcendence of the beautiful as an ordering of a confused reality, has as its metaphysical substructure a concept analogous to Sartre's unrealizing power of the imagination. Or at least the analogy holds so long as we accept Sartre's phenomenology of the imagination; for then form and real existence are incompatible. And Sartre's notion of unreality is evident in extreme forms of aestheticism such as art-for-art's-sake, in which art is valuable precisely because it is not real.

There is a problem, however, in accepting Sartre's claim that his radical distinction between real and unreal explains that "celebrated disinterestedness of aesthetic experience" (*IM*, 277) which Kant developed. With his view of art as unreality, Sartre implies that all aesthetic appreciation is appreciation of the work as artifact, as a formal entity which can be appreciated aesthetically precisely because it is unreal and consequently not subject to the unlimited relationships that characterize any real object. Sartre, then, does not allow for Kant's contention that the aesthetic imagination is a "productive quality of cognition." Kant's definition of the "aesthetical idea" takes art beyond the purely formal: "By an aesthetical idea I understand that representation of the imagination which occasions much thought, without, however, any definite thought, i.e., any concept, being capable of being adequate to it; it consequently cannot be completely compassed and made intelligible by language."[7] Kant is aiming at a more complex view of the relation between art and reality. The notion of representation allows for form, while the idea of a meaning beyond conceptualization allows for theories like Mrs. Langer's of non-discursive meaning. The art work can relate to the complexities of real existence, so long as the perceiver does not judge the work by evaluating the moral or the scientific validity of the representation. He can see the work as related to reality so long as he does not judge the work in terms of that relationship.

III

A possible allusion in the title *What Is Literature?* to Verlaine's sarcastic line in "Art poétique," "*Et tout le reste est littérature,*" signifies Sartre's shift in concern from the purely aesthetic to the intermediate realm of "*littérature,*" a realm which becomes for Sartre primarily that of the novel. While Sartre's concept of the activity of the imagination does not completely change, it now appears in a surprising new light. The philosophical freedom of imagination as productive of unreal images changes to the existential notion of the situated freedom of the imagination as an ethical instrument in human communication. Sartre's new "engaged" aesthetic is the product of two important modifications of the philosophy in *Psychology of the Imagination.* Sartre makes a radical distinction between pure arts (that is, those in which the essential purpose is the making of a purely aesthetic object) and the novel which, because it is in prose, is essentially a communicative art. Second, he develops the correlative notion of situation, which makes it possible for Sartre to realize the idea of communication.

The difference between poetry (that is, literature as appeal to the imagination) and prose is a difference in the intention of consciousness: "What defines the imaginary world and also the world of the real is an attitude of consciousness" (*IM*, 27), and "prose is first of all an attitude of mind" (*WL*, 14). The intention of mind in prose is not to create a material analogue which is recreated by the reader in the unreal, but to communicate. And communication implies commitment to reality. In poetry, as the French literary tradition conceived it and as Sartre believes, language seeks to become a part of the unreal object by containing within itself the sensuous quality of the words and all the ambivalent meanings the word can create, while in prose language seeks absolute transparency: "Prose is, in essence, utilitarian" (*WL*, 13); since prose is employed in discourse, "the words are first of all not objects, but designations for objects" (*WL*, 14). The language of poetry seeks to escape the real, while the language of prose has for its essential function signification, a focusing on and elucidation of reality.

What Sartre is searching for in his distinction between poetry and prose is something like Mrs. Langer's notion of "radical of presentation"; however with Sartre the radical is not the formal medium but the intention. He knows that the novel is different from expository prose because its function is not to present ideas but the feelings of ideas (*LE*, 32). He is also aware that a continuum exists between the poles of pure poetry and pure prose. But he insists that a barrier exists which makes it impossible to go from poetry to prose by a continuous series of intermediate forms (*WL*, 31). Prose cannot fulfill its primary function if, as in Joyce's *Ulysses*, the words are turned into objects whose relations are primarily to one another; nor can poetry fulfill its essence when the world intervenes to impede the "dance of the intellect among words."

Sartre's proof for this essential difference is that prose, unlike poetry, is considered successful if it leaves us remembering an idea or a scene without our remembering the specific words in which the idea is given. The distinction is well illustrated by Sartre's discussion of one of Genet's poems. Sartre criticizes a particular line because it is explanatory and drags into "prosaism" a poem that "had asserted nothing" and stood on "the amazing cohesion of its monosyllables which is cemented by the rhythm." Sartre then points out how the poetry degenerates because logical significations now prevail. He concludes that Genet "is not meant for producing brief formulas 'translated from silence' but for grappling with language . . . he is a discursive writer" (*SG*, 433–41).[8]

If prose is reality centered, we must ask ourselves how Sartre conceives of the human involvement in reality, a question which leads us to a consideration of Sartre's concept of "situation." We have already seen the first, or epistemological, dimension of situation by which the imagination in order to determine a tree must unrealize in turn both tree and world. The ethical dimension occurs when one wishes to make a moral judgment. Any moral judgment is an act of consciousness which requires an unrealizing. For the oppressed Negro to say he hates his inferior citizenship necessitates his imaginative projection of a world in which his inferior citizenship is not a reality. He must go beyond the world in order to evaluate it. Thus Sartre can say, "To speak is to act; anything which one names is already no longer quite the same; it has lost its innocence" (*WL*, 16). It has lost its innocence because in bringing it to consciousness the determiner has been forced to isolate it and project it against a world in which the thing named either need not exist or may exist in another way. To see what something is, is to see it in terms of necessity—either it need be that way (itself a relational judgment) or it may exist in another way.

We have gone far enough to see why the revelatory nature of the novel is so important to Sartre (see below), but there are further implications of "situation" we must explore to understand the role of the writer in *What Is Literature*? There remains an obvious objection to the example of the Negro above: "We decide every day that we don't like things, and, while we might unrealize in order to express our dissatisfaction, aren't most of our unrealizings simply daydreams and therefore irrelevant as ethical concerns or even as proof of anything but abstract freedom?" Sartre would reply, in a development from *Psychology of the Imagination*, that in a sense we are correct. Practical freedom "supposes a commencement of realization in order that the choice may be distinguished from the dream and the wish" (*BN*, 483). A novelist who communicates daydreams does nothing for his own or for the reader's freedom.

The relation of freedom to reality is important to Sartre for several reasons. It leads to the concept of situation and it underlies the proper balance of being, having, and doing (a balance distorted by aestheticism which is concerned only with the link between being and having and neglects that between being and doing—a link basic to the act of communication). Sartre begins from a position like that of Stevens and Santayana; neither man nor outside reality has any meaning because there is no God and no human essence. Only man can create meaning, because meaning is a problem only for a freedom. The question becomes, how does man create meaning both for things and for himself? Stevens and Santayana would say, by creating a believable myth; but Sartre wants a solution more applicable to ethical choices. Remember, if freedom is meaningful it resides only in acts, at least in the commencement of acts. So the only meaning man can create for himself that is existentially applicable (and not possibly a daydream) is the meaning he creates by his acts. Sartre's summary phrase for this is "existence creates essence."[9]

Let us turn again to the example of the oppressed Negro. He has several possible ways of choosing his existence and thus giving it and himself meaning. First, he can be not even aware of a situation in which, were he aware of other possibilities, he would realize that he is oppressed. If the human being is defined by freedom, this lack of knowledge keeps one at a sub-human level of existence. Then there is the choice we have seen of his condemning his world by relating it to a daydream. The choice here is itself free, but because it does not result in meaningful action which is the proof of freedom, it is a free choice to deny freedom. This Negro is freely defining himself as a slave. Sartre calls the free choice to avoid the responsibilities of action which freedom demands, a choice made in bad faith. The choice of a realizable means of correcting the situation, on the other hand, is a choice which, when accompanied by action, defines the person as fully human.

Sartre's idea of situation enables us to clarify a few general characteristics of *What Is Literature?* First of all, we see the basis for the negative and constructive role Sartre posited for the French writer in 1957. The end of writing is "spiritualization, that is renewal. . . . The writer will renew it [the world] as it is, the raw sweaty, smelly, everyday world, in order to submit it to freedoms on the foundation of a freedom" (*WL*, 152). The writer's situated presentation of a world will be the means of making the reader aware that he is free and that there are concrete projects in which he can materialize and define his freedom:

> It is by means of the book that the members of this society would be able to get their bearings, to see themselves and see their situa-

tion. But as the portrait comprises the model, as the simple presentation is already the beginning of change, as the work of art, taken in the totality of its exigencies, is not a simple description of the present but a judgment of this present in the name of the future, finally, as every book contains an appeal, this awareness of self is a surpassing of self. The universe is not contested in the name of simple consumption, but in the name of the hopes and sufferings of those who inhabit it. Thus, concrete literature will be a synthesis of Negativity, as a power of uprooting from the given, and a Project, as an outline of a future order. [*WL*, 152–53]

Second, we see what has happened to Sartre's imagination with respect to the prose work as reality centered. Since the novel signifies, the imagination of the novel reader functions, not as the unrealizer of artistic objects, but as the epistemological and ethical agent of the human project in the world. The novel because it is reality presented to the imagination becomes an aid in the reader's freeing and consequently determining of himself: "If perception itself is action, if for us, to show the world is to disclose it in the perspectives of a possible change, then, in this age of fatalism we must reveal to the reader his power in each concrete case of doing and undoing, in short, of acting" (*WL*, 285).

Sartre, then, with respect to the novel wants to go one step beyond Northrop Frye's statement, "The simple point is that literature belongs to the world man constructs, not to the world he sees; to his home not his environment."[10] Sartre concretizes the mythic imagination and applies it to perception or disclosure. For in prose the imagination is not completely free; it is situated, it signifies the real world. Since the act of naming is also the beginning of imagination's role of providing a basis for change, the world man constructs and the world man sees are inextricably combined. The novel concretizes the human imagination in the service of the spiritualization of mankind. Whether one decides to change the world presented or not, he has defined himself in terms of it and must accept responsibility for it.

Finally, we should now be able to see the coherence of Sartre's argument in *What Is Literature?* The first chapter, "What Is Writing?," defines literature as communication, that is, as a projection of the real which employs art in order to enable the reader to re-create this world in its capacity for change. Also, because the writer is a man talking to other men about the real world, he is situated in the world he shares with his readers. "To be situated is to be engaged," that is, to be involved in the problems of the present in which history is being made. The second chapter, "Why Write?," outlines two essential aspects of writing: the author writes not for himself, but to be seen as necessary in relationship to the world, and he writes in order to reveal a part of reality so that man may realize it and give it meaning in terms of himself and himself meaning in terms of it. For this writing to be possible, the freedom of the reader is necessary—both to constitute the world of the work of art as being and as capable of being given meaning and freely to accept the author's existence as necessary in the world.

In the chapter "For Whom Does One Write?" Sartre tries to show how earlier "*littérature*" was determined by the world the writer felt his audience could re-create and how, if the writer is not in communication with all men, the world he creates will be incomplete. For if a writer is not at one with all men, it is almost impossible for him to embrace the total human condition in his work. And the impossibility of pure communication between beings from different social structures forces the writer to adapt the integrity of his vision to the practical demands of trying to reach as many men as possible. If a writer hopes for a total literature, he must be capable in reality, not just in idealistic terms, of imagining all men as his readers. Such a situation is possible only in a classless society, so the writer committed to the essence of his art must be committed to the development of a classless society.

The final chapter describes the present role of the writer in bringing about the ideal situation for literature. Sartre also points out directions which the novel must take if it is to fulfill its essence and lead to the eventual goal of literature of the human totality. Communication is possible only if the world of the novel is like the real world, that world in which the reader freely judges as he perceives. The attempt to convince the reader or to align his passions takes the reader as an object to be used by another—the method of propaganda—and not as a free subjectivity.

IV

The preceding summary indicates merely the logical structure of Sartre's argument. We must now put flesh on the skeleton. Let us return to Abrams's four perspectives for classifying aesthetic theories. Evidently we should begin with the reader, since Sartre's psychology of reading is the basis of his program for the author: "It is by choosing his reader that the writer decides upon his subject" (*WL*, 65).

We have already seen several indications of why for Sartre any attempt to enslave his readers threatens a writer in his very art (*WL*, 58);

but there are two aspects of Sartre's description of the freedom of the reader which demand elaboration. First, how does the reader reconstitute the author's communication so that he sees both himself and the world as capable of change? The reader of prose, unlike the reader of a poem, does not merely reconstitute an object already present in a material analogue that "everyone can grasp" (*IM*, 275). Sartre says that the appearance of the work of art (by which I take Sartre to mean exclusively the novel; cf. note 8 and the context of the citation) "is a new event which cannot be explained by any anterior data" (*WL*, 40). Since the novelist signifies and does not make, "to write is to make an appeal to the reader that he lead into objective existence the revelation which I have undertaken by means of language" (*WL*, 40). The objective existence of the world of the novel is possible because the novel does not exist in language (as does the poem) but is given through language in a silence which is the significance the reader creates beyond the terms of the specific description by the author (*WL*, 38). Only in this way can Sartre affirm that the reader is not given diversions but obsessions, "not a world 'to see,' but to change." (*WL*, 231).

A good example of the need for the reader's freedom is Sartre's discussion of Richard Wright's potential audience. Wright can be read by literate Negroes, and he may further serve their freedom by clarifying their own personal situations. It is more difficult for white readers, no matter how sympathetic, to read him because they are the Other and cannot completely re-create Wright's world. The illiterate Negro, of course, cannot read Wright at all, but neither can the white racists "whose minds are made up in advance and who will not open them" (*WL*, 72–74). The various responses are caused because "reading is an exercise in generosity, and what the writer requires of the reader is not the application of an abstract freedom but the gift of the whole person, with his passions, his prepossessions, his sympathies, his sexual temperament and his scale of values" (*WL*, 45). In order for the "world of the novel, that is, the totality of men and things," to offer its "maximum density," "the disclosure-creation by which the reader discovers it must also be an imaginary engagement in the action; . . . the more disposed one is to change it, the more alive it will be" (*WL*, 55). Limitations of freedom —ignorance, prejudice, and the like—are limitations on one's imaginary engagement in the action.

The second aspect stems from the first. If when men are free they can engage their particular selves in re-creating the same world, it is possible to discern another benefit of the novel. For Sartre, as for Kant,[11] the novel is a symbol of morality because in reading it a man "strips himself in some way of his empirical personality and escapes from his resentments, his fears, and his lusts in order to put himself at the peak of his freedom. This freedom takes the literary work and, through it, mankind, for absolute ends" (*WL*, 264–65), that is, as pure subjectivities and not as objects to be manipulated in a world constructed by an empirical personality. Thus universal communication and universal consideration of the other as an end is a possibility, but only when men bring about the classless society in which the obstacles of ignorance and resentment are obliterated to the extent that the novel can have a universal appeal.[12]

The novelist is situated and "engaged" in two ways—as a man who gives his existence meaning by declaring his vocation as a novelist, and as a professional involved in a work whose realization depends on the freedom of men: "A blacksmith can be affected by fascism in his life as a man, but not necessarily in his craft; a writer will be affected in both, and even more in his craft than in his life" (*WL*, 58).

As a man, the novelist must define his situation in social time. Because "man must be invented each day" (*WL*, 287), the way in which a person creates himself is the creation of the meaning he gives to man. Thus, simply in his role as man, the writer must serve the cause of freedom for all men (*WL*, 58). As a writer, he has further obligations to defend the freedom. Writing "is an act of confidence in the freedom of men" (*WL*, 57). As we have seen, the writer, if he is professionally concerned, must work for the freedom which is required if his readers are to reconstitute properly the world signified by the work. "Actual literature can only realize its full essence in a classless society" (*WL*, 151). Second, without the reader's freedom not only the novel but the justification for the novelist's existence would be destroyed. Since the writer himself decides the rules of production by which the work is made, *he* can never find anything but himself in the work (*WL*, 36). Only when the reader accepts the gift of the work and freely re-creates the world signified by the guidelines of the writer is the artist's existence recognized as necessary and valuable (*WL*, 54). Finally, the writer as professional must align himself with "the dignity of language" because the truth value of words (as signifiers) is absolutely necessary to the novel. Thus he cannot align himself with propagandistic political systems which distort language for their own ends (*WL*, 250–58).

Sartre suggests several interesting applications of the writer's engagement in defending freedom. We have already seen how his work serves as a mirror in illuminating individual freedoms and as a presentation to the imagination of a world to be changed. Two other notions which must be explored are Sartre's idea of the concrete universal and his concept of the role of the writer in man's task of creating in history a "city of ends."

In connection with the first Robert Belvin attacks Sartre for not reconciling the particular historical situation and the universal dimensions of the work which would make it a classic.[13] Sartre does, in fact, grapple with the problem. The end of literature, he says, is a "literature which unites and reconciles the metaphysical absolute and the relativity of the historical fact" (*WL*, 216). But this literature of the concrete universal is difficult when there is a divorce between the writer's potential and his actual public. Only in a new society would Richard Wright not have to alter his subject to adapt it to the different possibilities his audience has of imagining the world he communicates. Further, as long as the real public comes from a particular class, the writer risks "confusing the interests and cares of man with those of a small and favored group." If society were classless, the writer would necessarily be speaking about all men when speaking about himself; he would "really have to write about the human totality" (*WL*, 150).

On the novelist's commitment to the city of ends which is first indicated in the nature of aesthetic joy, it is sufficient to let Sartre speak for himself:

> But if we start with the moral exigence which the aesthetic feeling envelops without meaning to do so, we are starting on the right foot. We must *historicize* the reader's good will, that is, by the formal agency of our work, we must, if possible, provoke his intention of treating men, in every case, as an absolute end and, by the *subject* of our writing, direct his intention upon his neighbors, that is, upon the oppressed of the world. But we shall have accomplished nothing if, in addition, we do not show him—in the very warp and weft of the work—that it is quite impossible to treat concrete men as ends in contemporary society. Thus, he will be led by the hand until he is made to see that, in effect, what he wants is to eliminate the exploitation of man by man and that the city of ends which, with one stroke, he has set up in the aesthetic intuition is only an ideal which we shall approach only at the end of a long historical evolution. In other words, we must transform his formal good will into a concrete and material will to change *this world* by specific means in order to help the coming of the concrete

> society of ends. For good will is not possible in this age, or rather it is and can be only the intention of making good will possible. [*WL*, 269–70]

Since the writer has as his essential role to evoke change, and since the goal above is the one Sartre sees as the most desirable definition man can give to himself, and the historical direction most conducive to a literature of the human totality, Sartre feels he can advise the French novelist that "we must militate in our writings in favor of the freedom of the person and the socialist revolution" (*WL*, 270).[14]

With Sartre's aesthetic imagination the work and the universe are radically distinguished; with the committed imagination the two are one. More precisely, since the committed imagination comes into being by the act of naming, the universe and the work are one because both come into existence from a specific point of view which inserts a meaning as it brings the world to awareness. The result of Sartre's new view of the imagination is that he must deny for the novel the same type of beauty that exists in works of the aesthetic imagination. The image or product of the imagination is capable of sustaining a form because it contains only a limited number of relations (*IM*, 11) in a unity that is separated from the plurality of interrelationships which characterize the world of reality. Because the novel, on the other hand, presents a world which the reader can always create more profoundly, the novel should be "as inexhaustible and opaque as things" (*WL*, 40). Beauty can no longer be defined "by the form, or even by the matter, but by the density of being" (*WL*, 223).

It is interesting that Sartre's criterion of beauty in the novel leads him to many of the critical doctrines of the aesthetic tradition whose ontology and whose emphasis on form Sartre denies. For example, Sartre uses Hemingway, a writer who continually insisted that novels were "made," to illustrate that density of being is achieved by the "multiplicity of practical relations which the reader maintains with the characters" (*WL*, 233). Indeed, the multiplicity of practical relations is, except for the demand that the relations be with the real world, very similar to Kant's "aesthetical idea" and to Bergson's "intensive manifold." Notice also that Sartre insists that preordained form destroys the novel (*WL*, 201; *LE*, 23) and that the novel must be "pure presentation" (*WL*, 45) with characters who seem free from any manipulation by the author for thematic or dogmatic ends (*WL*, 223). The similarity is possible because Sartre conceives that reality is grasped in the act of knowledge much in the same way that a novelist in the aesthetic tradition like Henry James thinks a novel is comprehended in the act of reading. While James conceives characters as not reducible to any one interpretation, Sartre insists that reality itself can never be completely grasped by any one mind; there are no privileged subjectivities. As aesthetic contemplation is continual elucidation of relationships, Sartre conceives that human comprehension of reality is a continual determination of meaning. So Sartre can call for a literary world which approximates the "aesthetical idea" while making the literary world created in its entirety an appeal to the practical reason, to the moral being of the reader.

V

There remains the task of evaluating Sartre's aesthetic, a task for which one feels inadequate because so few serious attempts have been made to clarify the relation between the art work and reality, the problem which lies at the heart of both Sartre's aesthetic and his engaged imaginations. Final evaluation of Sartre must rest on whether one can make the radical distinction between imagined object and communicated object. However, an examination of various attempts to criticize Sartre and their implications may help focus for us some of the problems he raises. Most of the criticism of Sartre's literary aesthetic concentrates on two points—the prose-poetry split and Sartre's insistence on the commitment of the writer to his present audience and to problems facing the contemporary world.

Iris Murdoch summarizes the obvious objections to Sartre's radical distinction between prose and poetry: "Poetic language may be transparent and discursive, and prose whether in literary or in everyday use may be opaque and rhetorical."[15] Robert Belvin reserves his criticism for the idea of non-rhetorical prose: "Sartre's utilitarian definition of literature excludes precisely everything which is literature."[16]

Our own background inclines us to accept these objections, but we ought first to see the twofold attack Sartre mounts against them. In the first place he employs a dialectic analysis of history in order to explain the origin of the idea that the novel should be a work of art and not a medium of communication. The nineteenth-century writer came to the idea that the novel was art because he sought a means of separating himself from a bourgeois society whose ideology of hypocritical morality opposed the moral requirements of literature. Since his possible audience was all bourgeois, he had no way of defining himself except in terms of an absolute audience, hence the concept of ideal beauty (*WL*, 111–12). The impossibility of communication kept him from realizing the essence of prose, an essence Sartre hopes he has intuited. The second reason that Sartre denies ornate prose (and, by implication, the art novel) is that the essence of prose is communication, and communication is negated by the "rhetorical" (as Miss Murdoch uses the term) and the poetic. Prose is a tool, a means; the more opaque it becomes, the less it can serve its essential function. There is another dimension of the idea of prose as means. All means are important only insofar as they realize an end. And an end, as we saw in our analysis of situation, is always a human project by which man defines himself and his world. So prose is engaged. Poetry, on the other hand, reverses the end and means relationship; "the world and things become inessential . . . for the act which becomes its own end" (*WL*, 29n).

A practical application of Sartre's doctrine of the novel would not, as Mr. Belvin says, exclude all literature (in the normal sense of the word, not Verlaine's) that is literature. What it would do is deny that the poetic novel, in which words do not function as signifiers, is a novel. If "pure disinterested intuition of the word" (*WL*, 30) occurs, as it does, for example, in *Ulysses*, the work does not function as a novel; but this does not mean it is not a work of art. Whether a work of bad craft can be a novel, I do not know. However, the pains which it takes to create a vision of the world that really does contribute to freeing the individual make me think it is impossible.

Here we see the deeper problem arise, the problem of the possibility of making ontological distinctions between the unreal and the real. Despite Joyce's art and his poetic use of language, isn't there a sense in which his novel communicates? Isn't his use of the Ulysses myth an attempt to present an insight into the existential condition? Isn't Eliot's "The Wasteland" also successful both as a formal object and as an attempt at communication? Yeats's "Circus Animal's Desertion" is a complaint that the poet's concern for form frequently distorts the essential reality, "the foul rag and bone shop of the heart," he is trying to communicate.

The problem is central in modern aesthetics. New Criticism in its purest forms and symbol-oriented criticism like that of Cassirer stress the artifact at the expense of the reality. Many thinkers like Poulet, Bachelard, and Maritain (in practice though not in theory) stress the reality content in literature so heavily that they lose sight of the art object. Perhaps the two best analyses of the problem are offered by Susanne Langer with her insistence that form is the only way to capture feeling, and Northrop Frye. Frye is interesting because he makes a distinction similar to Sartre's, but perhaps in more defensible terms. He admits that all language signifies, but suggests that in the literary object the sign value of the words is directed inward toward the object (thus a tragedy presents a whole drama about life) while the direction of the signs in nonliterary verbal structures is outward toward the world.[17] But at the root of the conception which allows a systemization of all literature, there must be, according to Sartre's concept of the imagination, an unrealizing of all literature. Frye's idea of the direction of signification provides a good description of what happens in the reading experience we call aesthetic, and yet we still require a description of the way a particular work of art illuminates our own existential condition.

The second objection is that Sartre, in calling for a literature of contemporary problems, misunderstands the universal appeal of literature. William Barrett puts the objection most precisely when he points out that commitment may work in various degrees and on various levels. Proust, for example, gives a more illuminating picture of the breakdown of a social class than any committed writer: "To exist deeply in one's own time is not the same as to exist in the spotlight."[18]

Kaelin tries to exonerate Sartre from the charge of limiting the sphere of the novel by insisting that Sartre's idea of engagement is not a critical canon, but a moral one derived from an analysis of the profession of writing.[19] I hope my analysis of the engaged imagination has shown that Kaelin's view is not entirely valid. The logic of the novel of communication implies that the writer must portray a particular aspect of the world as he sees it in order to free the reader and produce a world to be changed.

Sartre's logic, however, is limited. It is at best doubtful that reality can be reduced to reality of the immediate situation. Moreover, Sartre's notion that the morality in which the work is conceived necessarily implies the way the work will be received is perilously close to being another version of the intentional fallacy. Take *King Lear*, for instance. Whether Shakespeare conceived it as an art object, as a mode of engagement, or as a means of hastening his retirement in affluence at Stratford, the play communicates "the human condition in its totality" (*WL*, 216). In spite of its lack of a specific relation to "the modern condition," *King Lear* is perhaps the best example in literature of a work which, on its ethical level, provokes the intention of "treating men, in every case, as an absolute end" (*WL*, 269). Admittedly *Lear* does not show that "it is quite impossible to treat concrete men as ends in contemporary society" (*WL*, 269), but the connection between the universal idea and the contemporary situation is one which the reader's imagination ought to be able to make.

Sartre would probably grant these objections. But at this point he might retreat from the aesthetic and bring in the moral argument that Shakespeare was an exception and that most works written for an absolute audience remain on library shelves. He might also point out that many people read and enjoy *Lear* without relating it at all to their present condition, a phenomenon which cannot occur with a contemporary setting such as Wright's novels have, because if the reader reconstitutes the work, the world described loses its innocence and must in some way be incorporated by him into his self-definition. And Sartre's final remark would in some way repeat the statement "None of these lovers of glory [i.e., the aesthetes, but the remark would also hold true for the work not immediately committed to a particular situation] asked himself in what sort of society he would be able to find his recompense" (*WL*, 120). If one does not become engaged now, totalitarianism may produce a society in which neither the aspiring writer nor Shakespeare may be read.

The danger in Sartre's position is that the cry for engagement may actually weaken the moral impact of art. Frequently it is the writer who avoids immediate commitment who most profoundly understands and portrays the situation. A writer like Shakespeare, while he may not present a specific situation in a way that calls forth immediate action, communicates the values which go beyond situation and are the bases of all action.

The question of engagement, however, remains of vital importance to those who are professionally involved in literature. For if the writer is to be free from specific social obligations because his work transcends history, someone less essential as an individual to society and equally committed to the value of literature must preserve and develop the freedom of readers to read. The relation of freedom to reading is especially important if one agrees with Sartre's description of the engaged imagination, but even without this agreement it seems apparent that poverty, social injustice, propaganda, and totalitarianism are all threats to the promulgation and preservation of literature. The teacher-critic especially has the potential in and through the university to form a society in which "reading" is available for all. Here, then, is Sartre's essential value for modern aesthetics: he raises for us the important questions, both theoretical and ethical, about the relation to life of literature and literary men.

NOTES

1. Eugene Kaelin, *An Existentialist Aesthetic* (Madison, 1962), p. 123.

2. Quotations from Sartre are from the following works:

(IM): *L'Imaginaire* (Paris: 1940); *The Psychology of the Imagination*, trans. unknown (New York: Washington Square Press, 1948)

(BN): *L'Etre et le néant* (Paris: 1943); *Being and Nothingness*, trans. Hazel Barnes (New York: Washington Square Press, 1956)

(WL): "Qu'est-ce-que la littérature?," in *Situations, II* (Paris: 1948); *What Is Literature?*, trans. Bernard Frechtman (New York: Harper & Row, 1949)

(SG): *Saint-Genet, comédien et martyr* (Paris: 1952); *Saint-Genet: Actor and Martyr*, trans. Bernard Frechtman (New York: Braziller, 1963)

(Sit.): *Situations, IV* (Paris: 1964); *Situations*, trans. Benita Eisler (New York: Braziller, 1965)

(LE): *Situations, I–III* (Paris, 1947–49); *Literary Essays*, trans. Annette Michelson (New York: Collier Books, 1957)

3. Sartre moves from phenomenology to existentialism as his thought develops from *L'Imaginaire* to "Qu'est-ce-que la littérature?" Thus in the later work he is more hesitant to claim essential realities and more aware of history. Thus he realizes that his suggestions are only temporal and incomplete steps in a process.

4. The implications of the following passage from *Psychology of the Imagination* are not worked out until *Being and Nothingness*: "The unreal is produced outside of the world by a consciousness which *stays in the world*, and it is because he is transcendentally free that man can imagine. But, in its turn, the imagination, which has become a psychological and empirical function, is the necessary condition for the freedom of empirical man in the midst of the world" (*IM*, 271).

5. Coleridge's example of the water insect is familiar. For Kant's theory see *Critique of Judgment*, trans. J. H. Bernard, 2nd edition (London, 1914), p. 198: "Thus we feel our freedom from the law of association (which attaches to the empirical employment of the imagination), so that the material supplied to us by nature in accordance with this law can be worked up into something different which surpasses nature." Sartre, however, does not grant that the art work as product of imagination "surpasses nature." It is the ethical imagination for Sartre that most clearly "surpasses nature."

6. Bernard, trans., *Critique of Judgment*, p. 198.

7. Ibid., p. 197. In a later essay, "The Artist and His Conscience," Sartre approaches the idea of non-discursive meaning when he distinguishes meaning (pure arts) from significance (the novel). See *Sit.*, pp. 216–17.

8. I am presuming from the first chapter in *What Is Literature?* that Sartre is consistent in his poetry-prose separation. That Sartre is inconsistent (for example, he uses painting, which in Chapter 1 he made an art of the imagination, to illustrate the effects of prose [WL, 40] and he frequently uses the term "work of art" where logic would demand that he use "novel") seriously threatens my argument. But since Sartre's explicit statements support the imagination-prose split and since Sartre, even after *What Is Literature?*, refers to both music and sculpture as non-signifying arts (*Sit.*, 191–99, 216–17), I feel that the inconsistency is accidental and that the description I give of the two imaginations is essentially correct.

9. In *L'Imaginaire* Sartre defined "situations" as "the different ways of apprehending the real as a world" (p. 268), still an epistemological projection. Sartre's summary definition of "situation" in *Being and Nothingness* is unintelligible for most readers without a glossary (p. 487), but the following formulation is more understandable: "Human reality cannot receive its ends . . . either from outside or from so-called inner nature. It chooses them and by this very choice confers upon them a transcendent existence as the eternal limit of its projects. From this point of view . . . human reality in and through its very upsurge decided to define its own being by its own ends" (*BN*, 443). Sartre uses the fact of fatigue as an example: fatigue is a fact, but since it only presents itself to human subjects, it is always realized as a meaning. Thus two people equally fatigued will react differently. But both may project the same future or unreality in which they define their fatigue; i.e., the goal of the inn at the mountain top. For one man, however, fatigue is bearable because it is the sign of the body overcome, while for the other fatigue is a cause to rest because he chooses his body over the projected goal or over the desire to overcome the body. Each has defined himself by giving meaning to a brute reality (*BN*, 454–57).

10. Northrop Frye, *The Educated Imagination* (Bloomington, 1964), p. 27.

11. Kant says the aesthetic is a symbol of morality because "it gives pleasure with a claim for the agreement of everyone else" (Bernard, trans., pp. 250–51).

12. This notion of universal subjectivity, or the "City of Ends," represents an important advance for Sartre over *Being and Nothingness* where it was impossible for even two people, since each is free and each constructs his own world in which the other is an object, to take one another as ends. And he continues the notion to make it the basis of his

wedding of existentialism and non-Soviet Marxism in *Search for a Method,* trans. Hazel Barnes (New York: Vintage Books, 1963), p. xxvii: "The ultimate ideal for mankind would be a world in which all men worked together in full consciousness to make their history in common."

13. Robert Belvin, "The Problem of the Literary Artist's Detachment As Seen by J. Benda, J.-P. Sartre, and Thierry Maulnier," *Romanic Review,* XLVII (1956), 271.

14. We must remember that Sartre's specific program comes only after assurances that he is addressing only the French writer in 1947, a man writing for a primarily bourgeois society. It is the essence of situation that Sartre cannot make recommendations for artists in other countries whose particular situation he does not know.

15. Iris Murdoch, *Sartre: Romantic Rationalist* (New Haven, 1953), p. 72.

16. Belvin, "The Problem of the Literary Artist's Detachment," p. 281.

17. Frye, *Anatomy of Criticism* (Princeton, 1957), pp. 74–78.

18. William Barret, "The End of Modern Literature," *Partisan Review,* XVI (1949), 45–46.

19. Kaelin, *An Existentialist Aesthetic,* p. 119.

Georges Poulet's "Criticism of Identification"[1]

J. HILLIS MILLER
THE JOHNS HOPKINS UNIVERSITY

I

PRIOR TO CRITICISM, and the origin of it, is the act of reading. The special virtue of reading, for Georges Poulet, is that it gives a man unique access to another mind: "without leaving oneself, without abandoning one's own interiority, the person who, as they say, 'plunges' into reading, by this fact alone sinks within the depths of a second interiority, with which his spirit coincides."[2] To plunge into a book does not mean entering an impersonal realm created by words. It means entering another consciousness, for "the consciousness of the reader, and, *a fortiori*, the consciousness of that special type of reader who is the critic, have as their characteristic trait the habit of identifying themselves with a thought other than their own."[3]

A central theme of much literature, especially of fiction, is the interplay of consciousness with consciousness. One writer may be distinguished from others according to his assumptions about the way one person exists for another. For example, the relative opacity of person for person in Jane Austen's novels may be set against the relative transparency of Trollope's people to each other. The theme of intersubjectivity is rarely treated directly in Poulet's criticism. To read one of his essays is usually to be transported into a consciousness which exists almost as if there were no other minds in the world. Nevertheless, his criticism comes into being only through an act of reading which is the complete entry of the critic into the mind of the author criticized.

For Poulet the relation of two subjectivities in reading is rarely an interchange or dialogue, neither the marriage of true minds, in which each self enhances and supports the other, nor the implacable battle of mind with mind described by Sartre. The plunge into a book is achieved only in the perfect *coincidence* of the reader's mind with the "indescribable intimacy"[4] of the author's mind. Criticism derives from an act of rigorous self-dispossession. "To read or criticize," says Poulet, "is to make a sacrifice of all [our] habits, desires, beliefs."[5] Having abandoned all particular commitments, the reader becomes a neutral power of comprehension. This neutrality is not a lazy yielding to external forces. Literary criticism, in Poulet's view, "is possible only insofar as the critical thought *becomes* the thought which is criticized, insofar as it succeeds in re-feeling, rethinking, re-imagining the latter from within."[6]

In his essay on Marcel Raymond, Poulet compares the critic's act of self-sacrifice to those Christian virtues of self-effacement which, in the epochs of faith, made it possible for a man to empty himself of himself and become a vessel fit for the presence of God.[7] This receptivity is characteristic of all that group of critics of the so-called Geneva School. One quality, however, especially distinguishes Poulet: his *disinterestedness.* Like those seventeenth-century quietists whom he especially admires, Poulet does not ask anything for himself. Though he likes certain authors (the young Goethe, Byron, Chateaubriand, an aesthete like Pater) for whom the act of writing is a means of salvation, his own criticism has no Promethean or egotistical motive. The re-creation of the mind of the author in the mind of the critic is not performed for the sake of any good it may do the critic, but for the sake of the author criticized. If Poulet's criticism, like Raymond's, is the twentieth-century equivalent of a seventeenth-century book of devotion, it has not that last vestige of egotism present in the quietist's awareness that his effacement of himself before God is a way, perhaps the only way, to win a place in heaven. For Poulet the "absolute transparence with the soul of the other"[8] is an end in itself, not a means to some further end.

This gratuitousness may be seen in another characteristic which distinguishes Poulet's criticism. He never tries to reach, through his identification with the mind of an author, anything beyond or outside that mind. Almost all the other critics of his school, however self-effacing they are, secretly or openly try to attain through literature to something beyond literature. Albert Béguin seeks through poetry to possess "the full garden of things."[9] Having attained objects in the created world, he tries to reach, beyond them, their Creator. The criticism of Gaston Bachelard and Jean-Pierre Richard also goes through poetry to the material world, and experiences, from within, all the nuances of texture and substance which words borrow from things. Maurice Blanchot seeks through a patient and systematic destruction of words to reach a dark and devouring absence which those words reveal and hide. The fatal glance of Orpheus at Eurydice, model for all literature, is a look beyond literature and beyond the consciousnesses expressed in literature. Jean Starobinski, it seems, seeks through literature indirect access to himself, "that visage of ourselves which we cannot bear to look at except on the strict condition that we see it reflected in a play of mirrors."[10] Even Marcel Raymond, closest of all these critics to Poulet, reaches through literature to a silence beyond literature. He goes through consciousness toward a confused and obscure "subconsciousness" in which "things are no longer things, and objects, objects in such a way that consciousness and things, melted together, constitute a universal non-duality, within which the immanence of the divine everywhere shines."[11] Physical objects, a transcendent or immanent deity, the hidden self of the critic, the being at the base of all beings—these critics seek, through identification with the mind of an author, to attain something otherwise unattainable, something which transcends that mind and differs from it in substance. For these critics literature is in one way or another a form of mediation.

Not so for Poulet. He wants to reach, through his "criticism of pure identification,"[12] the mind of the author and nothing beyond that. Material objects, other people, God in his various modes, all are present in Poulet's criticism, but only as they have been turned into words, that is, into a form of consciousness. Everything that exists must exist as contained in the globular bubble of the mind of the author, and that bubble is never allowed to burst. For Poulet criticism "must define itself primordially as a taking into consciousness [*prise de conscience*] of consciousness."[13] What criticism is in the beginning it remains to the end: consciousness of consciousness and nothing more.

II

Having identified himself with another mind, what does the reader do then? Though reading is in one sense a purely verbal activity, since it consists in the assimilation by the reader of the meanings of words, in another sense it is mute. Reading reaches, beyond words, an ineffable presence of one consciousness within another. When the reading is over, this presence vanishes, leaving the mind of the reader once more empty, ready to be invaded and possessed by another book, another mind.

Moreover, the presence of one mind to another in reading is vivid, but blurred, disordered. It is the result of the piling up of all the furniture of that other mind, like a storeroom full of a great mass of bric-a-brac, chairs, tables, sofas, lamps, all in pell-mell confusion. Reading, in short, is not yet criticism.

Criticism, for Poulet, is the putting in order and clarification of the identification attained through reading. Order and transparence are two fundamental needs of his mind. Transparence is attained only by *seeing through* the author, bringing to light the intimate reason for each quality of the consciousness expressed in his works. Though Poulet likes a consciousness which is semi-opaque, a half-darkness penetrated with difficulty, this may be because such a mind is a challenge to his powers of clarification. Even when he talks about darkness or irrationality, he transforms muddle into clarity by demonstrating its plausibility. To show its plausibility means to show its connection to all the other salient motifs in the author's work. Transparence is attained only through a demonstration of the mutual implication of all the characteristics of the consciousness being criticized. If obscurity pains Poulet, so equally does any discontinuity, any description of an author which limits itself to a listing, without connection, of motifs. All the contents of the bubble of consciousness must be shown to be acting and reacting on one another, in reciprocal interchange. The works of an author make up a complex, three-dimensional structure, a palace of crystal filling the mind and integrated organically in its interplay of part with part, aspect with aspect.

Two fundamental assumptions of Poulet's criticism can be seen in this: the notion that all the works of an author form an indissoluble unity and the notion that the mode of interconnection of the parts of this unity is dialectical. Criticism, like all literature, is temporal, hence sequential. Dialectic is one way of defeating the mutual exclusion of words and moments. All the stages of a dialectical progression are present at once in any stage, and the development does no more than unfold the implications of some moment chosen as the beginning. These implications are not the necessary and determined ones of a logical progression. They are free and unpredictable, in the sense that any one stage might have been followed by other stages than the ones which actually occur, and yet the sequence seems, in retrospect, inevitable. Dialectic is a way of presenting the complexities of the palace of crystal from all its aspects, as though a consciousness were slowly revolved, still continuing its own intrinsic movement, until, finally, through time, time is transcended, and an atemporal unity is revealed.

The special quality of Poulet's dialectic can be seen in the fact that he has written more than one essay on the work of several writers. There are two essays on Pascal, two on Rousseau, two on Balzac, two on Baudelaire—and each of these is a full study of the ensemble of the author's work. Even though each consciousness is one space, not a house of many mansions, and even though the contents of this space may be finite, nevertheless there are many ways of proceeding from one place to another in a critical essay. Poulet's two essays on Rousseau (or Balzac, or Baudelaire) are the same and yet different. The same intuition of the unity of the author's work governs each essay, but the itinerary through that work is different. Sometimes the same quotations are used in both essays, but, approached from a new direction, they reveal a new aspect of their inherence in all the other motifs, as, in *A la recherche du temps perdu*, the towers of Martinville remain the same and yet seem different when approached by a novel route. If limpidity is a characteristic of Poulet's criticism, this transparency is achieved through an agility in making existential associations rather than through the solemn march of logical inference. This means that an indefinite number of valid critical essays could be written on the same writer.

The fluid structure of dialectic is sharply opposed to the objective structure which some critics find essential in literature. For Poulet, the structure of a single work is something supplementary and superficial, since "subjectively literature has nothing formal about it."[14] No objective form can hold or express so protean a force as a living mind.

> It is a characteristic of the work at once to invent its structures and to go beyond them. I should even say to destroy them. Thus the work of an author is certainly the collection of the individual works he has written, but in the degree to which, following one after the other, they replace one another and reveal in that very fact a movement of liberation from structures.[15]

If the school of criticism to which Poulet belongs defines criticism as "a sort of prolongation and deepening of poetic thought,"[16] the means of this extension is the language of the critic. Language is used in three interconnected ways in Poulet's criticism. It is first "the indispensable medium by means of which the 'critical' identification takes place."[17] The poet's words are the initial means of this identification, but the critic's own words complete it. The critic's language is a grappling of one mind with another which ultimately attains complete assimilation. The sign of this assimilation is the coincidence of the language of the critic and the language of the author. If Poulet's criticism makes much use of direct quotation, the status of quotation is defined by the fact that the critic's language is as much as possible in the style and vocabulary of the author. Poulet's criticism is first of all mimesis, and the duplication of an author's mind in a critic's mind is accomplished when the critic can, as it were, speak for the author, alternately in the author's language and in the critic's language, for the two languages have become the same. In this coincidence comes to the surface the connection of Poulet's criticism with the romantic strategy of role-playing. Like Keats, Browning, or Dilthey, Poulet wants to relive the inner lives of other people, as if they were his own life.

Nevertheless, a critical essay by Poulet is not a curious kind of ventriloquism. Such a criticism would be "a crude sort of mimicry,"[18] an impoverished reduplication of the poet's voice. If criticism is to be "literature about literature,"[19] if it is to prolong and deepen literature, it must add something to it. This addition is never, in Poulet, that distant and detached "view from above" which Starobinski sometimes recommends. Such detachment would separate critic from author and make intimate comprehension impossible: "A critic who does not wish or who is unable to attain the properly subjective comprehension of which I speak, is condemned by this fact to see and to express beings and things only from the outside."[20] Poulet is completely unwilling to detach himself from the author in hand, to judge from a distance according to criteria other than those of the author himself, to put in question the validity, sanity, authenticity, or plausibility of anything he finds in the author's work. The critic must never withdraw from the mind of his author, but his own language may deepen the poet's language, that is, define it more precisely, and it may prolong that language, prolong it by establishing connections and implications which the poet may never have stated explicitly. Deepening and prolonging are in fact the exact equivalents of that clarification and putting in order which are the habitual needs of Poulet's mind in its relation to other minds.

Clarification is attained by intense concentration on one or another aspect of the author's work. As long as Poulet remains within one area of an author's thought it is as if nothing could be more important than the exact definition of the quality of that area. This definition is performed by a series of ever finer distinctions which gradually closes in on the specific nuance of the motif in question and pins it down with the sharpest possible precision. This relentless approach toward ever finer and finer clarification is like getting a microscope into focus, as more powerful lenses are substituted one for another. In the end, an area heretofore blurred or invisible fills the entire field of vision with all its delicate details laid bare. Habitual in the language of Poulet's criticism is a sequence of distinctions; when one is rejected as too coarse, it is replaced by another sharper one, until finally the requisite precision is attained: "Then occurs the strange apparition, in the depths of the self, of the thought, is that enough to say? no, of the life, more still, of the *being* of another."[21]

Along with clarification goes putting in order. If Poulet has a great power to concentrate on a single passage in an author's work, in order to establish its exact flavor of meaning, an essay of his is concentrated in yet another way. Unlike Jean-Pierre Richard, Poulet rarely attains density in his criticism by minute attention to the texture and substance of material images. The material world may enter into poetry, but by the time that world has become poetry it is disembodied. Density in an essay by Poulet results chiefly from an extreme compression of the author's thought or feeling. Such an essay seeks to put within the limits of a brief study the essential structure of an oeuvre which may include dozens of volumes. The energy of Poulet's intelligence appears as much in an extreme firmness of dialectical structure as in his power to distinguish subtle nuances of feeling or thought. Firmness of structure is attained by a great power of reduction. Passages from different books by an author, written at different times of his life, are set side by side, so that their similarity can be seen. All the apparent heterogeneity of a multiform author like Balzac or Baudelaire is reduced to a manageable number of motifs. These motifs are put in a sequence showing how each leads to the next and how all are connected. The critic may confirm his coincidence with the mind of his author when he discovers, in a work before unread, the explicit expression of a connection which he had seen to be present latently. If Poulet dislikes the sequence of mere addition, no words are more important in his criticism than words of dialectical connection: "but," "then," "or," "therefore," "nevertheless," "however," "in other terms," "that is to say," "moreover," "not only . . . but also."

III

Clarification and ordering, deepening and prolonging—these are the ways in which Poulet's criticism goes beyond mimetic doubling. A problem arises at this point. If the work of an author is like a transparent crystal, and if all can be shown to follow naturally from a beginning, where, exactly, is the proper place to begin? Perhaps there is no proper beginning, so that the sequence of an essay is arbitrary. Starting anywhere, the critic will ultimately be led everywhere, for all the aspects of an author's mind exist simultaneously, and each implies the rest. Poulet would be dissatisfied with this uncertainty. One of the strongest penchants of his mind leads him to search for the true beginning of his author's spiritual adventure.

The *Cogito* is that true beginning. It is for this reason that the theme of the *Cogito* has such importance in Poulet's work. No concept occurs more constantly than that of the *Cogito,* and almost all his essays begin with an attempt to establish the unique version of the *Cogito* which is the starting point for the author in question. Poulet names Marcel Raymond as the first critic "who has applied the principle of the *Cogito* to the critical knowledge of literary thoughts and works, and who has made that criticism begin in a *moment* of the same nature as the moment of the *Cogito,* since the being discovers himself there in the activity of his present thought."[22] If Raymond was the first to use the *Cogito* as an instrument of criticism, Poulet is surely the critic who has most systematically studied all its varieties.

It is easy to see why the *Cogito* should be important for Poulet. A criticism directed exclusively toward the consciousness of others will want to identify the quality of the other mind in its purest form, not as it is modified by one content or another, but as it exists in itself. If consciousness is a kind of "interior depth"[23] which may be occupied by all the contents of consciousness, that inner space is not a hollow shell, neutral, unqualified; it is "an ambient milieu, a unifying field."[24] Each consciousness has its own precise texture or tone. This texture or tone is the invariant which persists through all the diverse experiences of the self. It is an irreducible X, necessary coefficient of all the things that consciousness is conscious of. Since the invariant note distinguishing one man from all others is hidden or distorted when consciousness is engaged with some object, the critic will want to surprise it at a moment when nothing exists but a naked presence of consciousness to itself. This is the moment of the *Cogito.*

For Poulet this moment is radically original and originating. A criticism oriented entirely toward consciousness cannot allow consciousness to have any cause or source outside itself. Consciousness appears from nowhere. It is a beginning before which it is impossible to go. In assuming this Poulet shows himself to be the heir of a certain mode of idealism.

If nothing is prior to consciousness, if nothing causes it or explains it or supports it in being, then consciousness is, from the point of view of human existence, the origin of everything else, and "an act of selfconsciousness" is the "invariable point of departure for every human existence perceived from within."[25] The moment of the revelation of the self to itself, before the assimilation of any of its objects, is the true beginning not only because nothing exists before it, but also because the moment of the *Cogito* is the ground or foundation of everything else. Everything follows from it, as a tiny cube of paper unfolded may be a map of the world, or as a colorless button grows, in a glass of water, into a magic Japanese garden full of flowers, trees, and shrubs. If the *Cogito* has this marvelous power of expansion, the critic will want to catch it "in the surging forth and genetic exercise of this power," in the moment before it explodes into form, when it exists "in a nearly virginal state, not yet invaded and, as it were, masked by the thick heap of its objective contents."[26]

The proper beginning for the critic's reliving and reconstruction of the inner experience of an author must always be the *Cogito*, but the *Cogito* exists not only in its Cartesian or rationalist form, the putting in doubt of all the contents of the mind in order to reach a clear and distinct thought which proves that the self exists. The *Cogito* exists in a multitude of versions, a different one for each age or author, and Poulet has in his criticism identified a great variety of these: the Christian *Cogito* in all its modes, the intellectualist one, the romantic or sensationalist *Cogito*, the *Cogito* of Mallarmé, and so on, down to the last page of *Les Métamorphoses du cercle*, which ends with a definition of the *Cogito* of Jorge Guillén.

The supreme importance of the moment of self-awareness makes Poulet especially delighted by passages where an author describes his awaking from sleep. If the moment of waking is like a repetition of the creation of the world, so that the waker is seized with an astonishment before things comparable to that of Adam or Miranda, waking is also a daily repetition of the *Cogito* and is a fresh enactment of the discovery of the self. From the waking of Montaigne, of the statue of Condillac, or of Rousseau, to the waking of Poe, Proust, or Béguin, Poulet follows the theme of "the moment of awakening," and in each case waking is the way in which the *Cogito* is intimately known. The *Cogito*, for Poulet, is no theoretical abstraction, but is always the most immediate and inward of experiences.

IV

The universality of the *Cogito* solves the problem of the starting point for both Poulet and Raymond, but Poulet differs radically from Raymond in his use of this instrument of criticism. Raymond's criticism goes against the stream, as it were. It works backward from the mass of motifs and details which fill a consciousness toward the virginal moment when consciousness is as yet empty of all but itself. To attain identification with this moment is Raymond's ultimate aim, for in that moment only, a moment on the frontier between consciousness and unconsciousness, the critic has a chance to reach a sense of the confused co-presence of all things and people in the universe. Poulet, on the other hand, goes out from the moment of the *Cogito* to follow the adventures of a mind at grips with its objects. The crystalline bubble of consciousness is made up of the engagement of a mind with things, and the critic must go with his author as he assimilates the world. Poulet wants to see just how far a particular author will take him and follows without questioning to the farthest distance he can reach while still remaining inside the sphere of a single mind.

Consciousness may engage itself with physical objects, with time and space, with other consciousnesses, with God. In his criticism Poulet explores each of these modes of relation, but all tend to be transformed into one or another of the endless possible interchanges of subject and object within the inner space which Poulet calls "the interior distance." In this allegiance to the primacy of the subject-object relation Poulet shows himself once again the inheritor of romanticism and idealism. From Montaigne, Descartes, and Rousseau, to Coleridge, Fichte, or Amiel, on down to Yeats, Claudel, or Proust, the continuity of literature and philosophy since the Renaissance is marked by the dualism of subject and object, self and world. Taken as a whole, Poulet's criticism may be said to approach a recapitulation of all the varieties of experience possible within the limits of this dualism.

Only if it is true that this tradition is coming to an end in our day is it possible to give assent to a curious passage about *Les Métamorphoses du cercle* in a review of 1963 by Maurice Blanchot: "I asked myself, having closed this book, why there closed with it the very history of criticism and of culture and why it seemed with a melancholy serenity to dismiss us and at the same time to authorize us to enter into a new space."[27] Without sharing Blanchot's desire to destroy all the forms of subjectivity which Poulet so cherishes, it is possible to say that certain contemporary authors, like Jorge Guillén or William Carlos Williams, have gone beyond the division of subject and object, as they have gone beyond the tradition of a transcendent power dwelling beyond the world. Such writers hardly represent the end of culture, but they contradict some of the habitual assumptions of Poulet's criticism. Poulet is not unaware of this:

> Guillén's poetry separates itself sharply from the rest of European poetry. It does not begin from the interior, but from the exterior. It situates that which is, not in the central hollow of a consciousness, but in the peripheral manifestation of a tangible reality. . . . A singular relation, which seems to reverse the habitual direction of thought. What? everything then no longer springs forth from the interior? What? it is no longer *beginning from the center* that life is born and propagates itself?[28]

The "What?" here might be defined as the moment of encounter with a new tradition, reversing earlier habits of thought. Since the essay on Guillén forms the conclusion of *Les Métamorphoses du cercle*, that book does not so much celebrate the funeral of literature and criticism, as move toward the confrontation of a new age, an age in which consciousness will no longer be defined as "that interior vacancy within which the world redisposes itself."[29]

So habitual is this image of an interior milieu to Poulet that his thought may be defined as fundamentally spatial. Though his earliest book is entitled *Etudes sur le temps humain*, time is there often treated in terms of a relation of the mind to objects which are presented to it across a kind of subjective distance. The notion of interior distance provides the title for his next book, *La Distance intérieure*, and in his more recent work he has yielded overtly to the spatializing tendency of his criticism. In *Les Métamorphoses du cercle* writers from Parmenides to T. S. Eliot are presented in terms of relations, within the spheric bubble of the mind, between center and periphery. The center is the *Cogito*, source of all, and at various places within consciousness all the objects of consciousness are located in a moving totality which sometimes expands to infinity and sometimes contracts to a point, but always remains enclosed in itself. Through the whole history of Western thought Poulet explores the varieties of spatial relation: distance, closeness, or union; continuity or discontinuity; condensation or dilation; thickening or rarefaction—all the categories by which center and circle may be separated, identified, or brought into some form of association.

Throughout all this development two states of consciousness are most important for Poulet. As long as there is distance there is a failure of consciousness to coincide unequivocally with itself. One way to avoid this has been discussed: the *Cogito*, reduction of all to a central point. The other possibility is an expansive diffusion of that point until it includes everything, as, according to an image which Poulet especially likes to find in his authors, a stone dropped in water will start a series of concentric circles radiating outward to infinity. Poulet could say of many of his authors what he says of Amiel: "Particular activities are here only a middle term between the unextended depth of a life seized in the eternity of its principle and, on the other hand, the expansion of an existence dilating by means of thought to coincide with the full dimensions of the universe."[30] In his latest books as in his earlier ones Poulet pursues the dream of a *totum simul*, the enclosure by consciousness of all existence, in an infinite moment of expansion transcending time and space. If Jean Starobinski in his early criticial essays yields to "the sin of angelism,"[31] a central motif in Poulet's criticism is the desire to be not like an angel, but like a God. In his essay on Gérard de Nerval, Poulet observes that "all thought which draws its life only from itself is unable to suffice to itself," and that "human thought cannot endure being substituted either for the totality of the real or for its simplicity."[32] Nevertheless, Poulet is fascinated by writers who approach as close as is humanly possible to a divine self-sufficiency. For this reason, perhaps, Rousseau holds a place of special importance in his work, for Rousseau was the first man to achieve a state of expansive revery in which the self, dwelling in a realm where only the solitary mind and its objects exist, possesses all, and therefore "suffices to itself, like God."[33] With each of his authors Poulet goes as far as he can toward the attainment of this *totum simul*, human equivalent of divine simultaneity and ubiquity. His essays often end at the stage closest to this ultimate victory, or in the recognition of a failure to win it or hold it.

Failure is in fact more important than temporary success. For Poulet, human consciousness, both in its widest expansion and in its contraction to the purity of the *Cogito*, is marked by a sense of "existential insufficiency, the feeling of contingency and incapacity."[34] Hence the importance in his criticism of the theme of continuous creation. Unless some power sustains the self it will be powerless to bring into existence its own future. Each man is "called by an immense demand, [but] discovers within himself an immense weakness."[35]

V

When the critic has gone as far as he can with an author, the essay is over. The silence after the ending marks the evaporation of that union of critic's mind and author's mind which has made the essay possible. After coincidence, separation. Having investigated to its limit the effect of being occupied by the consciousness of another person, the critic's mind returns to attentive vacancy. He must turn now to another author, and, once more forgetting all other writers, begin again the process which will culminate in a critical essay.

It is not true, however, to say that all other authors are forgotten. There is in Poulet's criticism a constant comparison between one author and another. He rarely uses it to show how two authors are alike, but almost always to identify more precisely the uniqueness of the author at hand. The notion of the singularity of each consciousness is central in Poulet's criticism, and this is often shown by the juxtaposition of ideas or motifs from two authors, as a color can be more exactly identified if it is set against a different hue. Just as a comparison with another author, within the body of an essay, will make possible more precise definition of a certain motif, so the setting side by side, within the covers of a single book, of essays on a number of authors is a way of demonstrating that no two consciousnesses are alike. Poulet has an intense dislike for any blurring or smudging of the integrity of a writer's thought. If he concerns himself with the history of ideas, it is chiefly with "that still neglected part of the history of ideas which we could call the history of consciousness,"[36] and it seems that a study of the history of consciousness must be based on the Leibnizian assumption that each mind is unique and isolated from all the others.

In spite of the importance of this assumption, however, there is a counter assumption of equal importance. This new assumption provides an escape from an apparent dilemma. If each consciousness excludes all the others, how can the critic include a number of essays together in a book, and by implication possess a group of minds at once? "It is impossible to escape from this difficulty," says Poulet, "except by imagining for each epoch a consciousness common to all the contemporary minds. It is within this general consciousness that the individual thoughts and feelings are bathed."[37] At any one time each consciousness, however particular, participates in the general consciousness. Its particularity consists in the unique version or organization it makes of ideas common to the age, not in its power to think ideas unheard-of in that time and place. This notion is, in Poulet's earlier books, present overtly only in the prefatory chapter to *Etudes sur le temps humain*, but *Les Métamorphoses du cercle* contains a number of chapters of a kind new in Poulet's criticism: essays on ancient and medieval thought, on the Renaissance, on "the baroque epoch," on the eighteenth century, and on romanticism. The presupposition of these essays is that the consciousness of an age forms a closed unity, a crystalline sphere much like that of a single mind. Such a collective mind can be seized by the same consciousness of consciousness which grasps the mind of a single author, and it can be followed through its structure by the same kind of dialectical route.

Enclosing the consciousness of an age is the genius of a language or of a culture. It may be that Poulet is motivated in his reading and criticism by a desire to follow through all its changes the flowering of the French language as an expression of the varieties of human existence. Outside the French language there is Western culture as a whole. Like T. S. Eliot, Poulet has a strong sense of the oneness of Western civilization and thinks of it as an immense consciousness which contains in moving simultaneity the thought of all the members of that culture from the early Church Fathers to the latest authentic poet who adds his work to the whole and thereby changes that whole in every part. From the single writer to the mind of an age, to all the writings in one language, to all of Western culture—each of these larger wholes encloses the next smaller and forms its milieu. Taken together, they are so many concentric circles of consciousness, each inside the next larger, like a Chinese carving.

Why should Western culture form the largest bubble of all? Can it not be said that Poulet's criticism implies the notion of the unity of the consciousness of all mankind in its historical development? The history of literature can therefore be defined as "a history of human consciousness."[38] The model of history suggested by *Les Métamorphoses du cercle* is that of a progressive diversification, from the relatively homogeneous thought of antiquity, the Middle Ages, the Renaissance, and the eighteenth century to the explosion into individuality in the nineteenth and twentieth centuries, when every important writer deserves a full essay to himself. Significantly, the chapter on romanticism twice ceases to be a rendering of the consciousness of an age and for a time concentrates on an individual mind, that of Coleridge and that of Goethe. But though the recent history of consciousness is more diversified it still remains continuous. All individual consciousnesses still dwell together within an embracing general mind, and Balzac and Baudelaire belong as much to the same age as Montaigne and Pascal belong to theirs.

Poulet's sense of the continuity of history does not lead him to be tempted by Dilthey's notion of an exhaustive reliving of all possible human points of view, so that man might go through history beyond history. No, for Poulet the human spirit is inexhaustible in its potential variety, and its development is always incomplete, still moving toward the realization of its infinite possibilities. If this is the case, then the literary critic can never hope to reach an equivalent of the *totum simul* of God. The best he can do is to make a concentration, re-creation, and coordination of all mankind's thought so far. Through this strategy he can move with that ever-developing consciousness as it approaches toward a completion it can never attain. The critic can perhaps exhaust the mind of a single writer, for each individual mind may be finite, but criticism can never come to the end of the human mind in its totality. That mind will always be open-ended, unfinished.

Recognition of the essential historicity of Poulet's criticism will lead to a final definition of it. History, for Poulet as for the romantics, is not a linear development, but a spherical expansion. A criticism which recreates history will also be spherical, not, like the thought of Jacques Rivière and Robert Browning, asymptotic, but not less an approach toward infinity. As a curve sweeps toward its asymptote, Rivière moves always closer to that coincidence with the mind of another person which he never quite attains, and Browning sees all human history as a gradual movement toward the plenitude of God. Poulet's criticism remains faithful to its exclusive commitment to human consciousness, and, for this, an image of three-dimensional enclosure is more appropriate. Like a sphere dilating toward the infinity it will never reach, his criticism follows the mind of mankind as it uncovers the limitless riches of interior space.

VI

The preceding parts of this essay were written in 1963. It may stand as an introduction to the scope of Georges Poulet's criticism and as an outline of its theoretical presuppositions. In what follows I shall take notice of the many books and essays Poulet has published since 1963,[39] and I shall try to proceed further in an interpretation of the significance of his work.

Poulet's recent publications have filled out the contours of his lifework in several ways. New programmatic statements have confirmed his commitment to a "criticism of consciousness": "I wish to save at any price the subjectivity of literature," he says,[40] and he defines his kind of criticism firmly as "above all, a criticism of participation, better still, of identification. There is no true criticism without the coincidence of two consciousnesses."[41] The literary text is a means by which the critic can achieve an identification with "a consciousness which is in the work,"[42] and his criticism is an expression of the results of this identification.

The publication of *Le Point de départ* and *Mesure de l'instant*, the third and fourth volumes of the *Etudes sur le temps humain*, has made clearer than before the monumental and inclusive nature of Poulet's work, its unity as an attempt to relive from within and to express in criticism more or less the whole range of French literature from the Renaissance to the present, placing it in the context of a less complete treatment of ancient and medieval literature, and of major modern writers in other European languages: Goethe, the English romantics, Poe, Whitman, Henry James, Guillén, and so on. In fact *Les Métamorphoses du cercle* is only somewhat arbitrarily excluded from the *Etudes sur le temps humain* (on the grounds, presumably, that its leitmotif is a spatial rather than a temporal form). The five volumes together, *Etudes sur le temps humain, I, La Distance intérieure, Les Métamorphoses du cercle, Le Point de départ*, and *Mesure de l'instant*, form a single comprehensive work consisting of seventy essays on various writers, groups of writers, or literary periods. Most of the essays are on single authors, and each follows a dialectical itinerary through the interior space of the author in question, drawing quotations from the whole range of his writing to trace out a spiritual adventure leading the author from some beginning in an awakening to consciousness toward an end of triumph or defeat. The seventy essays may be thought of as juxtaposed side by side in a spatial panorama, somewhat as, in Poulet's interpretation of Proust in *L'Espace proustien*, the various times of Marcel's life are set side by side in *A la recherche du temps perdu* like the paintings of different events from a saint's life in a triptych. To borrow another Proustian metaphor, the five major volumes of Poulet's criticism are like five bays within the voluminous interior of a cathedral, the smaller books on Proust, Constant, etc., forming adjacent chapels. The introduction to each major volume identifies the special commitment of that collection within the all-inclusive themes of literary time and space: the range of literary experiences of human temporality in the first volume of *Etudes*, the exploration of the distance within literature between consciousness and what it is conscious of in *La Distance intérieure*, the inexhaustibly renewed movement of the mind's spherical expansion and contraction in *Les Métamorphoses du cercle*, the special commitment of twentieth-century poets to the genetic energy of the moment in *Le Point de départ*, and in *Mesure de l'instant* the power of the instant, as it has been "measured" by various writers, to move between nullity and totality. Each volume is organized within itself chronologically. Each moves through an historical trajectory, sometimes from the Renaissance to the present, as in the eighteen essays going from Montaigne to Proust by way of Descartes, Pascal, Molière, Corneille, Racine, Madame de La Fayette, Fontenelle, Abbé Prévost, Rousseau, Diderot, Benjamin Constant, Alfred de Vigny, Théophile Gautier, Flaubert, Baudelaire, and Paul Valéry in the first volume of *Etudes*, or as in the twenty essays of *Les Métamorphoses du cercle* going from "La Renaissance" to Rilke, Eliot, and Guillén, by way of "L'Epoque baroque," Pascal, "Le Dix-huitième Siècle," Rousseau, "Le Romantisme," Lamartine, Balzac, Vigny, Nerval, Poe, Amiel, Flaubert, Baudelaire, "La 'Prose' de Mallarmé," Henry James, and Claudel, or as in the fourteen essays of *Mesure de l'instant* going from Maurice Scève through Saint-Cyran, Racine, Fénelon, Casanova, Joubert, "Les Romantiques anglais," Madame de Staël, Lamartine, Stendhal, Michelet, Amiel, and Proust to Julien Green. Sometimes the trajectory is less inclusive, as in the movement from Marivaux to Mallarmé by way of Vauvenargues, Chamfort, Laclos, Joubert, Balzac, Hugo, Musset, and Maurice de Guérin in *La Distance intérieure*, or in the concentration on nine recent writers in *Le Point de départ*: Whitman, Bernanos, Char, Supervielle, Eluard, Saint-John Perse, Reverdy, Ungaretti, and Sartre.

This recapitulated historical movement in each of the volumes, going over and over the same periods of literary history from the Renaissance to the present has brought more clearly into the open the historical schema assumed in Poulet's critical enterprise. For him European literature took a new turn in the Renaissance when consciousness became conscious of itself with a new acuteness in writers like Montaigne and Descartes. In the seventeenth century Poulet is especially interested in those religious writers (Pascal, Saint-Cyran, Racine, and Fénelon) who experienced with most intensity the contingency of the human spirit in relation to a divine transcendence. This distant deity must intervene continuously, creating the soul anew from moment to moment and preventing it from falling into nothingness. Poulet sees the eighteenth century as the time when belief in the sustaining power of God fades. Man finds himself alone, in the moment, forced to create a duration and a self through expansive revery, through feeling, or through affective memory. The romantic writers, from Rousseau on, seek to create, in rare moments of secular ecstasy, a human equivalent of the divine *totum simul.* In the twentieth century this historical movement is continued by a tendency to "break with every *a priori* conception of time," to reject all but the living moment of experience. Twentieth-century authors use this moment as a point of origin on the basis of which the writer must "invent or rediscover [a] duration."[43]

When this historical pattern gradually emerges as a structuring constant, it becomes clear that Poulet considers each writer limited to some degree by the time in which he is born as to the possible spiritual experiences open to him. At the same time there is a contrary recognition of the complexity and multiplicity of each writer. This is implied in the increasing number of examples of Poulet's power to return to a writer treated in an earlier essay and to find something new to say about him. In *Mesure de l'instant*, for example, there are new essays on Racine, Joubert, Amiel, and Proust, all of whom had been treated at least once before. Works published since 1963 make even more evident the fact that for Poulet a great writer is inexhaustible. The voluminous imaginative space of a writer like Proust may always be entered again from a different point and traversed anew by a different route.

Poulet's recent work, finally, has more clearly exposed the deeper commitments of his enterprise, the assumptions which lie beneath those he overtly affirms in his statements about the nature of criticism. It is not wholly true to say that Poulet is to be distinguished from other critics in his group (Albert Béguin, say, or Marcel Raymond) by his disinterestedness, by the fact that he is unwilling to use the transparency of one mind to another attained in criticism "as a means to reach some further end."[44] Though Poulet differs from his colleagues in the breadth and catholicity of his sympathy, in his openness to a wider variety of writers, nevertheless his criticism is motivated, one begins to suspect, by a covert personal quest, a quest of whose guiding assumptions he may not be entirely conscious. As Paul de Man has recently asserted, it may be that each writer or critic has a blind spot which is the pivot around which his whole work turns, its hidden energizing source. In Poulet's case, this central concern may govern more or less covertly the search he has conducted by way of other writers for answers to questions which are his own. This aspect of his work is one factor which justifies defining it as authentically a work of literature in its own right, perhaps one of the most important of our time. In these areas, moreover, Poulet's work is most problematical and raises in its own way those questions which are most crucial in twentieth-century literature, philosophy, and criticism. What, in Poulet's case, is the genetic concern? And what, in his case, is the unspoken system of assumptions establishing the rules according to which the exploration of literature is conducted?

VII

Poulet inherited from Bergson, a philosopher who much influenced his earliest work,[45] the distinction between inauthentic spatialized time and authentic duration. In his own writing, however, this theme takes the form of a concern for the opposition between a human time of transient flowing and the all-embracing fixed time of the divine eternity. The search for an escape from the human time of evanescence to a time of plenitude governs Poulet's exploration of literature. He finds some version of this search in most of the various writers he studies. His criticism is therefore not so much a series of studies of human time as it has been experienced by major authors since the Renaissance as it is a study of the various attempts made by these authors to escape from the fluidity and instability of everyday time—escape through the discovery of a transcendent power outside time by the Christian writers, or through the discovery of a sensationalist equivalent of the *totum simul* of God by a writer like Rousseau, or through a dismissal of all other times but the present instant in certain modern writers. In some cases Poulet finds an expansion of the self to include all the universe, in others a reduction of the self to a self-sufficient point. In all these variations the constant is an escape by one form or another of spatialization from the transitivity of time.

This search for an escape from temporal flowing may also be defined as the search for some authentic point of departure, some solid beginning from which all else will follow. To escape from fluidity one must find some motionless rock in the flux. Poulet's criticism makes the a priori assumption that this beginning before, behind, or below which one cannot go is to be found in consciousness, in the authentic *moi*, in the self as it is to itself when it is deprived of all its contents. In each of his essays he attempts to "go back in the work of the author all the way to that act from which each imaginary universe opens out."[46] This act is a moment of self-consciousness. Such a moment, says Poulet, is the true point of departure for every human existence.[47] An important letter of 1961 defines in detail the quality of this act of self-awareness and specifies the tradition to which it belongs:

> I should readily consider that the most important form of subjectivity is not that of the mind overwhelmed, filled, and so to speak stuffed with its objects, but that there is another [kind of consciousness] which sometimes reveals itself on this side of, at a distance from, and protected from, any object, a subjectivity which exists in itself, withdrawn from any power which might determine it from the outside, and possessing itself by a direct intuition, infinitely different from the self-knowledge which is the indirect result of our relations with the world. In other words, I should say that subjectivity [in criticism] is the consciousness of the critic coinciding with the consciousness of the thinking or feeling person located in the heart of the text (of every literary text), in such a way that this double consciousness appears less in its multiplicity of sensuous relations with things, than prior to and separate from any object, as self-consciousness or pure consciousness. . . . As you have seen, in this I remain faithful to the Cartesian tradition.[48]

Here is that *Cogito* which Poulet seeks to identify initially in each of his essays as the source of everything of importance in the author in question. He tries to identify it in a moment of "double consciousness," the pure intuitive grasp of the unique affective tone of the mind of the author by himself, doubled in the intuitive insight into that self-reflecting mind by the receptive mind of the critic. Both in this pure subjectivity without content and in all the transformations it goes through when it opens out to the world "in the multiple effects of its fecundating power,"[49] one quality is assumed by Poulet to be fundamental: the quality of *presence*. This condition is the basic test of authenticity which Poulet applies to the various experiences he finds recorded in literature. It persists as a constant among the motifs which recur in proliferating variety throughout his criticism—as the presence of the mind to itself in the "indescribable intimacy" of the genetic moment of self-consciousness; as the presence of one consciousness to another in the coincidence of two minds which takes place in the reading which precedes criticism; as the priority accorded to the instant, to the present, to immediate experience within the presence of the present; as the presence of objects to the mind in the instant of sensation or perception; as the presence of past moments of sensation to the now of consciousness in that recovered present of affective memory which Poulet finds in so many of his authors; as the presence of the whole world to the mind in the immediacy of the *totum simul* which imitates in the finite and fleeting consciousness of man the infinite and eternal consciousness of God. If Rousseau's importance lies in the fact that in his writing "for the first time there appears in literature a text which claims to retrace, not as a didactic development nor as a mystic vision, but as an experience personally lived, the *totum simul* of the Alexandrians and the scholastics,"[50] the English romantic poets, in the essay on them in *Mesure de l'instant*, are described as all seeking in one way or another a human version of the divine *totum simul*, "a personal, subjective eternity; an eternity for their own use";[51] of Paul Claudel Poulet says in *Le Point de départ* that no one "has more amply depicted the *totum simul* of that eternity at once cosmic and human."[52] From the presence to itself of consciousness in the contentless point at the origin of the mind's adventures to the most expansive revery in which the mind contains all existence in panoramic simultaneity, the priority and supreme value of the present and of presence are everywhere assumed in Poulet's criticism.

This means the implicit acceptance, in spite of the prolonged meditation which Poulet has applied to the theme of time in literature, of a spatial model of temporality, a model determined by the Christian-Platonic inheritance of the Western tradition of metaphysics. Poulet finds this spatialized time in multiplied variations in the writers he discusses from the Presocratics to Proust. It is no accident that in spite of his commitment to an exploration of human time spatial images become increasingly dominant in his criticism, as in the notion of interior distance, or in the title image of *Les Métamorphoses du cercle*, or in the concept of juxtaposition in *L'Espace proustien*. Poulet is correct in claiming that this spatial image of time is a fundamental constant in our tradition, occurring in countless variations among philosophers and writers. A spatial model of time is, for example, present in Plato's *Timaeus*, in Aristotle's *Physics*, in Book Eleven of St. Augustine's *Confessions*, and on down even to Edmund Husserl's *Vorlesungen zur Phänomenologie des inneren Zeitbewusstseins* in our own century.[53] The continuity of this image of time is suggested by the fact that Husserl praises St. Augustine's Book Eleven at the beginning of his own discussion of time.[54]

The spatiality of this Christian-Platonic image of time, accepted for the most part without question by Poulet when he encounters it in his writers, is systematically associated with the acceptance of presence as an original category from which other categories are derived. Plato,

Aristotle, Augustine, and Husserl all build their image of time on the priority of the present, viewing past and future as presents which once happened or which will one day happen. In such a view, temporality, however complex its structure, is still a pattern of interrelated presents or "now-points," as in Husserl's diagrammatic representation of the "running-off phenomena" of time in the *Vorlesungen*.[55] This view of time is traditionally associated with the contrast, so frequently referred to by Poulet, between the *nunc fluens* of human time, to which only one present moment can be present at a time, and the *nunc stans* of God's eternity, to which all moments are perpetually present in an all-inclusive spatialized now, guaranteeing the substantial presentness of those moments which, to a given human experience, are not at present present. For Poulet, as for the tradition generally, each man wishes intuitively to obtain an experience of all times as immediately present. He wants to achieve in one way or another something like the *nunc stans* of God.

This priority of presence in Poulet's criticism is associated, finally, with a tendency to take language for granted in literature. For the most part he does not put the language of his authors in question, hold it at arm's length and analyze it, interrogate it suspiciously for distinctions between what it apparently says and what it really says. He does not scrutinize the language of his texts for the covert assumptions of its metaphors, its tense structures, its silences. Part of Poulet's generosity toward his authors is a taking for granted not only of the authenticity of their experiences, but also of the authenticity of the words in which they have expressed these experiences. It is scarcely an exaggeration to say that for Poulet the language of the works he discusses is seen as a perfectly transparent medium through which the mind of the author passes into the mind of the critic. If Poulet apparently accepts without question the Western tradition of presence he also accepts the Western tradition of representation or mimesis. His relatively infrequent stylistic analyses tend to assume that the language of literature is the undistorting mirror of a state of mind which precedes it and can exist in full authenticity without it. Consciousness, it seems, is the genetic source of literary language, and words like "express," "reflect," or "imitate" are usually present when Poulet calls attention to some characteristic of an author's style. I shall cite two from the abundant examples of this which could be given. Speaking of the habit of ejaculatory syntax in Gide's writing, Poulet says: "Better than any other syntactical form, the exclamation expresses the moment, responds to it in instantaneous echo, marks it, in its springing forth, with an exclusively present life."[56] Writing of Proust, he says: "*Au-devant, devant!* [Beyond, before!] Few adverbial expressions appear more frequently in the work of Proust and express more precisely at once the forward élan of the spirit and the perpetual impossibility for that spirit to attain its goal."[57]

Here one can better identify the role of citation, so important a feature of Poulet's procedure in criticism. If the critic must use as much as possible either the writer's own terminology or a neutral vocabulary which will not impose an alien screen between the reader and the mind of the author in question, this is because it is assumed that in the citation the minds of author, critic, and reader of the criticism coincide in a perfect presence of three consciousnesses to one another. To put in question the power of language to make possible this merger of minds would be to put in question the quality of presence, as a category of space, time, and consciousness, which is the true point of departure in Poulet's criticism.

VIII

The right of this quality of presence, however, to be called the basis which has priority over all forms of absence or distance has been challenged by much recent philosophy, literature, linguistics, and criticism. Under the aegis of such nineteenth-century predecessors as Marx, Freud, and Nietzsche recent writers of many different orientations have addressed themselves to what is sometimes called the "deconstruction of metaphysics." In one way or another all the forms in which the priority of the present and of presence appears in Poulet's work have come under attack.

The Freudian concept of the unconscious, for example, puts in question the notion that consciousness is a beginning or basis which cannot be gone beneath. Freud's unconscious is a region of the mind which never was present to consciousness and which can never be brought wholly out of obscurity into the bright realm of the mind's presence to itself. The concept or word "consciousness," or even consciousness itself, it is often suggested today, is generated as one element in a systematic interplay of linguistic elements which is the ground of the mind, rather than the other way around. The "I" or "me" which seems to prove its own existence in the *Cogito* may be no more than a grammatical term of a peculiar sort, as Emile Benveniste has suggested recently and as Nietzsche in a somewhat different way had already proposed in 1885: "It is within and by language that man constitutes himself as a *subject* [*comme sujet*]," says Benveniste, "because language alone in reality founds, in *its* reality which is that of being [*de l'être*], the concept of the 'ego.' "[58] "We used to believe in the 'soul,'" states Nietzsche, "as we believed in grammar and the grammatical subject; we used to say that 'I' was the condition, 'think' the predicate that conditioned, and thinking an activity for which a subject *had to be* thought of as its cause. But then we tried, with admirable persistence and guile, to see whether the reverse might not perhaps be true. 'Think' was now the condition, 'I' the thing conditioned, hence 'I' only a synthesis which was *created* by thinking ['*ich*' *also erst eine Synthese, welche durch das Denken selbst gemacht wird*]."[59]

Many recent linguists and literary critics, to take another such topic, inherit the tradition of Saussure, who denies that meaning preexists language or that a word can be a sign pointing toward some idea or thing which was present before the word was invented. Language, according to such thinkers, creates meaning in the differential relation of sounds or signifiers to one another. This means that language is never a matter of immediate presence, nor a matter of mimetic representation. Meaning arises from the reference of one signifier or phoneme to another, in the interplay of their differences. Meaning in language is always deferred, always in movement away from the present toward the no longer or the not yet. If language constitutes consciousness rather than the reverse, then such critics are right to argue that the structural, syntactical, and metaphorical details of languages are the proper subjects of literary criticism, not the state of mind which they generate rather than reflect. The concept of representation or of imitation has in fact been subjected to a searching criticism by such recent writers as Roland Barthes, Jacques Derrida, and Gilles Deleuze.[60]

To take another of Poulet's motifs, the search for a point of departure in literature or in life has recently been questioned by such thinkers as Michel Foucault. Here Nietzsche is again a forerunner, the Nietzsche who in *Jenseits von Gut und Böse* describes the radical thinker who believes that behind every beginning there is another beginning more original still: "He will suspect behind each cave a deeper cave, a more extensive, more exotic, richer world beyond the surface, a bottomless abyss beyond every 'bottom,' beneath every 'foundation' [*ein Abgrund hinter jedem Grunde, unter jeder 'Begründung'*]."[61] Foucault, speaking of the nineteenth-century revolution in interpretation initiated in part by Nietzsche, has spoken recently of a "*refus du commencement*," a refusal to believe that it is in any way possible in an act of interpretation to go back to a beginning before which one cannot go.[62]

As for Poulet's founding of criticism on an act of reading which attains an identification or overlapping of two minds, Emmanuel Levinas has based his recent work on a belief in the radical otherness of the other person. Another mind is so alien, so impenetrable, that it is never possible by any means to lift the veil which hides the other from me. This means that I can never confront the other person as an immediate presence, only encounter indirect signs and traces of his passage.[63]

A critic like Paul de Man, to turn to another structuring motif of Poulet's criticism, would put in question the concept of literary history on which Poulet's interpretations of literature appear to be based. For de Man and other present-day critics, literary history is not a sequence of self-enclosed "periods," each with its own unique set of assumptions determining the themes of literature written during that time. The human condition remains the same throughout history, de Man would argue, and the great writers of every epoch rise above the superficial configurations of thought in their age to express in authentic language the human predicament, in particular the abysses in man's experience of temporality.[64]

Martin Heidegger, finally, in the most celebrated twentieth-century analysis of time, *Sein und Zeit*, has subjected the spatialized model of time coming down from the Greeks and the Church Fathers to a penetrating criticism. For Heidegger authentic human time is never an experience of unmediated presence, but is a complex structure of "ecstasies" in which time arises from the not yet present future. Each dimension of time reaches out toward the others and forms an incomplete system moving toward a finite totality it never attains while a man is alive. "Temporality," says Heidegger, "temporalizes itself as a future which makes present in the process of having been [*Zeitlichkeit zeitigt sich als gewesende-gegenwärtigende Zukunft*]."[65] On the basis of this conception of time Heidegger argues that the Platonic or Christian idea of time as a succession of nows which is grounded in the static and infinite eternity of a God to whom all times are co-present arises as a false projection from the inauthentic everyday conception of time as an infinite succession of equivalent nows stretching before and after in a spatial row. So Heidegger affirms in a footnote in *Sein und Zeit* that

> the traditional conception of "eternity" as signifying the "standing 'now' " [*nunc stans*], has been drawn from the ordinary way of understanding time [*aus dem vulgären Zeitverständnis geschöpft*] and has been defined with an orientation toward the idea of "constant" presence-at-hand [*der "ständigen" Vorhandenheit*]. . . . If

> God's eternity can be "construed" philosophically, then it may be understood only as a more primordial temporality which is "infinite."[66]

Time as presence, the other as presence, the presence of consciousness to itself, language as the pure reflection of the presence of consciousness, literary history as a history of consciousness, the possibility of reaching an original presence from which all the others derive—each of these forms of presence has been rejected by a central tradition of modern thought. Perhaps the most radical and comprehensive of these attempts to dismantle metaphysics from within is that being mounted by Jacques Derrida.[67] All the apparent assumptions of Poulet's criticism are interrogated by Derrida and found wanting (though without specific reference to Poulet), for example in the more or less comprehensive taking of position in his recent essay, "La 'Différence.' "[68] The privilege accorded to the "living present," says Derrida,

> is the ether of metaphysics, the element of our thought insofar as it is caught in the language of metaphysics. It is impossible to escape from the limitations of such an enclosure except by interrogating today that value of presence which Heidegger has shown to be the ontotheological determination of being; and therefore by interrogating that value of presence, by a putting in question the status of which must be altogether singular, we interrogate the absolute privilege of that form or of that epoch of presence in general which is consciousness as the will to language [*comme vouloir-dire*] within its presence to itself.[69]

IX

It would seem that the tradition represented by Derrida and that represented by Poulet must be set against one another as an irreconcilable either/or. A critic must choose either the tradition of presence or the tradition of "difference," for their assumptions about language, about literature, about history, and about the mind cannot be made compatible. The more deeply and carefully one reads Poulet's criticism, however, the more clearly it emerges that it challenges its own fundamental assumptions and that as his work gradually develops it encounters in its own way the same problematical issues which are central for a critic like Derrida. It encounters them through the pursuit of its own avowed goals, that is, the reliving from within of the spiritual adventures of major Western writers in an attempt to see whether any of them has been able to find an escape from the flowing of time and in an attempt in each case to discover the point of departure within consciousness from which all aspects of the work in question have derived. As Derrida has repeatedly affirmed, the "deconstruction of metaphysics" takes place within metaphysics and remains within metaphysics, since we have no language but one version or another of the Western metaphysical tradition. However different in tone and attitude a critic like Derrida is from Poulet, their procedures are, in one way at least, the same. Derrida, like Poulet, calls for a reliving of the fundamental texts of our tradition, in his case a following through of the basic metaphorical strands which make up the texture of these texts. Far from going "beyond metaphysics" now, says Derrida, "it is necessary . . . to remain within the difficulty of this passage [back through the metaphysical tradition], to repeat it by way of the rigorous reading of metaphysics wherever it normalizes Western discourse and not only in the texts of 'the history of philosophy.' "[70] Poulet's criticism may be described as one form of such a rigorous reading, and in making a concentrated image of the literary tradition since the Renaissance, Poulet, however indirectly, puts that tradition to the test.

Moreover, if Poulet's "rigorous reading" is motivated covertly by a desire to discover an escape from the flowing of time in a stable point of departure, the result of this search is failure. In no writer, for more than an illusory moment, does he find what he seeks. Again and again in his criticism he experiences by way of his re-experience of the experience of others the inability of consciousness ever to reach back to its *point de départ*. He discovers the existence within the mind of a fathomless abyss, a deeper bottom beneath every bottom. Poulet's exploration of the *Cogito* of each of his writers leads to the recognition that the *Cogito* is the experience of a lack of a beginning, of an irremediable instability of the mind. The search for a beginning leads to a discovery of the impossibility of ever reaching an origin. This coincides with a revelation that the present moment of consciousness, from which all else follows, is undermined by absence and is a movement which can never be stopped in its reaching toward an ungraspable totality. Unlike Derrida, Poulet has no desire to "deconstruct" metaphysics. Quite the reverse. He wants to prolong it and to maintain it. But in reliving it from within he has participated in that deconstruction by encountering the instability of the foundation on which the tradition is based: consciousness and the present. "I believe," says Poulet in perhaps the most revealing statement he has made about the outcome of his study of literature,

> that in prolonging in its very interiority the spirituality of all the authors, one comes to glimpse something which exceeds them, to establish a convergence. . . . [T]he profundity of the interior [of the mind] is such that one can never see the edge or the end of it, and, as in the case of Pascal, there is a transcendence of the center.[71]

This transcendence of the center is the absence of any attainable origin. However far back or far below one goes, the center still eludes the searcher. Beneath the deepest deep a deeper deep still opens, and the authenticity of literature is constituted by this experience of failure to reach the bottom. "I am above all attracted," continues Poulet,

> by those for whom literature is—by definition—a spiritual activity which must be gone beyond in its own depths or which, in being unable to succeed in this, in being condemned to the consciousness of a failure to go beyond itself [*un non-dépassement*], affirms itself as the experience and verification of a fundamental defeat.[72]

This insight into the fact that the central movement of literature is an experience of failure explains the crucial importance for Poulet of writers like Pascal, Rousseau, Baudelaire, and Proust, those problematical authors in whom especially appears in one way or another the insufficiency of consciousness to sustain itself or in whom, as in the case of Rousseau, the attempt to make it sustain itself has been most heroic. Marcel Proust is above all other writers important here as an indication of the inner drama of Poulet's criticism. He has returned many times to Proust, in the climactic essay of *Etudes sur le temps humain, I,* in a book-length essay, *L'Espace proustien,* in the admirable recent essay included in *Mesure de l'instant.* There are crucial pages on Proust at the end of the introduction to *Le Point de départ,* and in the preliminary essay in *Les Chemins actuels de la critique* Poulet salutes Proust as the founder of "thematic criticism," that criticism which, having "plunged into the apparent disorder which almost always constitutes the collection of works by the same author, discovers there . . . the *themes* common to all these works."[73] To follow the sequence of these essays on Proust is to trace by way of a series of salient points the development of Poulet's work, and it is to discover that if Poulet in his own way questions the value of presence and the definition of consciousness which seem to be postulates of his work, he also, in spite of appearances, does not view as trivial the fact that literature is made of words. His distaste for the objective study of literary language springs from a desire to protect what is most unsettling about literature from those who would turn it into a fixed spatial structure which can be held at arm's length and safely studied as an external object. To turn a work of literature into an object in this way is to be unable to experience it from the inside and thereby to be unable to discover the record it contains of the failure of the mind ever to coincide with its point of origin. The relation of consciousness to language, when this failure is recognized, comes to be seen as no longer that of a passive mirroring of a preexistent state of mind in words. Language is rather the instrument by which the mind explores its own depths, discovers there is no attainable point of origin within it, and ultimately recognizes that language itself must be used as the means by which the mind attempts to constitute its own continuity and duration over the unfathomable gulf within itself.

Poulet's first essay on Proust explores the way in which in *A la recherche du temps perdu* a fragile and wavering present self founds itself on a recovery of the apparently solid ground of its own past. *L'Espace proustien* looks upon the vast expanse of *A la recherche* as a spatial panorama of events recorded in language and juxtaposed in the present within the covers of a book. The essay in *Mesure de l'instant* reveals a new Proust, a Proust oriented toward the future, toward a prospectivity which will be created from instant to instant in the act of writing, that is, through language. *A la recherche*, says Poulet, leads to a decision

> to draw from past existence a future work, in such a way that the final decision of the hero becomes the initial point of a new novel, the point of departure of a new future. . . . The Proustian novel does not lead up to a simple grasp of the past as past. It creates its own future; it reestablishes . . . the primacy of the prospective élan in the expression of a duration.[74]

This insight into the indispensable, and yet precarious, function of language as the true "point of departure" of literature, this recognition that language is an instrument of revelation and creation rather than merely of reflection or mimesis, had already been affirmed in *Le Point de départ*, where Poulet speaks of the special discovery in twentieth-century literature of the naked present as that on the basis of which it is necessary for literature "to invent or recover that [lost] duration."[75] This invention or recovery, continues Poulet, is "a work not impossible, but difficult, and in which the defeats are more frequent than the victories. There are numerous examples in the literature of the twentieth century of durations sketched out, aborted, exploded, in short of non-durable durations."[76]

Of those writers who have best demonstrated the difficulty of creating a duration through words none stands, for Poulet, above Proust, but Poulet's criticism is itself such a construction. Far from being a mere representation of the work of others, it is the creation of a duration out of all the detached moments of experience recorded in words and strewn here and there in all the books. This creation, like Proust's creation of *A la recherche du temps perdu*, moves forward with language toward a never-completed future in the act of recapitulating and organizing the past:

> One cannot . . . understand the literary work except by placing oneself in the *nisus formativus* by which, as it gradually unveils itself to the eyes of the reader, it reveals to him at the same time how it moves from instantaneousness, that is to say, from the detached sequence of the sensible events which constitute it, to a structural temporalism, that is to say, toward the gradual cohesion which takes hold of the different parts, puts them in positive or dialectical relation to one another and brings into the open with the same stroke the ideological and stylistic constants and the formal sequences. . . . Contrary to what one supposes, time does not go from the past to the future, nor from the future to the past, in traversing the present. Its true direction is that which goes from the isolated instant to temporal continuity. Duration is not, as Bergson believed, an immediate given of consciousness. It is not time which is given us; it is the instant. With that given instant, it is up to us to make time.[77]

All Poulet's investigation of literature approaches toward this affirmation of the reciprocal dependence of consciousness and language in the progressive unfolding of the creative act. Mind and words balance and sustain each other in a wavering at the point of origin which can never be stilled. In saying this Poulet moves beyond any spatialized conception of time to confront the fact that the true beginning of both subjectivity and language, if the concept of origin may still be preserved, is the insecurity of human temporality, the fissures and dislocations which open up for man within time.

NOTES

1. The first five sections of this essay are a somewhat shortened and revised version of an essay originally printed as "The Literary Criticism of Georges Poulet" in *Modern Language Notes*, LXXVIII, 5 (December, 1963), 471–88, here reproduced with the kind permission of the Johns Hopkins Press. At that time Poulet had published three books: *Etudes sur le temps humain* (Edinburgh: Edinburgh University Press, 1949; Paris: Plon, 1950); *La Distance intérieure* (Paris: Plon, 1952); *Les Métamorphoses du cercle* (Paris: Plon, 1961). These three books have been translated into English and published by the Johns Hopkins Press. In 1963 Poulet had also published three of the essays on French (or in these cases Swiss) critics of his group which are ultimately to form part of the "Essai sur la pensée critique de notre temps" which he is preparing: "La Pensée critique d'Albert Béguin," *Cahiers du Sud*, 360 (1961), 177–98; "La Pensée critique de Marcel Raymond," *Saggi e ricerche di letteratura francese* (Milan: Feltrinelli, 1963), pp. 203–29; "Le Pensée critique de Jean Starobinski," *Critique*, XIX, 192 (Mai, 1963), 387–410.

Sections six through nine of this essay attempt to extend what I originally wrote in the light of work Poulet has published since 1963. Since then five books and a number of essays have appeared: *L'Espace proustien* (Paris: Gallimard, 1963); *Le Point de départ* (Paris: Plon, 1964); *Trois Essais de mythologie romantique* (Paris: Corti, 1966); *Mesure de l'instant* (Paris: Plon, 1968), and *Benjamin Constant par lui-même* (Paris: Seuil, 1968). Though the book on contemporary criticism has not yet appeared, several additional essays likely to form part of that study have been published in the interim: "Bachelard et la conscience de soi," *Revue de Métaphysique et de Morale*, LXX, 1 (Janvier-Mars, 1965), 1–26; "Bachelard et la critique contemporaine," *Currents of Thought in French Literature: Essays in Memory of G. T. Clapton*, ed. J. C. Ireson (New York: Barnes and Noble, 1966), pp. 353–57; "La Pensée critique de Charles du Bos," *Critique*, XXI, 217 (Juin, 1965), 491–516: "Maurice Blanchot, critique et romancier," *Critique*, XXII, 229 (Juin, 1966), 485–97. In addition Poulet has directed an important conference at Cerisy-la-Salle on criticism, the transactions of which have been published as *Les Chemins actuels de la critique* (Paris: Plon, 1967), with an introductory essay by Poulet on his immediate predecessors in criticism—Thibaudet, Jacques Rivière, Charles du Bos, Ramon Fernandez, and Marcel Proust. A new book on Baudelaire, *Le Visage de Baudelaire* (Geneva: Skira, 1969), has recently appeared.

Further discussion of Georges Poulet's work has also been published since 1963. A good study in English of his criticism is included in Sarah

Lawall's *Critics of Consciousness: The Existential Structures of Literature* (Cambridge, Mass., 1968), pp. 74–135. There is a criticism of Poulet in Geoffrey Hartman's "Beyond Formalism," *Modern Language Notes*, LXXXI, 5 (December, 1966), 550–55. I have discussed Poulet's work again briefly in "The Geneva School," *The Virginia Quarterly Review*, XLIII, 3 (Summer, 1967), 477–82 (also available in *The Critical Quarterly*, VIII, 4 [Winter, 1966], 313–16). An admirably full and perceptive essay on Poulet by Paul de Man, entitled "Vérité et méthode dans l'oeuvre de Georges Poulet," has appeared in *Critique*, XXV, 266 (July, 1969), 608–23.

2. Poulet, "La Pensée critique d'Albert Béguin," p. 178. I am responsible for the translations of citations from Poulet's criticism which appear in this essay.
3. Poulet, "La Pensée critique de Marcel Raymond," p. 203.
4. Ibid., p. 209.
5. Ibid., p. 203.
6. Poulet, "Réponse," *Les Lettres nouvelles* (24 juin, 1959), p. 10.
7. Poulet, "La Pensée critique de Marcel Raymond," p. 204.
8. Poulet, "La Pensée critique de Jean Starobinski," p. 408.
9. Poulet, "La Pensée critique de Albert Béguin," p. 178.
10. Poulet, "La Pensée critique de Jean Starobinski," p. 409.
11. Poulet, "La Pensée critique de Marcel Raymond," p. 228.
12. Poulet, "La Pensée critique de Jean Starobinski," p. 408.
13. Poulet, "La Pensée critique de Marcel Raymond," p. 208.
14. Poulet, *La Distance intérieure*, p. ii.
15. Poulet, *Les Lettres nouvelles* (24 juin, 1959), p. 12.
16. Poulet, "La Pensée critique de Marcel Raymond," p. 225.
17. Ibid., p. 224.
18. Poulet, "La Pensée critique de Jean Starobinski," p. 408.
19. Preface by Georges Poulet to Jean-Pierre Richard's *Littérature et sensation* (Paris, 1954), p. 9.
20. Poulet, *Les Lettres nouvelles* (24 juin, 1959), p. 11.
21. Poulet, "La Pensée critique de Marcel Raymond," p. 205.
22. Ibid., p. 210.
23. Poulet, *La Distance intérieure*, p. i.
24. Ibid.
25. Poulet, "La Pensée critique de Marcel Raymond," p. 209.
26. Ibid., p. 208.
27. Blanchet, "Ars Nova," *La Nouvelle Revue Française*, 125 (Mai, 1963), 886–87.
28. Poulet, *Les Métamorphoses du cercle*, pp. 515–16.
29. Poulet, *La Distance intérieure*, p. ii.
30. Poulet, *Les Métamorphoses du cercle*, p. 339.
31. Poulet, "La Pensée critique de Jean Starobinski," p. 397.

32. Poulet, *Les Métamorphoses du cercle*, p. 263.
33. Poulet, *Etudes sur le temps humain*, I, 176.
34. From a letter of 1963.
35. Poulet, *La Distance intérieure*, p. 251.
36. Poulet, "La Pensée critique de Marcel Raymond," pp. 212–13.
37. Poulet, *Les Lettres nouvelles* (24 juin, 1959), p. 12.
38. Ibid.
39. See note 1 above for a list of these.
40. Poulet, *Les Chemins actuels de la critique*, p. 251.
41. Ibid., p. 9.
42. Ibid., p. 55.
43. Poulet, *Le Point de départ*, p. 37.
44. See my essay, "The Geneva School," p. 477.
45. As Paul de Man has shown in his discussion in the article cited above in note 1 of Poulet's pseudonymous novel, *La Poule aux oeufs d'or* (Paris, 1927), and of his uncollected periodical essays of the early 1920s.
46. Poulet, *Trois Essais de mythologie romantique*, p. 11.
47. See the discussion of the *Cogito* in section III above.
48. From a letter to this author.
49. Poulet, "La Pensée critique de Marcel Raymond," p. 208.
50. Poulet, *Etudes sur le temps humain*, I, 174.
51. Poulet, *Mesure de l'instant*, p. 164.
52. Poulet, *Le Point de départ*, p. 34.
53. For recent discussions of the complexities of Husserl's position on this point see Gérard Granel, *Le Sens du temps et de la perception chez E. Husserl* (Paris, 1968), and also Jacques Derrida, *De la grammatologie* (Paris, 1967), pp. 97–98, and his *La Voix et le phénomène* (Paris, 1967), especially pp. 93–96.
54. For the English translation see Edmund Husserl, *The Phenomenology of Internal Time-Consciousness*, trans. James S. Churchill (Bloomington, 1964), p. 21: "For no one in this knowledge-proud modern generation," says Husserl of Augustine, "has made more masterful or significant progress in these matters than this great thinker who struggled so earnestly with the problem."
55. Ibid., p. 49.
56. Poulet, *Le Point de départ*, p. 9.
57. Poulet, *Mesure de l'instant*, 315.
58. Benveniste, *Problèmes de linguistique générale* (Paris, 1966), p. 259.
59. Nietzsche, *Jenseits von Gut und Böse*, Section 54, *Werke*, ed. Karl Schlechta, II (Munich, 1954), p. 616; English trans. by Marianne Cowan, *Beyond Good and Evil* (Chicago, 1955), pp. 62–63.
60. See, for example, Roland Barthes, "L'Effet de réel," *Communications*, 11 (1968), 84–89; Jacques Derrida, "La Théâtre de la cruauté

et la clôture de la représentation," *L'Ecriture et la différence* (Paris, 1967), pp. 341–68; Gilles Deleuze, "Simulacre et philosophie antique," *Logique du sens* (Paris, 1969), pp. 292–324.

61. Nietzsche, *Jenseits von Gut und Böse*, Paragraph 289, p. 751; Cowan, trans., p. 232.

62. Foucault, "Nietzsche, Freud, Marx," *Nietzsche* (Paris, 1967), pp. 187–92.

63. See, for example, "Le Temps et l'autre," *Le Choix, le monde, l'existence* (Grenoble, 1949), and *Totalité et infini, Essai sur l'extériorité* (The Hague, 1961): "If one could possess, seize, and know the other, he would not be the other."

64. See de Man's essay on "The Rhetoric of Temporality," in *Interpretation: Theory and Practice* (Baltimore, 1969), and see also his comments on the historical assumptions of Poulet's work in the essay on Poulet in *Critique*, cited above. De Man argues that the historical schema of Poulet's criticism is apparent rather than real.

65. Heidegger, *Sein und Zeit*, tenth ed. (Tübingen, 1963), p. 350; English trans. John Macquarrie and Edward Robinson, *Being and Time* (New York, 1962), p. 401.

66. Ibid., p. 427; p. 499.

67. In addition to the three books mentioned above Derrida has published "La Pharmacie de Platon," *Tel Quel*, 32, 33 (1968), pp. 3–48, 18–59; "La 'Différence,'" *Bulletin de la Société Française de Philosophie*, 62e année, 3 (Juillet-Septembre, 1968), 73–120; "ΟΥΣΙΑ et ΓΡΑΜΜΗ," *L'Endurance de la pensée* (Paris, 1968), pp. 219–66; "La Dissémination," *Critique*, 262, 263 (Mars, Avril, 1969), 99–139, 215–49.

68. See above.

69. Derrida, "La 'Différence,'" pp. 89–90.

70. Ibid., p. 96.

71. From a letter of 1963.

72. Ibid.

73. Poulet, *Les Chemins actuels de la critique*, p. 23.

74. Poulet, *Mesure de l'instant*, p. 335.

75. It is worth noting, however, that a fundamental question is begged in the either/or here. Invent or recover, which is it?

76. Poulet, *Le Point de départ*, p. 37.

77. Ibid., p. 40.

Gaston Bachelard's Theory of the Poetic Imagination: Psychoanalysis to Phenomenology

NEIL FORSYTH
UNIVERSITY OF CALIFORNIA, BERKELEY

WHEN GASTON BACHELARD DIED IN 1962, he was probably best known to students of the philosophy of science for his work in the French post-Cartesian tradition. But at present he is also becoming well known for his studies of the literary imagination and the theory of criticism. He continued to teach the philosophy of science at the Sorbonne until his retirement in 1955, always maintaining his early interest in the rational intellect. But gradually he became interested in the problem of the non-rational imagination, partly as a result of his studies of rationalism, but also through the influence of such writers as Bergson and Husserl. While insisting upon the radical separation of the intellect and the imagination, he ultimately became chiefly concerned with the imagination. As his interest in it grew, he first attempted to study it objectively in the same way he had approached the intellect, and he developed a psychological theory of the imagination based on the schema of the four alchemical elements. Eventually he became dissatisfied with this approach, and adopted a position best understood as a variant of twentieth-century phenomenology. The central course of his development, then, is from the objectivity of psychoanalysis to the subjectivity of phenomenology.

Bachelard begins his book *L'Air et les songes* with a quotation from Joseph Joubert that is significant not only for the development of his own critical theory but for much contemporary French criticism: "The poets should be the chief study of the philosopher who wants to understand man." As he admits in the introduction to the same book, he is studying literature not as an end in itself, from an aesthetic position, but because it can lead to something else, to an understanding of the human psyche.

As Blake said, "Imagination is not a state, it is human existence itself." One will be more readily convinced of the truth of this maxim if one studies, as I am going to do in this work, the literary imagination, the spoken imagination, that which, keeping to language, forms the temporal tissue of spirituality, and which consequently separates itself from reality.[1] The principle themes of Bachelard's work are sounded here. He is making a study of the imagination, and in particular of the literary imagination, since that presents the best evidence; it is the "temporal tissue of spirituality." And, far from adopting a scientific approach to reality, he is studying that which "separates itself from reality."

Bachelard's study of the literary imagination is in fact a study of the subjective consciousness; it evolves gradually into the completely subjective method of his final period, the phenomenology of the imagination. There is the same distinction here that we find Georges Poulet (himself heavily influenced by Bachelard) setting up in his series of essays on what he calls "the interior distance," a distinction between an objective and a subjective approach to literature.

> Objectively, literature is made up of formal works, the contours of which stand out with greater or lesser clarity. They are poems, maxims, plays, and novels. Subjectively, literature is not at all formal. It is the reality of a thought that is always particular, always anterior and posterior to any object; one which, across and beyond all objects, ceaselessly reveals the strange and natural impossibility in which it finds itself, of ever having an objective existence.[2]

If we relate this obscure statement to Bachelard's thought, it may become a little clearer. Poulet is approaching in his own way what Bachelard was tackling—the subjective consciousness as it can be studied in literature.

Bachelard too had ignored the formal, objective aspect of literature. He set out to understand not the formal imagination, but the material imagination. It is in this context that we should view the statement he made in a tape-recorded interview: "A poem without unity but with ten beautiful images, well that suits me. You see, my role is very modest, and I don't claim to be a professor of literature. I don't have enough culture for that."[3] With Bachelard we are watching the very first stages of the imagining process, we are back at the roots of being; we are studying not the formal synthesizing imagination but the imagination of matter, which is always fresh. We are ultimately studying the imagination rather than literature. But why does he use literature for his study at all? He attempts to explain this in his introduction to his two books on the terrestrial imagination. His interest in literature is more particularly an interest in the literary image, and we shall watch that interest later as it grows into the central concern of his philosophy. For Bachelard it is through the essential novelty of the poetic image that we are led back to the root of things.

> This novelty is evidently the sign of the creative power of the imagination. An imitative literary image loses its animating power. Literature has to surprise. Of course, literary images can exploit some fundamental images—and my work in general consists in classifying these fundamental images—but each image which comes under the writer's pen must have its own differential of novelty. A literary image says what will never be imagined twice. There might be some merit in copying a painting. There is none in repeating a literary image.[4]

We need to remember here that the most powerful tradition in twentieth-century French poetry, in strong contrast to contemporary Anglo-American trends, has been toward a poetry that puts its emphasis on the revelatory power of the image itself, on the fresh, surprising quality of the poetic image, the poetry of Surrealism. Bachelard at times sounds a lot like the philosopher of Surrealism, but he is not bound by its limits, since he is using the surrealistic image for his own purposes. He has this to say in the Introduction to *La Terre et les rêveries de la volonté*:

> To reanimate language by creating new images, that is the function of literature and poetry. . . . Every new literary image is an original use of language. To feel its action, it is not necessary to have the knowledge of a linguist. The literary image gives us the experience of a creation of language. . . .
>
> We are now in a century of the image. For better or worse, we are more than ever undergoing the action of the image. . . . In the fire and brilliance of literary images, the ramifications multiply; words are no longer simply terms. They do not terminate in

> thoughts; they have the future of the image. Poetry makes the sense of a word ramify by surrounding it with an atmosphere of images. It has been demonstrated that most of Victor Hugo's rhymes excite images; between two rhyming words plays a sort of metaphorical bond: thus images are linked together thanks simply to the sonority of words. In a freer kind of poetry like Surrealism, language is a full ramification. The poem is a cluster of images. [pp. 6f.]

Of translations, two are particularly significant: *La Poétique de l'espace,* is from his last period,[5] and the other, *La Psychanalyse du feu,*[6] represents the transition from his first to his middle period, from his strictly philosophical concerns to the literary studies that will fill the last years of his life. There is a considerable difference between these two books, indeed they represent almost the opposite ends of Bachelard's development—objective and subjective optimism—although both reflect the constant presence of optimism. In the first one he is optimistic about the possibility of objectivity; in the later he is tracing the completely subjective path by which he discovers his own happiness.[7] When we look more closely at *La Psychanalyse du feu* later we shall see that the transition from one kind of thinking to the other is already in evidence there.

I

The original concern of Bachelard's thought was a scientific one, a search for pure objective knowledge of the external world. This search involved a careful examination of our own attitudes to whatever is the subject of our investigation. In order to advance in the knowledge of an object, we must guard ourselves, it seems, from knowing it. The assumption is that final and pure objectivity of knowledge is going to be something strange, and we need to keep a careful watch that we do not attribute the least recognizable trait to the object. The search is for pure, external, and impersonal truth, and it is consequently a denial of all subjectivity. His chief work on this subject is *La Formation de l'esprit scientifique*, published in 1938, but as he himself was to say later, it was badly named;[8] the subtitle is more significant: "A Contribution to the Psychoanalysis of Objective Knowledge." In it he is concerned about demonstrating this problem: "The scientific mind must align itself against Nature, against what is in us and outside us, the impulse and instruction of Nature."[9]

La Psychanalyse du feu grew out of this epistemological concern, and it was published in the same year. In it he makes a very similar statement:

> Scientific objectivity is possible only if one has broken first with the immediate object if one has refused to yield to the seduction of the initial choice, if one has checked and contradicted the thoughts which arise from one's first observation. [P.F., 1]

The important word here is perhaps "seduction," and we should notice that it is the imagination which has this seductive power. The aim of this scientific method is to detach the observer from the object, to remove all the affective and imaginative qualities from the mind, to achieve the purely objective functioning of the intellect, to attain to "the perfect limpidity of a thought that, because it has been thoroughly psychoanalyzed, has become exclusively objective."[10] It is a sifting, purifying process; separating objectivity from all the impurities of subjectivity. The surprising result of this attempt becomes clear in *La Psychanalyse du feu*: when you psychoanalyze the process of objectivization you also psychoanalyze the subjective life. If you remove all the elements of subjectivity from objectivity, you don't just have pure objectivity, you have pure subjectivity as well. The implications of this fact are important for Bachelard's development.

> Bachelard recognizes that if one eliminates from every mental phenomenon the appearance of objectivity that it offers to the contemplator, a spiritual substratum remains. It is this which is going from now on to occupy his attention: no longer an integral objectivity which discovers itself to the mind only after every trace of subjectivity has disappeared, but on the contrary an interior life whose significance can only be understood when the mind, having, conditionally or not, abandoned the search for objective truth, contemplates the subjective reality in itself, in its substantial simplicity and in itself.[11]

From this article by Poulet on Bachelard we may notice in passing how much like his own studies does this analysis of his mentor sound. But he is expressing something that is central to Bachelard's thought. It might help to understand it if we use an analogy from the smelting process, which is also rather appropriate in view of the paradox we will discover in Bachelard's discussion of the relation between fire and the purifying process. Smelting separates out all the impurities from iron and leaves you with a molten mass of pure ore; but you are also left with a pure heap of impurities. It is just a matter of which pile you direct your attention to. Bachelard moves more and more from the study of one pile, the activity of the intellect, to the other, the activity of the imagination, always keeping the two entirely separate.

La Psychanalyse du feu represents the transition between these two stages of Bachelard's thought. It grew out of his concern with establishing a method for achieving this scientific objectivity, and thus primarily deals with exposing the fallacies of our convictions about fire. Yet it is, he says,

> no longer the axis of objectivization but that of subjectivity that I would like to explore in order to illustrate the double perspectives that might be attached to all problems connected with the knowledge of any particular reality. [P.F., 3]

By the time he had completed the book he had become aware of the importance of the subjective power, the power of the imagination, so that he could write a conclusion looking forward to the possibility of creating a new kind of literary criticism, one which would study the true source of psychic and poetic production, the imagination, through the images it creates.

In the larger context of Bachelard's entire oeuvre we can see *La Psychanalyse du feu* as the book which looks both backward and forward, and which established the distinctive pattern of the rest of his philosophical work. It is not so much that he made radical revisions in his theory as that he expanded it enormously. His consciousness now has two faces. Instead of trying to eradicate all the imaginative fallacies that cluster around scientific observation, he begins to look at the imagination as an important activity of the human psyche. The polarity of the intellect and the imagination remains central to his thinking, but the relationship between them is reversed.

After *La Psychanalyse du feu* he can say:

> We need to examine all the desires we have to leave what one sees and what one says in favor of what one imagines. That way we shall have the chance to give back to the imagination its role

> as seducer. By the imagination we abandon the ordinary course of things. To perceive and to imagine are as antithetical as presence and absence. To imagine is to absent oneself; it is to start out toward a new life. [A.S., 10]

The imagination is still the seducer, but it is no longer the corrupter. It is worth studying in its own right, it is even healthy: "A being deprived of the function of the unreal is a neurotic just as much as one deprived of the function of the real" (A.S., 14).

La Psychanalyse du feu, then, begins the middle period of Bachelard's writings. He is no longer so concerned with the need for scientific thinking to be objective, though he still remained a philosopher of science, which he taught at the Sorbonne until his retirement.[12] His primary interest now is with the four kinds of material imagination, more especially as they manifest themselves in literature. The four elements of ancient science and its philosophy have no objective value for modern science, but they are important to the imagination. They are a priori archetypes of the mind, rooted in the human unconscious; all imaginative activity is conditioned by them. When we apply this to the poetic imagination in particular, we arrive at a theory of the four humors or temperaments, a theory of imaginative polarization, so that every poet may be inscribed in one of these four categories, according to which of the larger images he prefers. Bachelard summarizes the theory in *L'Air et les songes*:

> I am considered to have initiated the notion of a law of the four material imaginations, a law which attributes *necessarily* to the creative imagination one of the four elements: fire, earth, air, and water. Of course, several elements can intervene in the make-up of a particular image; there are composite images; but the life of images has a more demanding purity of relation. As soon as the images present themselves in order, they designate one material as first, one basic element. The physiology of the imagination, even more than anatomy, obeys the law of the four elements. [A.S., 14]

If we look back to *La Psychanalyse du feu,* we can see the theory in its initial stages, apparently when it first occurs to Bachelard. Fire had originally been chosen as the object he would use for his study, not because he had any idea of a theory of the four elements, but because it is the most obviously double of the objects that produce images: as well as being something objectively and in itself, it is very obviously beset with subjective fallacies, as Bachelard had discovered in his studies of alchemy. But as he studied our reactions to fire he became aware of the possibilities. The entire passage deserves to be quoted since it stands at the beginning of the efforts that were to mark the next ten years of his life.

> If our present work serves any useful purpose, it should suggest a classification of objective themes which would prepare the way for a classification of poetic temperaments. We have not yet been able to perfect an overall doctrine, but it seems quite clear to us that there is some relation between the doctrine of the four physical elements and the doctrine of the four temperaments. In any case, the four categories of souls in whose dreams fire, water, air, or earth predominate, show themselves to be markedly different. . . . Reverie has four domains, four points from which it soars into infinite space. To surprise the secret of a true poet, of a sincere poet, of a poet who is faithful to his original language and is deaf to the discordant echoes of sensuous eclecticism, which would like to play on all the senses, one word is sufficient: "Tell me what your favorite phantom is. Is it the gnome, the salamander, the sylph, or the undine?" Now—and I wonder if this has been noticed—all these chimerical beings are formed from and sustained by a unique substance: the gnome, terrestrial and condensed, lives in a fissure of the rock, guardian of the mineral and the gold, and stuffs himself with the most compact substances; the salamander, composed all of fire, is consumed in its own flame; the water nymph or undine glides noiselessly across the pond and feeds on her own reflection; the sylph, for whom the least substance is a burden, who is frightened away by the tiniest drop of alcohol, who would even perhaps be angry with a smoker who might contaminate her element, rises effortlessly into the blue sky, happy in her anorexia. [P.F., 89ff.]

This theory does not of course mean that people are rooted in a particular substance, but that "these primitive images orient psychological tendencies; these were the sights and impressions which suddenly aroused an interest in what is normally devoid of interest, which gave an interest to the object" (P.F., 90). For that "normally" we might read "objectively" and thus we are back to our original distinction between the subjective and the objective activity of the mind. The theory of the four material imaginations is a theory which attempts to classify the subjective projections that we make onto the outside world. For example Hoffman and Poe, writers that one might imagine to be alike in the character of their imagination, are in fact very different; their attitude toward alcohol is entirely dissimilar:

> The alcohol of Hoffman is the alcohol which flames up; it is marked by the wholly qualitative and masculine sign of fire. The alcohol of Poe is the alcohol that submerges and brings forgetfulness and death; it is marked by the wholly quantitative and feminine sign of water. [P.F., 91]

We are to assume that objectively alcohol is the same substance both for Hoffman and for Poe; but subjectively it is entirely different. There it is conditioned by the humor, by that a priori category of the human psyche which conditions all our imaginative life.

II

Two doctrines begin to emerge here in Bachelard's middle period that are going to be of central importance, and which he carries to their extreme in his final books. The first is a discovery that the central concern of his literary studies should be the poetic image; that his theory of the four material imaginations is taking us back to the roots of our being, and that what is found can be studied as it reveals itself in the image. The second is the notion, which we see only in embryo in *La Psychanalyse du feu*, that the state of mind in which the imagination is freest to create these images is "reverie."

The image is to be studied in its dynamic freshness. This is the century of the image, and Bachelard makes the most of that fact: "The poem is essentially an aspiration towards new images" (A.S., 8). He considers the dynamics of the image, that is, the way the image echoes in the psyche, gathering nuances. "The value of an image is measured by the extent of its imaginary halo" (A.S., 7). This dynamism can most clearly be seen in relation to aerial images, since they are the most obvious. The image and, in particular, the aerial image, has a liberating function. I quote from the Introduction to *L'Air et les songes*, where he claims that the aerial imagination is the best example of the imagination of movement, of this dynamic imagination.[13] It is interesting to note how far he has already (1943) come from the position of *La Psychanalyse du feu*; indeed, he begins to sound like Sartre in attributing such value to the unrealising function of the mind:

> Like many problems of psychology, studies of the imagination are impeded by the false light of etymology. One always wants the imagination to be the faculty of *making* images. But it is more often the faculty of *unmaking* the images furnished by the perception. It is above all the faculty of freeing us from the initial images, of *changing* images. If there is no changing of the images, an unexpected union of images, there is no imagination, there is no *action of imagining.* If an image that is *present* does not make us think of an image that is *absent,* if one occasional image does not set going a whole host of wandering images, an explosion of images, there is no imagination. There is perception, a memory of perception, a familiar memory, the customary colors and shapes. The basic word which corresponds to imagination, is not *image* but *imaginary.* The value of an image is measured by the extent of its *imaginary* halo. Thanks to the *imaginary,* the imagination is essentially *open, escapist.* Within the human psyche it is the experience of opening, the experience even, of *novelty.* [A.S., 7]

And it is the poem which responds to our need for novelty, for the freshness "which is a characteristic of the human psyche."

These dynamics only take place properly when the image is entirely fresh, and at this stage in Bachelard's thought there is an important reason for this demand for novelty in the image. He is not studying metaphors, which are standardized images and therefore lifeless, lacking in dynamism; nor is he studying those images that have been developed in myth and become domesticated, downgraded into what Heidegger calls the *Gerede.*[14]

> There is a big difference between a literary image which describes a beauty that has already been realized, a beauty that has reached its full form, and a literary image that works in the mystery of matter and which wants more to suggest than to describe. [T.R.V., 8]

The mystery of matter. It is only by the freshness of the individual poetic image that the imagination gets back to matter, that a harmony is established between the self and the thing, a harmony that implies an innocence, a happiness that is very dear to Bachelard, and which lies at the root of his theory of reverie.

Several problems begin to arise here. First, although Bachelard wants each image to be new and fresh, he establishes categories for his images that are as old as the human psyche itself, that are embedded in the human unconscious as archetypes. He comes to discuss this problem in his later period, and indeed this is perhaps the central issue that is forcing him toward the phenomenological method. We should now extend the discussion to include that final period, since we are dealing with the problems that he attempts to face there.

He attacks the problem of the freshness of the image at the beginning of the long and important statement of his poetics which serves as an introduction to *La Poétique de l'espace.* He talks here of the non-causal relation of the image, as it emerges, to the unconscious archetypes. The image is "a sudden salience on the surface of the psyche" (P.S., xi); but the onset of the image is not caused by the poet's unconscious. "The poetic image is not the result of an inner thrust. It is not an echo of the past." It would apparently be taking a very simplistic view of the workings of the mind if one regarded the unconscious as the cause of phenomena in the conscious mind. We can see in this attitude the increasing concern of Bachelard not to explain away the phenomena of the imagination as sublimations of certain facts of the unconscious. This is the anti-reductionism that is a common feature of the phenomenological reaction against classical psychoanalysis, a reaction that we discover as early as *La Psychanalyse du feu.* If anything, Bachelard may be suggesting here that the causal relation is the other way round; if the image is not caused by the past, if the fact of its newness cannot be explained by relating it to an archetype, it is still true that it is only by means of this newness that its archetypal nature is revealed. The image, in fact, may cause reverberations that are the echoes of the past: ". . . through the brilliance of an image, the distant past resounds with echoes" (P.S., xiii). At any rate, we can see what is involved in the movement of Bachelard's thought. He is becoming increasingly aware of the inadequacy of previous theories to explain the observed facts of mind, and in particular to explain the *surprising* nature of the poetic image; he is moving away from his studies of the material imagination to a study of the image in all its uniqueness, a movement from psychoanalysis toward phenomenology.

If we find that the problem of the poetic image is pushing Bachelard toward his later method, even more so does the closely related doctrine of the state of mind in which the poetic image emerges, the state of reverie. Indeed, his last major work, *La Poétique de la rêverie,* is devoted to the subject, and represents the culmination of a trend toward the subjective method; it is almost a reverie on reverie. Let us look at two important statements in which the method of this last period is announced, and which repudiate his earlier approach:

> In my earlier works on the subject of the imagination I did in fact consider it preferable to maintain as objective a position as possible with regard to the images of the four material elements, the four principles of the intuitive cosmogonies; and faithful to my habits as a philosopher of science, I tried to consider images without attempting personal interpretation. Gradually, this method, which had scientific prudence on its side, seemed to be an insufficient basis on which to found a metaphysics of the imagination. The prudent attitude itself is a refusal to obey the immediate dynamics of the image. [P.S., xiv]

As well as restating his position on the utter polarity of the two aspects of the consciousness, the intellect and the imagination, Bachelard eventually adopted entirely different methods for studying them.

> Far be it from me to try to weaken this polarity . . . I have already found it necessary to write a book in order to exorcise the images which, in a scientific culture, pretend to engender and sustain concepts. . . . But on the other hand, in stating my faithful devotion to images, I would not dream of studying them from the point of view of concepts. The intellectual criticism of poetry will never get to the seat [*foyer*] where poetic images are formed. . . . The image can be studied only by the image, dreaming the images as they gather in reverie. It is nonsense to pretend to study the imagination objectively, since one only really receives the image if one admires it. Even in comparing one image with another, one risks losing one's participation in its individuality.[15]

The reference here is back to his early period, to *La Formation de l'esprit scientifique*, out of which *La Psychanalyse du feu* grew. We can see now how far he has come. He has established two opposite poles in the activity of the psyche; one is the objective knowledge he was searching for in his first books, knowledge that is to be achieved by the heightened activity of the rational intellect; the other is the subjective "living" of the poetic image in the moment when it is formed, in the state of reverie.

The notion of reverie has developed considerably from the time of its introduction in *La Psychanalyse du feu*. If we look back for a moment to that book, we can see that the idea changes even there. It begins simply as the state of the mind observing the fire, the state which he is trying to overcome. It is the fireside reverie that he calls the "futility of reverie" (P.F., 4) because it engenders all those false subjective notions about fire. But he soon realizes its importance in the study of poetry. It becomes the poetic state of mind, and we find Bachelard looking upon his book as a basis for determining the objective conditions of reverie, and thus establishing an "objective literary criticism" (P.F., 109). From the simple state that the mind invariably adopts before the fire, it becomes the whole state of the poetic imagination.

In *La Psychanalyse du feu* Bachelard differentiates reverie rather casually from the night dream, largely on the basis that reverie is always more or less centered on one object. He is only dimly aware of a distinction that was to become central to his later poetics: the fact that reverie is a consciousness, whereas the night dream is unconscious. In *La Psychanalyse du feu* Bachelard first becomes aware of the problem:

> As it happens, one of the advantages of the psychoanalysis of objective knowledge that we are proposing to carry out seems to be that we are examining a zone that is less deep than that in which the primitive instincts function; and it is because this zone is intermediary that it has a determinative action on clear thought, on scientific thought. . . .
>
> Since we are limiting ourselves to psychoanalysing a psychic layer that is less deep, more intellectualised, we must replace the study of dreams by the study of reverie, and more particularly in this little book we must study the reverie before the fire. [P.F., 12–14]

As the phenomenological method develops, Bachelard comes to insist more and more on this distinction between dream and daydream that we see here in embryo. There is a vital and absolute line to be drawn between the two, the line between consciousness and the unconscious, between the presence or absence of a *cogito*. It is a distinction which ultimately comes to be the difference between phenomenology and psychology.

> In brief, it boils down to this: to determine the essence of reverie, one should come back to the reverie itself. And it is precisely by phenomenology that the distinction between dream and daydream can be elucidated, since the fact that consciousness is involved in reverie is the decisive mark. [P.R., 10]

The theory has now become the center of Bachelard's poetics, and we need to trace briefly some of its implications in the final period of his life.

Reverie implies solitude, the state where man finally encounters things in their true reality. It is creative and not passive; in other words, it is not the state where man is gradually lapsing into the unconscious world of dreams. It is the supremely creative state in which the poetic image is formed (though we should beware of using the passive voice here, since Bachelard often says that "image" is the subject of the verb "to imagine"). All the senses awaken and harmonize in poetic reverie. It is this polyphony of the senses that the reverie listens to, and which the poetic consciousness must register. Poetic reverie writes itself, or at least promises itself to write. Bachelard's philosophical ambition is large, and he admits it: "to prove that reverie gives us the world of a soul, that a poetic image bears witness to a soul as it discovers its world, the world where it would like to live, where it is worthy of living" (P.R., 14).

> The reverie operating poetically maintains us in a space of intimacy which stops at no frontier—a space uniting the intimacy of our dreaming being to the intimacy of the beings we dream. . . . All the being of the world amasses itself around the *cogito* of the dreamer. [P.R., 140]

In reverie, there is no longer a "non-I"; the word "no" has no meaning any longer. We are plunged into an inside that has no outside. In reverie, the purest state of the imagination, we lose the distinction of subject and object.

> The act of the creative consciousness [of the reader's as well as the poet's, since in reverie the reader repeats the creative act of the poet] must be systematically associated with the fleeting product of that consciousness, the poetic image. At the level of the poetic image, the duality of subject and object is iridescent, shimmering, unceasingly active in its inversions. [P.S., xv]

Reverie becomes a cosmic reverie, a completely unified existence. "The simplest hearth enfolds a universe" (P.R., 166).

It is in this state of reverie that the poetic image is formed. Bachelard's phenomenology concentrates on the emergence of the image in the individual psyche. The image has no past, it is a totally new event in the consciousness. And yet the strange fact is: it is communicable, it has a quality of trans-subjectivity. This communicability of the image is the subject that Bachelard later investigates. It comes to mean that the creative act of the poet's imagination, its intentionality, is repeated in that of the reader. The phenomenologist studies this fact of communication, but not as if he were in the world of science, the "real" world composed of external elements, perceived by the senses and coordinated by the intellect; he is in an unreal world, acting as a subjective power. That is, he is trying to fabricate within himself the world of the imagining man. One can only understand this imagining man by sharing his imagining, by reenacting the same act of imagination. The phenomenologist is, in fact, acting as the perfect reader of poetry—he becomes a poet himself. He has to keep himself from objectifying his own thoughts, his own act of consciousness. This is the problem, the paradox that we discover in the development of Bachelard's thought, and that we find in *La Psychanalyse du feu*—the problem that, in studying the subjective power objectively, you destroy its validity. And yet, how can you *study* something subjectively? In his phenomenological method, Bachelard answers the problem by attempting to become the subject, to *live* the subject.

Bachelard admits candidly that this involves leaving out of account all the "labor of composition." We noticed before that this was because of his distinction between the formal and the material imaginations, that he was not studying the synthesising power, but the image in its initial dynamism. An interesting development appears now in his later work. His study of the material imagination has become both concentrated and expanded. He is now studying the individual image as it emerges; and relating it to more categories than simply the four elements. But the old distinction reappears under a new guise. It is not the material imagination, but the "soul"; the formal imagination is now the "mind." He is studying the poetic image as it appears in the poet's soul, not as it is acted upon by the mind. We can see here, then, the development of Bachelard's earlier categories. He relates the notions of "soul" and reverie as essential to the poetic act.

> To specify exactly what a phenomenology of the image can be, to specify that the image comes *before* thought, we should have to say that poetry, rather than being a phenomenology of the mind, is a phenomenology of the soul. . . .
>
> The dialectics of inspiration and talent become clear if we study their two poles, the soul and the mind. In my opinion, soul and mind are indispensable for studying the phenomena of the poetic image in their various nuances, above all, for following the evolution of poetic images from the original state of reverie to that of execution. . . . To compose a finished, well-constructed poem, the mind

> is obliged to make projects that prefigure it. But for a simple poetic image, there is no project; a flicker of the soul is all that is needed. [P.S., xviff.]

A flicker of the soul. He quotes the poet Pierre-Jean Jouve to help make his point clearer: "Poetry is a soul inaugurating a form." Inaugurating it, not bringing it to its completion—that is the job of the talent, of the "mind," of what he used to call the formal imagination. In *La Poétique de l'espace* Bachelard promised to write a book on poetic reverie that would be a phenomenology of the soul, and that is how we must interpret *La Poétique de la rêverie,* his next book. It is in the soul, during reverie, that the poetic image emerges.

III

We have been following the development of the concept of reverie from its beginnings to its final enshrinement at the center of a poetic theory. We are going now to look back to that beginning, to a study in which the notion of reverie, and its accompanying idea of soul, seems false or at least an annoying interruption of the subjective psyche onto the objective world. As we look back, we move from the subjective study of the soul to the objective study of the rational intellect, but now, with hindsight, we can discern the fallacy that is at the basis of the earlier study. In viewing *La Psychanalyse du feu* we see the paradox that Bachelard became aware of himself only much later, yet which opened the way for the development of his future theory. This paradox exists in all the ways in which fire is linked to knowledge.

Although Bachelard was to interpret it as such later in his life, *La Psychanalyse du feu* is neither a study of the material imagination nor of the poetic image; those are the studies that grow out of it. It sets out, in fact, to be a contribution to the science of epistemology that had concerned Bachelard so much in his early period—a study of the general phenomena he had isolated in *La Formation de l'esprit scientifique.* The fact that the book does not finally come out like that is something for which aesthetics can be grateful, since it opened the way for the studies we have been outlining. There are, in a sense, two introductions in this book. One is his original project, the actual introduction which describes how he plans to test the particular phenomena of fire for subjective errors and eliminate them. By psychoanalyzing our convictions about fire, "we shall have many opportunities to show the dangers that first impressions, sympathetic attractions, and careless reveries hold for true scientific knowledge" (P.F., 3). But the other introduction is what, in retrospect, seems to be the true direction of the work. For he also sets himself another, very different, task, apparently rejecting the very psychoanalysis which had been his original objective.

> Petitjean was able to write that the imagination eludes the determinations of psychology—psychoanalysis included—and that it constitutes an autochthonous, autogenous realm. We subscribe to this view: rather than the will, rather than the *élan vital,* imagination is the true source of psychic production. Psychically we are created by our reverie—created and limited by our reverie—for it is the reverie which delineates the furthest limits of our mind. Imagination works at the summit of the mind like a flame. . . . We must then find the way to set ourselves at the place from which the original impulse is directed into various channels, doubtless led astray by its own anarchical tendency, but also impelled by the desire to charm others. [P.F., 110f.]

The rest of Bachelard's work is, in a sense, attempting to do just that—to find a way to set ourselves at the place at which the original impulse is formed.

We may notice here another important development or movement within the book, reflecting the overall trend we have been analysing. It sets out to be a study of the errors of the imagination; the tone is confident, ironic. Bachelard psychoanalyzes the subjective convictions related to the knowledge of fire phenomena, or "more briefly, a psychoanalysis of fire" (P.F., 5). He is attempting to establish "the secret persistence of this idolatry of fire," and consequently he examines documents from close to his own time. Since his purpose is to expose error, the most useful documents will be from pre-scientific literature, that is, documents which purport to be scientific but which, because of ignorance of modern scientific methods, are full of subjective illusions. But many of his examples are taken from poetry, initially for the purpose of exposing the subjective error more completely. But the literature of alchemy and the literature of poetry can only be lumped together as error like this when the focus is not on them so much as on what is left after they have been removed—the pure objectivity that Bachelard is pursuing. As soon as the focus shifts, as soon as he becomes more interested in what he is removing than what he is removing it from, he begins to realize that the poetic image is unique. There is a movement from considering literature as error to considering it in itself, from considering imaginative works as examples of something else, to considering them in themselves. He begins to turn his attention to the "pure heap of subjectivity" that we talked about earlier. This quite evidently is an important change of focus, and Bachelard is only partially aware in this book of its implications for a study of poetry. The poetics of this theory are to come later. But in the movement from pre-scientific to poetic literature, we can see its beginnings; we can see reflected here the movement from an objective pursuit of objectivity to the objective pursuit of subjectivity which we have been discovering in Bachelard's overall development. That is partly why the book is such a hodge-podge, since it represents the transition between the two interests.[16]

Bachelard groups the subjective values that we attribute to fire under separate heads that he calls "complexes," but in view of his anti-Freudian viewpoint we should consider them as something different from, though closely related to, the categories of classical psychology. They are networks of chain reactions, complexes of events within the mind that are set in motion merely by the contemplation of fire. There are several of these complexes, but only three of them need concern us here. In the theory of complexes are the seeds of what he is later to discuss as the "reverberation" of the poetic image. We imbue fire with values and attributes that it obviously does not have objectively. Among all phenomena, for example, it is the only one to which we can impute so definitely the opposing values of good and evil. "It shines in Paradise. It burns in Hell" (P.F., 7). The associations that we have with fire are both archetypal and personal, and there is no real problem here of the relation between those two aspects as there was to be later.

Let us look at the first of these complexes—the Prometheus complex. This is the basic complex associated with fire; and it is one that is closely linked with childhood. We avoid the fire because our father will rap our fingers if we get too close to it; thus the respect that we show to fire is originally a social respect, and it is our first *general* knowledge of fire. The Prometheus complex is an outgrowth of this and leads to our first *particular* knowledge of fire. In order to obtain it, we have to disobey our father, to outwit him. This is in fact a fundamental characteristic of man; it is the will to intellectuality. We can see already Bachelard's anti-reductionism here. Instead of explaining our desire to know about fire by the usefulness of the knowledge we are going to obtain, he looks at it in itself, as a will to know as much as our fathers do for its own sake. It may not be as basic an instinct as the Freudian Oedipus complex, but psychology must also study "minds of a rarer stamp" (P.F., 12). "The Prometheus complex is the Oedipus complex of the life of the mind" (P.F., 19). We are going to return later to this basic complex of our associations with fire, but it is noticeable that the linking of fire and knowledge is already apparent.

IV

There is an opposite complex associated with fire, and in this connection we can take account of Bachelard's more specifically literary interests. This complex is called the Empedocles complex, since it is the instinct for dying—the death wish. If the Prometheus complex is the wish to seize fire, an active wish, the Empedocles complex is the wish to be seized by the fire, an ultimately passive wish. Bachelard cites as an example a long and very Gothic fragment by George Sand, which is rather poor literature. This is significant because in bad literature the basic errors of the subjective mind that he is looking for are going to be more easily recognizable. At this point, Bachelard does not quote literature because he likes it, so much as because it helps him to expose the imaginative errors. But he follows this passage with an explicit comment about successful poetic works, and though we are here at the very beginning of Bachelard's literary criticism, we see a tendency that is going to come much more into evidence later.

> When one has recognized a psychological complex, it seems that one has a better and more synthetic understanding of certain poetic works. In point of fact a poetic work can hardly be unified except by a complex. If the complex is lacking, the work, cut off from its roots, no longer communicates with the unconscious. It appears cold, artificial, false. [P.F., 19]

Bachelard is talking here not exactly about form itself, but about a certain formal unity of the total poetic work, instead of what he comes later to concentrate on, the individual image. Even an unfinished work by Hölderlin, *Empedocles*, has a certain unity simply because it is grafted onto the Empedocles complex.

Secondly, the sole criterion here for the success of a poetic work seems to be the presence or absence of a complex, of some relation to the unconscious. Even when Bachelard narrows his theory, as it becomes more specifically literary, to a concentration on the poetic image itself, the same criterion seems to apply. The passage above sounds very similar to the previous citations from Bachelard's middle period, showing how he differentiated between image and metaphor; even in his final period, he still uses the same criterion—indeed, it is the only basis on which he presumes to judge literature.

Let us look forward for a moment to *La Poétique de l'espace*. Bachelard has just been analyzing what he calls "intimate immensity" in Baudelaire. It is one of the fundamental images of the psyche, and in the work of a great poet like Baudelaire, one can hear its call. This suggests, for one thing, that the purpose of poetry is to communicate these fundamental images (even with Baudelaire, who preceded "the century of images"), and also that we must judge poetry by whether it succeeds in doing so. In order to make his point clearer, he gives a passage from Taine's *Voyage aux Pyrénées* as an example of immensity that is not successful because it is not in touch with the fundamental image.

> "The first time I saw the sea," writes Taine, "I was most disagreeably disillusioned. . . . I seemed to see one of those long stretches of beet fields that one sees in the country near Paris, intersected by patches of green cabbage, and strips of russet barley. The distant sails looked like homing pigeons and even the outlook seemed narrow to me; painters had represented the sea as being much larger. It was three days before I recaptured the feeling of immensity."
>
> Beets, barley, cabbages, and pigeons in a perfectly artificial association! To bring them together in one "image" could only be a slip in the conversation of someone who is trying to be "original." For it is hard to believe that in the presence of the sea, anyone could be so obsessed by beet fields. [P.S., 199]

Two points need to be made here. First that the passage from Taine is treated a little like a statement by a client on the existential psychoanalyst's couch, and second, that there seems to be an implicit assumption that the presence of the sea, by itself, will produce the right associations. Thus any literature which does not reproduce those associations is not merely fiction, it is dishonest and therefore bad. There is a criterion of truth implied in the judging of literary works that we find almost explicitly stated in an earlier book, *La Terre et les rêveries de la volonté*:

> For me, the argument I want to discuss about the primitiveness of the image is immediately decided because I attach the true life of images to the archetypes whose activity psychoanalysis has demon-

> strated. Imagined images are sublimations of archetypes rather than reproductions of reality. And since sublimation is the most normal dynamism of the psyche, we shall be able to show that images come out of a true human depth. [T.R.V., 4]

Disregarding the difference, for the moment, between a work of Bachelard's middle and a work of his late periods we can see clearly enough the criterion implied, and the ultimate purpose of the study of literature. "I thought it possible, in the simple examination of the literary image, to discover an emergent activity of the imagination" (T.R.V., 7). Yet how can the critic be expected to achieve this task if the writer of literature lies about that "emergent activity of the imagination?"

Whether this is a justifiable reason for dividing literature into "good" and "bad," instead of some other category such as "useful for my purpose" or "not applicable to my purpose," is a complicated question. It involves deciding, for one thing, whether there is any better reason for dividing literature up in this way. The basis for the distinction is: does this image *work* or not? It is the same distinction, in effect, that Coleridge made between the fancy and the imagination: a good image for Bachelard, one of Baudelaire's for example, would be the product of the imagination in Coleridge's terms; a bad one, like that by Taine, would come solely from the fancy. There is, in fact, a good case for regarding Bachelard's work as an extension of Coleridge's theory. Whereas Coleridge was content to make such a distinction and examine a few favorite images in terms of it, Bachelard, with the advantage of twentieth-century psychological discoveries, and ultimately by the use of the phenomenological method, tries to explain in extreme detail *why* the Coleridgian category of the imagination produces great poetry, while the fancy can only associate objects like Taine's beets, barley, cabbages, and pigeons. In order to demonstrate the "why" of poetry, Bachelard examines the faculty that Coleridge associated with it, the creative imagination. Just as Coleridge was driven ultimately to metaphysical theories, so Bachelard gradually moves toward his later phenomenology, which he sometimes calls a metaphysics of the imagination. He states this explicitly in the final chapter on the phenomenology of roundness of *La Poétique de l'espace*, claiming that we have to "de-psychoanalyse" ourselves.

> Some five or ten years ago [that is, at about the time of the above quotation from *La Terre et les rêveries de la volonté*, in which images were specifically related to unconscious archetypes] in any

> psychological examination of images of roundness, . . . we should have laid stress on psychoanalytical explanations for which we could have collected an enormous amount of documentation, since everything round invites a caress. Such psychoanalytical explanations are, no doubt, largely sound. But they do not tell everything, and above all they cannot be put in the direct line of ontological determinations. When a metaphysician tells us that being is round, he displaces all psychological determinations at one time. He rids us of a past of dreams and thoughts, at the same time that he invites us to actuality of being. [Bachelard has already changed Jaspers' statement "*Jedes Dasein scheint in sich rund,*" to "*das Dasein* ist *rund,*" in order to abolish the doublet of being and appearance, when we mean the entire being in its roundness.] It is not likely that a psychoanalyst would become attached to this actuality enclosed in the very being of an expression. From his standpoint such an expression is humanly insignificant because of the very fact of its rarity. But it is this rarity that attracts the attention of the phenomenologist and encourages him to look with fresh eyes, with the perspective of being that is suggested by metaphysicians and poets. [P.S., 236f.]

That last sentence is perhaps as close as we can get to an understanding of the reason for the poetic quality of Bachelard's final metaphysical period, and we should notice how the poet's and the metaphysician's approach are equated. Both are an attempt to look with fresh eyes from a new "perspective of being."

If this was to be the final direction of Bachelard's thought, to explain the "why" of poetry in metaphysical terms, we can see why the method of *La Psychanalyse du feu* was inadequate. In retrospect, we can see this growing apparent.

V

After examining the Prometheus and the Empedocles complexes, *La Psychanalyse du feu* goes on to isolate several other complexes around the central archetype of fire: the associations of sex, alchemy, and alcohol. But for our examination of the central paradox of Bachelard's work, the most interesting is the last complex he studies, in which fire is seen as a purifying force, and ultimately as purity itself. We are back at the beginning again. The whole book is based on the assumption that in order to know something about fire we must first know something about the mind that claims to know fire, so that the problem of the knowledge of fire is a true problem of psychological structure. When we see how fire becomes a symbol of purity, how this becomes another of the complexes of fire, we assume some structure of the mind that makes it so, an impulse to purity. Freudian psychology is thus wrong, as Max Scheler had pointed out (P.F., 99), to reduce all love for spiritual things to a shrewdly sublimated sexual love; that is confusing the kernel and the shell, reducing the word "love" to a literal, not a metaphorical meaning. We should consider it rather as a true impulse to purity, and consequently as the impulse to repress impurities.[17] In fact, Bachelard justifies this kind of repression in very un-Freudian fashion; he talks about repression as a joyful activity, as the joy in accepting limitations that is inherent in all learning. The fire symbol has now come full circle in the course of the book; just as it began as the Prometheus complex—the impulse to intellectuality—so it now becomes, at the end, the symbol of joy in learning. It is now time to draw a conclusion from this close connection between fire and knowledge.

Bachelard does not fully realize the implications of his discoveries for his own epistemology. True, he does relate this learning pleasure to his own work:

> In our own field of study, through the application of psychoanalytical methods to the activity of *objective knowledge,* we have arrived at the conclusion that repression is a normal activity, a useful activity, better a joyful activity. There can be no scientific thought without repression. Repression is at the origin of concentrated, reflective, and abstract thought. Every coherent thought is constructed on a system of sound, clear inhibitions. There is a *joy in accepting limitations* inherent in all joy of learning. It is insofar as it is joyful that a well-founded repression becomes dynamic and useful. [P.F., 100]

In his joy at this new idea, Bachelard even goes on to apply it to methods of psychiatry. "The truly anagogical cure does not consist in liberating the repressed tendencies, but of substituting for the unconscious repression a conscious repression, a constant will to self-correction." But he was going beyond himself, and soon realized his mistake; in fact, he says exactly the opposite of this in *L'Air et les songes* (see A.S., 8). We are back with the original paradox, where the smelting analogy depicted the separating of objective from subjective. The problem can be stated as follows.

All the other subjective values attributed to fire have been dismissed as errors in the pursuit of objective knowledge, of the purification of the object from all subjective impurities. Yet now we find that the pursuit itself of purity, of objective knowledge, is a subjective value attributed to fire; it is our impulse to repress the subjective errors we make in the process of learning. Bachelard's book has been an objective study of subjectivity, that is, he has been treating subjectivity as an object. He has been using the psychoanalysis of fire as a means to expose the subjective errors that the seductive imagination is liable to lead the rational intellect into. But he has now discovered that the impulse to pure objectivity itself is an aspect of the imagination. Now if he has been clearing away as error all the other subjective and imaginative responses to fire should he not now also clear away this impulse to repress impurities as itself subjective, and therefore error? It would seem inevitable that he is led to this conclusion, yet he does not realize it until long afterwards, when he finally adopts the subjective method. Ironically, Bachelard seems to have been aware of this fact, even in *La Psychanalyse du feu,* though he did not make the connection with his own method. In his conclusion he refers to what later became the central statement of his phenomenology, the need to keep from objectifying oneself: "It is impossible to escape this dialectic: to be aware that one is burning is to grow cold; to feel an intensity is to diminish it; it is necessary to be an intensity without realizing it. Such is the bitter law of man's activity" (P.F., 112).

VI

We have been dividing Bachelard's work into periods, but now the rigid distinctions between the three periods begin to blur. One period *grows* out of another, there is no sudden reversal. Just as we saw the gradual transition from one study to another as we moved through *La Psychanalyse du feu,* so we can now see the confession of subjectivity that he makes at the outset of his final period (in the Introduction to *La Poétique de l'espace*) adumbrated in his second book on the material imagination in 1942, which is called, significantly, *L'Eau et les rêves,* and not *La Psychanalyse de l'eau.* He claims to be a rationalist, but if we listen carefully, as Bachelard would always have us do, we can hear the notes of his final period:

> Rationalist? I am trying to become one, not only in our culture as a whole but in the detail of our thoughts, of our imaginations. By a psychoanalysis of objective knowledge and of "imagified" knowledge, I became a rationalist in my view of fire. Sincerity obliges me to confess that I have not achieved the same objectivity with water. The images of water I live again synthetically in their first complexity, in often giving them my irrational adhesion.[18]

Between the beginning and the end, indeed, between the study of the intellect and the study of the imagination, there is an absolute polarity. From his last period, he looks back on his first period, the psychoanalytical period, with aversion. It is called "mere psychoanalysis," that criticism which makes a man out of a poet, but does not explain how to make a poet out of a man (P.R., 9). Nor does it explain what we have been calling the "why" of poetry.

So we were oversimplifying when we divided his three periods into the objective study of objectivity, the objective study of subjectivity, and the subjective study of subjectivity. But there is this basic movement from one extreme to the other, and we must see it as a progressive attempt to be honest about poetry. It is a movement towards phenomenology, because phenomenology is the only method which truly faces the reality of the poetic experience. It refuses to become objective to itself and thus destroy the unique validity of the poetic essence.

We have been examining the treatment of fire in Bachelard's *objective* method. By way of contrast, we can look at an example of how he talks *subjectively* about a literary fire in his last major work, *La Poétique de la rêverie.*[19] Bachelard has just quoted a beautiful passage, describing a fireside reverie, from the novel *Malicroix* by his favorite author, Henri Bosco. Though the method of this final period is subjective, we need to see that Bachelard still emphasises the communicability of the subjective experience.

> What other pages does one need to contemplate in order to understand that fire *inhabits* the house? In the utilitarian fashion one would say that fire makes the house habitable. An expression like that belongs to the language of those who do not know the reveries of the word "inhabit." Fire transmits its friendliness to the whole house, and thus makes the House into a Cosmos of warmth. Bosco knows that, says that: "The air expanding in the heat, filled all the corners of the house, pressing against the walls, the earth, the

> low ceiling, the heavy furniture. Life flowed around from the fire to the closed doors and from the doors to the fire, tracing invisible circles of heat that floated across my face. . . ."
>
> Someone will object, perhaps, as he reads this page, that the writer is not telling his reverie, but that he is describing his well-being in a closed room. But let us read better, let us read and dream, let us read and remember. It is of ourselves, dreamers, of ourselves, that the writer is speaking. With us too, the fire has kept company. We too have known the fire's friendship. We communicate with the writer because we communicate with the images we keep in the depths of our selves. We return to dream in those rooms where we knew the friendship of the fire. [P.R., 167f.]

The difference between this and his earlier approach, both to fire and to literature, is obvious. Far from dismissing the fireside reverie as the source of subjective errors which get in the way of our objective knowledge about fire, he is treating it as an example of the supreme poetic experience—the activity of the poetic imagination. Reading the literary description of a reverie, Bachelard partakes in that reverie. He describes it to us, and urges us to take part in it too, by the activity of our own imaginations. He wants us to share the happiness that comes from this kind of unified reverie. One is no longer lonely, no longer suffering existential *Angst*, or the sense of division within the self. "Outside time, outside space, before the fire, our being is no longer chained to a *Dasein.*" In reverie we flow with the well-being of the world, a well-being that "teaches me to be the same as myself" (P.R., 166).

This new kind of fireside reverie duplicates the poetic experience. It gets its importance partly from the sense of cosmic union, where "the soul is no longer ensconced in its corner of the world. It is at the center of the world, at the center of *its* world. The simplest hearth enfolds a universe" (P.R., 166). Thus Bachelard claims that the state of poetic reverie is healthful partly because it abolishes the distinction between subject and object, between the self and Nature. That distinction is a product of the intellect. He sounds very like Coleridge here, with the "coalescence of subject and object" through the activity of the imagination. What Bachelard is doing is taking over one of the central notions of the phenomenological movement (which itself owes much to the Kantian tradition which Coleridge drew upon): reality is an aspect of phenomena, it does not subsist in a division of the perceiver and the perceived. We need to notice how different this is from the Cartesian methods of his early period, which involved arriving at objective knowledge by a ruthless dismissal of all imaginative responses to the object. Where the initial desire was to separate subject and object, this final period praises their union. The former was a destructive attempt, but the latter describes the creative state.

> One could not say of the man of reverie that he is tossed into the world with a jolt. The world is entirely friendly to him, and he himself is the principle of friendship. The dreamer is the double consciousness of his well-being and of the happy world. His *cogito* is not divided into a dialectic of subject and object.
>
> The correlation of the dreamer to his world is a powerful one. . . . To doubt the worlds of reverie one must stop dreaming, come out of one's reverie. The man of reverie and the world of his reverie are very close, they touch, they penetrate each other. They are on the same level of being. . . . I dream the world, therefore the world exists as I dream it. [P.R., 134f.]

Even here Bachelard still takes account of that Cartesian suspicion, that doubt which one might feel outside the poetic reverie. But that doubt is an activity of the intellect, not of the imagination. Bachelard still wants to separate the two, but the emphasis is reversed. Now, in this subjective period, he wants to stop the intellect intruding upon the proper field of the imagination. This is the complete opposite of his earlier interest. His final denial of the objective method of literary criticism is closely related to this desire to keep the intellect out of the field of imaginative experience. The intellect functions properly only when it is being truly objective; thus its opposite, the imagination, can only truly realize itself in absolute subjectivity.

Evidently Bachelard recognized the impossibility of achieving either ideal, but he still felt the importance of trying to maintain the polarity of intellect and imagination. He tried not to make any comparative value judgments between them and he was happy in either pursuit, but in view of this kind of cosmic happiness which can be the result of imaginative experience, one can understand why he came to concentrate more and more on the studies of the imagination. The last years of his life were devoted to pursuing the happiness of the imagination, and in the quality of the two kinds of happiness we can see his preference for imaginative activity. The joy in learning which he had talked about in *La Psychanalyse du feu* was a repressive joy, it narrowed itself to meet the purity of its object. But the joy of *La Poétique de la rêverie* is an expansive joy, it flows outward to become as large as the cosmos. It has no object, for in this world there is no "non-I." The only way to be faithful to this experience of poetic union is to be a poet oneself, to repeat the subjective activity of the poet through the methods of phenomenology. In order to understand the unique world of the poet, you have to live that world yourself.

NOTES

1. Gaston Bachelard, *L'Air et les songes* (Paris, 1943), p. 7. Future references are included in the text, and abbreviated as A.S. All translations are my own except for citations from the two works already translated into English (see below).

2. Georges Poulet, *The Interior Distance*, trans. Elliott Coleman (Ann Arbor, 1964), p. viii.

3. Cited in C. O. Christofides, "Bachelard's Aesthetics," *Journal of Aesthetics and Art Criticism*, XX (1961–62), 268f.

4. Bachelard, *La Terre et les rêveries de la volonté* (Paris, 1948), p. 6. (Abbreviated as T.R.V. in future.)

5. Bachelard, *La Poétique de l'espace* (Paris, 1957). References are to the English translation by Maria Jolas, *The Poetics of Space* (New York, 1964), and abbreviated as P.S.

6. Bachelard, *La Psychanalyse du feu* (Paris, 1938). References are to the English translation by Alan Ross, *The Psychoanalysis of Fire* (Boston, 1964), and abbreviated as P.F.

7. This optimism is a dominant characteristic of Bachelard's thinking. Though there are times when his ideas sound a little like Sartre's, especially "the function of the unreal," he has none of Sartre's horror at what he takes to be a totally meaningless existence. Bachelard's reality is warm and friendly, like the fireside reverie which becomes so important for him.

8. In the tape-recording cited note 3.

9. Bachelard, *La Formation de l'esprit scientifique* (Paris, 1938), p. 23.

10. Georges Poulet, "Bachelard et la conscience de soi," *Revue de Métaphysique et de Morale*, LXX (1965), 4. (I have drawn considerably on this article for my argument.) Bachelard actually wrote a book called *La Philosophie du non* (Paris, 1940).

11. Poulet, "Bachelard et la conscience de soi."

12. He had wanted to teach literature, but was not allowed to since he held the chair of the philosophy of science, and the department could not have its man teaching literature.

13. We need not be concerned that the imagination of movement is also the dynamic imagination. Similarly, the material imagination is also the imagination of matter. Bachelard means exactly what he says—the materialization of the imagination. He is talking about a world in which there is no distinction between subject and object, nor between subjective and objective genitives.

14. See Mikel Dufrenne, "Gaston Bachelard et la poésie de l'imaginaire," *Etudes philosophiques*, N.S. XVIII (1963). This would mean that poetry has nothing to do with dead metaphors or the vulgar commonplaces that occur in everyday conversation. Bachelard would exclude, with Mallarmé, "les mots de la tribu." Compare this passage from *La Poétique de la rêverie*, p. 137: "What a relief the poetic image is in our language! If only we could speak this lofty language, climb with the poet into that solitude of the speaking being which gives a new sense to *the words of the tribe*, then we would be in a realm where the active man cannot enter, the man for whom the world of reveries is 'just a dream.'" There are many important affinities between Bachelard and symbolism; he too is talking about an image which both elicits and requires the activity of the reader to complete it.

15. *La Poétique de la rêverie* (Paris, 1960), p. 45f. (Abbreviated to P.R. in future references.)

16. Bachelard recognized its incompleteness later, in the tape-recording previously cited. He called it "ragged."

17. The word I am translating here as "true" is "*propre*," not "*vrai*," but I think the implication is clear enough.

18. Bachelard, *L'Eau et les rêves* (Paris, 1942), p. 3.

19. Fire remained one of Bachelard's chief interests, and his final work, *La Flamme d'une chandelle*, began as an attempt to write a poetics of fire, and thus return to the subject which, by alerting him to the importance of reverie, had begun his literary studies so long ago.

Northrop Frye and the Necessary Hybrid: Criticism as Aesthetic Humanism

PETER CUMMINGS
HOBART COLLEGE

I

THE WORK OF NORTHROP FRYE, already voluminous and still increasing in bulk, stands as a challenge to modern literary criticism. The pressure felt by critics to come to terms with the man and his work is illustrated by the recent volume from the English Institute, *Northrop Frye in Modern Criticism*,[1] in which the editor, Murray Krieger, writes,

> Whatever the attitude toward Northrop Frye's prodigious scheme, one cannot doubt that, in what approaches a decade since the publication of his masterwork, he has had an influence—indeed an absolute hold—on a generation of developing literary critics greater and more exclusive than any one theorist in recent critical history.[2]

Statements like this, taken together with less sympathetic views of his work, show quite dramatically how important and yet how troublesome a gadfly Frye has been to the critical community. And, as in the case of that earlier Athenian gadfly, Socrates, there have even been sidelong glances and informal mutterings which indicate a suspicion that Frye may be corrupting the youth who gather at his feet.

It is safe to say that Frye can well enough provide his own reply to the charges of these critics. For most readers, the first order of business is rather to delineate the basic perspective of Frye's work in the form in which it has been developed and applied in his major essays. If one takes a larger view of Frye's work, at the expense of course of its fascinating details, many achievements become apparent and their interrelations can be understood. But something of a paradox emerges as well, for in Frye's work the disinterested philosophy of aesthetic literary criticism and the socially conscious philosophy of humanistic criticism threaten to meet head-on as irresistible force and immovable object. Frye himself recognizes this antithesis. It is dealt with explicitly and self-consciously at several points in his criticism, and it is ultimately resolved in something like a mature and willing resignation. That is, Frye seems to conclude that the paradox is inevitable. Moreover, he concludes that the fundamental dualism of literature as both a disinterested art and a product of the engaged human imagination, makes it impossible for criticism to be perfectly consistent. But to be so it must become a hybrid of two distinct and apparently antithetical mental attitudes.

When Northrop Frye began his study of Blake in about 1934 as a graduate student under Herbert Davis at the University of Toronto, he probably did not realize it would change his life. That did happen, of course, as Frye readily admits, and we may look to his study of Blake's Prophetic Books for the single greatest influence on the formulation of his theory of literature and criticism. As he says in his article "The Road of Excess," referring to his books *Fearful Symmetry* and *Anatomy of Criticism*, "it was obvious to anyone who read both books that my critical ideas had been derived from Blake."[3] It will be interesting, then, to refer to *Fearful Symmetry* for a glimpse of the germ of Frye's theory before it reached the awesome and abundant flowering evident in *Anatomy of Criticism* ten years later. In the final chapter of *Fearful Symmetry*, called "The Burden of the Valley of Vision," Frye suggests by his title as well as direct description the task which the study of Blake placed on his shoulders. "We cannot understand Blake," writes Frye,

> without understanding how to read the Bible, Milton, Ovid and the Prose Edda at least as he read them, on the assumption that an archetypal vision, which all great art without exception shows forth to us, really does exist. . . . if he is right, the ability we gain by deciphering him is transferable, and the value of studying him extends beyond our personal interest in Blake himself.[4]

Frye goes on to suggest that in consequence of this archetypal vision, all symbolism in art and religion might be intelligible to all men and ultimately might yield something like an "iconography of the imagination." The consequences of this discovery would, in Frye's terms via Blake, be a humanistic cultural revolution which would absorb cultural differences and produce a visionary synthesis by which a culture's response to art would be deepened and broadened, and by which a certain "catholicity of outlook that Montaigne and Shakespeare possessed"[5] would be restored to the artist. Frye's humanistic penchant was thus made clear quite early. More on this later, however.

At this stage Frye was quite obviously willing to see the close relationship between the study of literature from this archetypal point of view and comparative religion, psychology, anthropology, etc. That is, he was willing to consider the possibility of psychological explanations for the presence of archetypes in literature. He says that the study of these disciplines taken together with the study of literature "will lead us to a single visionary conception which the mind of man is trying to express."[6] This catholicity of attitude toward separate disciplines as important keys to the nature of man recalls Ernst Cassirer's philosophy of symbolic forms. In Cassirer's work there is a similar interest in the consequences of studying varied human constructs such as language and myth for their symbolic manifestations of the nature of the human mind.

In addition, however, it is important to note that in *Fearful Symmetry* Frye is already treading the heavily guarded border between aesthetic and humanistic criticism. For while he says he is categorically against making the point that Blake's work presents a message for modern times, he insists that the "shivering virgin theory of art," or the view of art as a completely disinterested realm which must remain unpolluted by any relations with humanity, has nothing to be said for it. This willingness to emphasize both the *dolce* and the *utile* of literary experience is dramatically evident on Frye's part in the following passage from *Fearful Symmetry*:

> If it were possible to delight without instruction, there would be no qualitative difference between painting the Sistine ceiling and cutting out paper dolls; if it were possible to instruct without delighting, art would be merely the kindergarten class of philosophy and science.[7]

In *Anatomy of Criticism*, however, we can see significant changes in and further developments of these attitudes. For instance, Frye makes a drastic change in his attitude toward the coherence of literary criticism with psychology, anthropology, etc. In *Anatomy* he insists with a kind of aesthetic vehemence on the autonomy of archetypal criticism from these other disciplines, and claims a purely literary origin for archetypes. At one point in his later career Frye even subsumes comparative religion and depth-psychology under the study of literature as a total mythic form, and calls *The Golden Bough* and Jung's work on archetypes "primarily studies in literary criticism."[8] The reason for Frye's changed attitude is not a desire to claim complete originality for his system, but the far-reaching theory, presented in *Anatomy of Criticism*, that everything verbal, including the disciplines of psychology and anthropology, belongs to a total verbal universe, articulated in myths and structured by archetypes, which has grown up systematically with man's imaginative attempt to formulate a world apart from his natural environment that expresses his desires and dreams.

In *Anatomy* we see also that Frye fully develops his notions of the dual nature of literature and criticism, which were only embryonic in *Fearful Symmetry*. He goes far beyond the rather limited aphoristic pronouncement on instruction and delight we saw in that book. His understanding of the necessity of both aesthetic and humanistic attitudes deepens in *Anatomy*, and his syncretism of those attitudes is both sophisticated and convincing. In both *Anatomy* and *The Educated Imagination* of 1963, Frye elaborates the implications of the aesthetic position while exploring and amplifying the humanistic position. We shall see, however, that the humanistic element of his criticism is never merely imposed on literature from without, but is rather discovered within the imaginative dimension of literature itself.

II

In dealing with *Anatomy of Criticism* one soon discovers that its "Polemical Introduction" is as germane an introduction to the text which follows as any book has enjoyed. It is the seed of all that follows. In the introduction Frye describes his book as essays "on the possibility of a synoptic view of the scope, theory, principles, and techniques of literary criticism."[9] His polemic has started, then, since Frye is assuming that a synoptic view of literature is possible—an assumption against the grain of those who assume criticism is doomed to multiple and conflicting approaches.

Over the course of the whole introduction Frye's urbane polemicism is quite clear, and refreshing for the sharp swaths it cuts through the dense wood of criticism. Frye's bold iconoclasm is most evident, of course, in the major argument of the introduction, that criticism is an inductive science which must refuse to proceed on grounds outside literature itself. Criticism must be to literature what physics is to nature, says Frye; therefore it must proceed inductively from the nature of its literary data to the postulates of a critical science. As the central discipline of the humanities with its flanking disciplines of philosophy and history, literature has provided an all too convenient springboard into these other areas, as literary criticism up to now indicates. Frye suggests that literary critics might avoid literature's distracting neighbors by believing that "just as there is an order of nature behind the natural sciences, so literature is not a piled aggregate of 'works,' but an order of words."[10]

For Frye, then, there is inherent in the nature of literature a quality that enables the science of criticism which deals with it to be a systematic discipline. Taking this stand, Frye dismisses as invalid the Marxist, Freudian, Jungian, and existentialist schools of criticism, and all others which are founded on extra-literary bodies of knowledge. This has not quieted the critics, however, and M. H. Abrams has assigned Frye's theory to the category of those which are fostered by "important intellectual developments outside the field of literature."[11] Opinion may well be divided on this point, though, for while Professor Abrams seems not to have given Frye sufficient credit for proceeding as empirically as he does, neither has Frye given theorists such as Frazer, Freud, Jung, and Cassirer sufficient credit for important influences which they have very definitely supplied.[12]

Much of the energy behind Frye's attempt to make criticism a rigorous science—complete with postulates, axioms, a *modus operandi*, and autonomy from other disciplines—is his wish to distinguish genuine criticism from what turns out to be a history of taste fluctuating according to the climate of professional prejudices. In short, criticism for Frye must be disinterested to the point of steadfastly refusing to make value judgments, and in one of his more emotional moments in the introduction he vociferously deprecates all criticism which involves direct evaluation. This includes, he says, "all casual, sentimental and prejudiced value judgments, and all literary chit-chat which makes the reputations of poets boom and crash in an imaginary stock exchange."[13]

Frye's clearest statement of the reason for his disavowal of evaluative criticism came after *Anatomy* in 1963 in his article "The Road of Excess." In it he explains that there are fundamentally two kinds of response to a work of literature. The first is a "response in time," in which the reader follows the formal design of the work as it unfolds in dramatic, narrative, lyric, etc., time. This response is essentially precritical, according to

Frye, and involves an engaged, interested, emotional response to literature. To quote Frye, "the second kind of response is thematic, detached, fully conscious, and one which sees and is capable of examining the work as a simultaneous whole."[14] It is this second response which earns Frye's approval as the only one in which judgment based on temporary standards of taste is not inevitable. As Frye unqualifiedly says in *The Well-Tempered Critic* of 1963, "the fundamental act of criticism is a disinterested response to a work of literature in which all one's beliefs, engagements, commitments, prejudices, stampedings of pity and terror, are ordered to be quiet."[15] It is important to notice that Frye does not degrade the emotional response to literature in itself; he realizes it is primary and necessary. It is only when this response functions without justification as a basis of critical judgment that Frye attacks it. Always for Frye "criticism as knowledge is one thing, and value judgments informed by taste are another."[16]

At this point, however, it is necessary to raise the question of how far it is possible to separate one's personal and analytical responses to literature. Probably every honest reader will admit that there have been times when he has found it impossible. Moreover, W. K. Wimsatt has leveled at Frye the charge that despite his repudiation of value judgments he makes them throughout his work. In both his essay for the English Institute volume, "Criticism as Myth," and in his book *Hateful Contraries*, Wimsatt contends that Frye is vague and inconsistent on the subject of value in criticism. He notes that in *The Well-Tempered Critic* Frye says that "both intellect and emotion are fully and simultaneously involved in all our literary experience"[17]—a pronouncement which jars with Fyre's implications elsewhere that at a certain point emotion should stop and intellect take over. I suspect that Frye's answer to the problem might be, like T. S. Eliot's in a similar impasse, that the only solution is to be very intelligent. Later we shall see that Frye accepts evaluation, but evaluation of a fundamentally different sort than is normally understood by critics.

But whether or not Northrop Frye himself achieves the disinterestedness which he advocates for criticsm, it is clear, as we step back to see the larger pattern of his recommendations, that his ideal is a criticism which operates at an aesthetic distance from canons of taste and morality and so is able to regard the work as a pure imaginative creation. For Frye, only when criticism has achieved freedom from the tyranny of taste and fashionable prejudice, and when the work has been isolated for examination solely in the context of literature itself, only then may there be a discussion of the particular ways in which criticism is to view the work. Of course it is to be understood that by this time criticism has also disburdened itself of what W. K. Wimsatt calls the intentional fallacy. Frye is very outspoken on this matter. "The assertion," he says,

> that the critic should confine himself to "getting out" of a poem exactly what the poet may vaguely be assumed to have been aware of "putting in," is one of the many slovenly illiteracies that the absence of a systematic criticism has allowed to grow up.[18]

Frye's branding of this limitation of criticism with the memorable tag of "premature teleology" is a graphic illustration of the extent to which Frye is willing to assume an unqualified aesthetic position. In the consideration of a poem we must isolate it even from the potential distortion which a consideration of the poet's intention might be. Frye's defense of the autonomy of the art work extends even to a conception of the artist as mere efficient cause. That revision is possible in poems, and that revisions are better (not merely *seem* better) proves, says Frye, that poems are born of a coherent literary universe and not merely of the unpredictable will of an individual mind.

In Frye's denial of the validity of criticism which swings with scholarly preferences or seeks to surround the work with its worldly origins in the intentions of its author, one recognizes the influence of the aesthetic tradition. And, as one hears echoes of Kant and Coleridge in Frye's notion of the primacy of the human imagination, one recognizes the vital basis of this tradition. But this emerges more clearly in the essays themselves.

In the first essay of *Anatomy of Criticism* Frye presents an ambitious scheme for a history of Western literature. In it the first three elements —*mythos*, *dianoia*, *ethos*—of Aristotle's six elements of poetry are central. A classification of the hero's power of action in fictional literature (in which *mythos* is dominant), and the attitude assumed by the poet toward his audience in thematic literature (*dianoia* dominant), yields a series of five modulations of *ethos*, or five "modes." These modes—Myth, Romance, High mimetic, Low mimetic, and Ironic—may be seen as the body of original, pure myth which becomes ever more displaced throughout history. In this way, the five modes indicate the historical development of the fundamental nature of literature, for over the fifteen centuries of its history the basic character of European fiction has steadily moved down the list of the five modes. If Frye's system has any validity, then the cultural revolution which he speaks of at the end of *Fearful Symmetry*, with its unification of responses to art and the return of a catholicity of outlook to the artist, would replace the present Ironic and Satiric mode with a kind of Neo-High mimetic mode.

Frye's laudable purpose in proposing a history of literature based on a natural succession of five modes within literature itself is to remedy the present situation in which the critic must borrow a framework of events from the historian and a framework of ideas from the philosopher. With a framework structured from literature itself, Frye hopes to keep criticism autonomous and to make possible the display of individual works against the "total form" of literature as a whole.

In viewing Frye's theory in the first essay it is helpful to refer to Angus Fletcher's essay in *Northrop Frye in Modern Criticism*. Mr. Fletcher reminds us of the impossibility of a truly objective historiography, and suggests that we may understand Frye's particular distortion as "utopian." No one believes that literature conforms to Frye's five-mode structure; it does not and in the nature of things could not. But it would be pointless to challenge Frye's system on these grounds. Quite obviously Frye is up to something more than an accurate description of literary history. His essay is but one form of the endless human attempt to give order to the messy past, a kind of Stevens-like "blessed rage for order" in surveying the chaos of the literary scene. Frye's "metahistory" of literature is the imaginative creation of a meaningfully ordered pattern against which to display existing literary works. The question to ask about this kind of historiography is not whether it is right or wrong, but whether the order it attempts to create is an order which is meaningful according to one's own particular sense of the literary past. Fletcher sees Frye's history as utopian because he has introduced "sacred time" into linear history and has thus created an imaginative cycle or rhythm of change and recurrence. According to Fletcher, Frye's theory in this way becomes "periodic, festive, memorial and dancelike."[19]

In his second essay on ethical criticism Frye proposes a counter balance to historical criticism in which we study literary works "as we do the stars, seeing their relationships, but not approaching them."[20] By stressing the symbolic nature of literature and in turn the ahistorical and multi-leveled nature of symbolism, Frye can say that ethical criticism deals with literature as a communication from past to present and stresses the meaning of works as they reach beyond their particular historical modes to create an impact on the contemporary milieu. Frye's justification for this disregard of history is his belief that literature has a potential relation to present reality which grows out of the relationship between literary creation and the worlds of truth and fact.[21] In the glossary of the *Anatomy* a symbol is defined as "any unit of any work which can be isolated for critical study." Depending on the particular unit isolated, and depending on the critical distance at which one stands from the work, Frye suggests that the symbol may be seen in five distinct ways: as simple motif, as connotative sign, as an image, as a metaphor, and finally as a monad, or universal symbol.

We come to see in this rather relativistic series of approaches to a work that Frye is a staunch supporter of the notion of "polysemous meaning" in the tradition of Dante's letter to Can Grande. (Typical of Northrop Frye's ambition and tradition-breaking spirit, however, is his raising the number of interpretative levels from four to five—after renovating Dante's original four levels quite drastically, of course.) But Frye is aware of the serious consequences for criticism of the endorsement of polysemous meaning. It poses the choice to criticism between the proliferation of endless numbers of critical methods in a relativistic system, and a situation in which "we can go on to consider the possibility that there is a finite number of valid critical methods, and that they can all be contained in a single theory."[22] This idea of a single theory of criticism lies at the heart of Northrop Frye's work, and it is the detailed schematization of this vast idea which Frye places with such conviction before the reader in the *Anatomy*, especially in the third essay.

Frye's discussion of anagogic criticism, which closes the second essay, sets the stage for this major phase of his theory. There he posits the bold idea of the "total form" of the verbal universe in which literature participates. Frye sees literature as "existing in its own universe, no longer a commentary on life or reality, but containing life and reality in a system of verbal relationships."[23] In this view life must be seen as merely the "seed-plot of literature," the rank and chaotic garden of potential literary fruits which only the artist will nurture, and even totally create. The implications of such a notion recall that audacious Blakean inversion of all Western philosophy. In this attitude the work of art, which had been seen before as the artifact, the artificial imitation of an existing action in a real nature now becomes the living creation which has grown by the power of its own intrinsic organic energy out of the inert "seed-plot" of nature. Nature comes to be seen as a delusion, the "Ulro" of Blake's universe where only chaos and nothingness reign.

This Blake-Frye theory of art seems to go even beyond Kant in asserting the primacy of the human imagination. For although at times it seems to be founded on the assumption of a *Ding an sich* which supplies the data to be reworked by the imagination, at other times the creative artistic imagination and the order of words which it creates (and *from which* it creates again) seems totally distinct from any reliance on the phenomenal world. On the anagogic level, says Frye, we see that

> nature becomes not the container but the thing contained, and the archetypal universal symbols . . . are no longer the desirable forms that man constructs inside nature, but are themselves the forms of nature. Nature is now inside the mind of an infinite man who builds his cities out of the milky way.[24]

While on the one hand this element of Frye's theory has been subject to parody by Kenneth Burke,[25] it is, after all, the twentieth century, and it is well, in an age of scientific revolution and power politics which even now are operating in full disregard of artistic insights and human values, that we have among us a perceptive and eloquent critic who is asking us to regroup our scattered forces and discover what we can know of and do for imaginative man.

To return to the subject, then, the direction of Frye's argument on anagogic criticism is toward a proof of Sidney's contention that "nature's world is brazen; the poets only deliver a golden," and perhaps even beyond. For on this rarefied level there is the additional suggestion that nature's brass is completely fake while poetry's gold is genuine. At these, the highest esoteric reaches of Frye's critical theory, it is quite plain that his alignment with the aesthetic attitude toward criticism is strong. For Frye, criticism must see that the freedom and autonomy of the artistic imagination is absolute; it must view the product of that imagination as a phenomenon possessing an elusive *Zweckmässigkeit ohne Zweck* which frees it from the interests of the natural world, and because of this it must regard as unnatural any tendency to grade or even display the work against a system of values which grows out of the natural world. There can be no "should" or "must" statements directed by criticism to the artist, there can be no flinching at or restriction of the subjects or methods of art. In short, criticism has nothing to say to art, but everything to say for it. In all his strictures for criticism Frye's "hands off art" attitude is quite clear. Art must be and will be what it is. In his third essay Frye reinforces this aesthetic position, but at the same time his moving back to the ultimate critical distance from works of literature—the distance at which their informing archetypes are visible—

causes certain patterns to appear which indicate that another critical attitude may or even must be adopted.

III

In his third essay Frye proceeds swiftly to the heart of his subject by suggesting that the structural unit of literature is the archetype. Just as the structural principles of painting are derived from geometry, so "the structural principles of literature are to be derived from archetypal and anagogic criticism."[26] For Western literature the Bible and classical mythology provide what Frye calls "the grammar of literary archetypes." Myths and their archetypes, however, seldom appear directly in literature. Rather, they appear in displaced forms, displacement being by Frye's definition the adaptation of myth and metaphor to canons of morality and plausibility. This idea has led Frye in another place to describe literature as a whole as a "displaced mythology."[27]

The relation of this essay to the first two emerges here as we discern in it something of a practical application of the rather philosophic and aesthetic ideas of the first two. The five-mode historical structure introduced in the first essay represents the progressively greater displacement of myth from the Mythic mode, or the portrayal of the world of pure desire, to the Ironic mode, or the portrayal of the world which desire totally rejects. While Frye refused to rank the five methods of symbol analysis of the second essay, in the third he does select the fourth method, archetypal analysis, as being central to the pursuit of the fundamental structures of literature as a whole. Out of Frye's utopian historiography and his symbolic relativity has come a definite and meaningful method of looking at literature. The further relation between the first three essays is apparent in Frye's treatment of *mythos* and *dianoia* here. *Dianoia*, or the structure of imagery which surrounds it, indicates and becomes theme. Theme in turn may take the undisplaced forms of apocalyptic or demonic imagery (linked respectively with a religious heaven and a modern, existential hell) which make no attempt to conceal desire on the one hand or the revulsion of desire on the other. As it happens most often, however, imagery assumes one of several displaced or "analogical" forms. All of these types of imagery become evident by their particular treatment of a syndrome of seven categories which stretch from the divine world in a kind of chain of imagistic being down to the mineral and water worlds. (For an impressive application of this theory of imagery categories to practical criticism the reader is referred to Frye's article "Literature as Context: Milton's *Lycidas,*" along with others, in *Fables of Identity.*)

Now, when the *dianoia* or the complex pattern of imagery moves in narrative or mythic time, it begins to take on the form of one of four "pregeneric narratives" or *mythoi,* which are "broader than, and logically prior to, the ordinary literary genres."[28] These are the season-oriented structures of Comedy, Romance, Tragedy, and Irony and Satire. At this point, as Frye says, "a somewhat forbidding piece of symmetry turns up in our argument." Frye is referring to his discovery of six "phases" in each *mythos,* whose relations to the phases of adjacent *mythoi* defy simple description here. But we may condense the argument for the present purpose.

The important idea to grasp about the four *mythoi,* their six phases and seven categories of imagery, is that they are cyclical in nature. The sixth phase of any particular *mythos* moves toward an atmosphere similar to the first phase, and each of the seven categories of imagery, stretching from divine to water world, associate naturally with some form of rhythmical, cyclical process in nature, such as death and rebirth, day and night, waking and sleeping, etc. Moreover, the cyclical symbols are naturally divided into four major phases. The dominant quadripartite cyclical symbol here is, as mentioned, the seasonal year, the parts of which correspond to the four *mythoi.* Even from this abbreviated sketch of Frye's schema one must conclude that the symmetry is indeed fearful.

Without disrespect to Frye one probably may admit that the staggering details of these cycles and phases, and the precision with which Frye claims to have sorted them out, do tempt incredulity and even parody. W. K. Wimsatt has provided the latter when in speaking of these architectonics he says, "superimposed fourth-of-July pinwheels, with a reversing sequence of rocket engines, may give a dim idea of the pyrotechnics involved here."[29] Wimsatt registers his appreciation of Frye's importance, though, when he says, "the devil's advocate is not called in until the prospect of canonization is imminent."[30]

This leads us to the central objective of Frye's theory. His ultimate purpose in displaying these phase-cycles is the structuring of a giant *Urmythos* or central myth which the great documents of literature both create and in turn employ. It would be best to repeat Frye's own words at this point.

> The four *mythoi* we are dealing with, comedy, romance, tragedy, and irony, may now be seen as four aspects of a central unifying myth. *Agon* or conflict is the basis or archetypal theme of romance.

> . . . *Pathos* or catastrophe . . . is the archetypal theme of tragedy. *Sparagmos*, or the sense that heroism and effective action are absent, disorganized or foredoomed to defeat, and that confusion and anarchy reign over the world, is the archetypal theme of irony and satire. *Anagnorisis*, or the recognition of a newborn society rising in triumph around a still somewhat mysterious hero and his bride, is the archetypal theme of comedy.[31]

The central myth thus built up of conflict, catastrophe, defeat and transformation is the quest myth, the journey-of-life archetype, the goals of which are widely varied, some of them being wisdom, self-realization, universal love, fertility over the wasteland, and the Holy Grail.

The consequences of this archetypal structure for what we have delineated as Frye's aesthetic position are indeed serious. Though on the one hand we may see a kind of neo-Coleridgean faith in the organic unity of the creative imagination coming through in Frye's belief that the works of the imagination may be formed by an organic synthesis into a vast but totally coherent structure, on the other hand there are slight but clear indications in Frye's discussions of anagogic and archetypal criticism of an evangelistic attitude which threatens to become the "thus-we-see theory which finds the meaning of art in a set of moral generalizations inferred from it."[32] The quotation is from Frye himself in a passage condemning the "thus-we-see" theory of criticism. Up until now it appeared that what we have called Frye's aestheticism would resist this tendency. One wonders at times in Frye's system-making if there is not the germ of yet another "New Humanism" in the Irving Babbitt tradition, or even a renovation of culture under the prescriptive shadow of Matthew Arnold. Frye's empirical, aesthetic, and scientific approach to literature seems to have led him to the discovery of the type of criticism so central and comprehensive that proselytizing for it as the ultimate critical method threatens to become inevitable.

Before examining this problem, however, perhaps it will be best to mollify some readers and solicit others by saying the obvious, i.e., that there are several ways to react to Frye's all-encompassing system. We might sample several critical opinions of Frye's archetypal framework for literature to see some of these.

M. H. Abrams, in his review of *Anatomy*, has reacted rather strongly in announcing that "systems which are too elaborately symmetrical tend to keep order by tyrannizing over the unruly facts." He goes on to say that Frye's attempt to narrow the infinite particulars of literature down to the one and absolute type of unifying myth "yields a 'certainty,' indeed; but it is not the certainty of empirical proof, it is the security of an ultimate abiding place for the monastic compulsion of the human spirit."[33] David Daiches feels that for Frye criticism "becomes a technique of description by categorization and reduction . . . subsuming different works in a class, defining by showing the kind, not the quiddity."[34] And Mr. Wimsatt, arguing along the same lines in his previously cited essay "Criticism as Myth," describes Frye's archetypal method as a mythopoeist's literary cliché collecting.

Another complaint centering around Frye's notion of archetype is that by Robert M. Adams. No one, says Adams, can really say why literary images recur. "We certainly can not," he says, after a perceptive detection of circularity in Frye's argument, "invoke the concept of the archetype defined as 'a symbol which recurs frequently,' to provide an antecedent reason why certain symbols recur frequently."[35]

Still other critics have defended Frye's archetypal system. Geoffrey Hartman, in his essay for the English Institute volume, suggests that in the threat which technology represents in the form of the power to change man's environment and man with it, there is a real need for the "global perspective" in the humanities which Frye represents. Murray Krieger, in the same volume, defends Frye as a kind of Ariel spirit who defies the pull of gravity. In Krieger's view, we see Frye as something of a latter-day Sidney who attempts with all the empiricism he can muster to verify the man-mystic notion of a literary creator who reconstructs the rank, stale, and unprofitable world in response to human desire and the dream of man. Indeed, like Sidney, Frye seems ultimately to be engaged in showing that man as poet is "beyond and over all the workes of that second nature, which in nothing hee sheweth so much as in Poetrie: when with the force of divine breath, he bringeth things forth far surpassing her doings."[36] But lest these defenses seem too utopian and rarefied, there have been voices of pragmatic approval as well. Frye himself writes that "since the book appeared, I have received enough correspondence echoing Mr. Hartman's 'it works; it is teachable' to make me reasonably satisfied with its general usefulness." This seems to discredit what Murray Krieger says of the critics who tried to use Frye's system but found they "could not put him to their uses; they could only apprehend him aesthetically as having the unusable completeness of a poetic entity."[37]

One of the most level-headed criticisms of Frye's archetypal scheme is, oddly enough, Frye's own. Unfortunately, Frye has relegated his comments to the unnumbered and therefore often overlooked footnotes to his text. Commenting on the idea that in the primary or emotional response to literature readers often fail to identify the archetypes present in a work, Frye says, "Archetypal criticism, which can do nothing but abstract and typify and reduce to convention, has only a 'subconscious' role in the direct experience of literature, where uniqueness is everything."[38] This passage successfully anticipates the frequent objection to Frye's system that it ignores the uniqueness of each literary work, and even anticipates Wimsatt's description of archetypal criticism as cliché hunting. As a mere footnote, however, it is not enough in the open nor elaborate enough to stave off these charges.

But all these views, including Frye's own, are from the outside vantage point of critical analysis of Frye's theory. Should we follow the implications of the theory from within, however, by refusing to judge it and seeking only to understand it, we would not only discover the humanism of Frye's thought, but the natural and inevitable heuristic quality of that humanism. This aspect of Frye's criticism is never a program imposed from without, but rather the renovation of imaginative experience from within.

The drive of Frye's argument on the archetypal and anagogic levels of criticism is to posit literature as an "iconography of the imagination," to use his phrase from *Fearful Symmetry*. On an aesthetic level this would mean that literature is a world of sheer imaginative invention which is so totally different from, albeit derived from, the sub-literary world of nature that any attempt to establish links of meaning between these worlds would be doomed to inaccurate statements and charges of the misrepresentation of the nature of art. We are reminded here of Frye's belief that literature is autonomous, has reference only to its own world, and ultimately that nature becomes not the container but the thing contained by an imaginary construct which engulfs it. On the other hand, Frye's 1951 article "The Archetypes of Literature" stresses the ritual origin of mythic narratives, and the oracular, epiphanic origin of mythic significance or theme, indicating that the primitive "sources" of literature's sources were the facts of life, and still may be. In other words, archetypal criticism may be "a kind of literary anthropology, concerned with the way that literature is informed by pre-literary categories such as ritual, myth and folk tale."[39] If so, then literature must be the iconography of the completely *human* imagination—where "human" implies the social, moral, physical, and spiritual complexities which must originally have given rise to those rituals of rhythmic and cyclical configurations and the timeless moments of oracular insight.

We begin, then, with Frye's discussion which closes the third essay, to stress the notion which Frye introduced in the second essay. In that instance Frye stated that criticism should proceed with symbol analysis on the assumption that a potential relationship exists between literary creation and the worlds of truth and fact—in short, the human world as opposed to the imaginative world in isolation. As Frye shows in the fourth essay and his "Tentative Conclusion," the literary universe is bound up of necessity with the entire verbal universe because any rhetorical organization of grammar and logic partakes of the nature of literature, and because everything verbal may possibly be founded on the same structural archetypes that the study of literature has located.

In the beginning of the fourth essay Frye makes his most explicit statement of the structural organization of the *Anatomy*, and in the process schematizes the origin of the dilemma which we have before us and the dilemma criticism must always face—that is, the problem of the relation of the art work to the realms of the autonomous operation of the imagination on the one hand, and human life on the other. In his schematic description Frye places the poetic symbol midway between two sets of three categories, one set on the side of social action or moral sense and the other on the side of thought or pure intellect. We see the poetic symbol hung between idea, precept, and dream on the one hand, and event, example, and ritual on the other. In this separation of the categories, out of which it is clear that poetic images do arise, into aesthetically and humanistically oriented groups, we have a clear representation of the dilemma which has existed so long about the nature of the literary work of art.

Once again, then, it appears that Frye has in his perspicacious way anticipated such criticism as both Geoffrey Hartman and W. K. Wimsatt make of Frye's schizophrenia in dealing with literature. They and many others have noted Frye's combination of approaches rather than his choice of a single approach, and they have been troubled by the contradictions this produces. But Frye had already quite carefully explained the conceptual and pragmatic reasons for adopting antithetical views toward literature. He explains again in his response to their essays:

> Mr. Hartman also notes in me a combination of interests which are partly scientific (perhaps the wrong word, though mine) and partly evangelical (certainly the right word, though not mine), the same mixture of detachment and engagement which exists in most areas of the humanities. These two aims are contradictory, but as they are both essential, they have simply got to contradict: this is part of the paradox that Mr. Wimsatt speaks of as inherent in criticism.[40]

Frye's recognition of this dichotomy in the nature of criticism is nothing new, but his handling of the ramifications of the situation is unique.

We have seen how Frye's literary universe expanded into a total verbal universe. But literary criticism is the means by which we are able to learn about and understand this verbal universe, since literature provides the structural principles for it. Like Cassirer, who dealt with the phenomenon of language in his first volume of *The Philosophy of Symbolic Forms*, Frye understands the absolute primacy of the word and the way in which it not only signals reality, but becomes reality. When we understand all this Frye suggests that we will have taken the first step toward a cultural revolution of the most fundamental sort.

In order to understand Frye's humanistic and educational thought, in order to keep from too soon dismissing it as a delusion or a program which has palpable designs on its subjects, one must understand Frye's defense of the intimate ties which literature, as something like a form symbolic of the human imagination, has with life. In his essay "Reflections in a Mirror," Frye states quite simply the belief which lies behind what has been called his "evangelistic" attitude. He writes, "literature is not ultimately objective: it is not simply there, like nature; it is there to serve mankind."[41] How logical this is. Nature was at first "simply there" but in his primitive situation man went to work on it in the form of rituals and myths, transforming it in his mind to conform with the serviceable notion of nature which his desires conceived. Were the products of this imaginative activity still simply there, it is sure that man would perform operations on them again. The mind of man loathes a void and an isolated entity; there must be use and purpose in the elements of man's existence, as nothing less than the whole shape of history indicates. The world of art as the prized realm it represents for man cannot be the island of isolation, the home of the "shivering virgin," no matter how beautiful she is. Because man has surrounded himself so closely and so lovingly with the world of art it seems fair to conclude that it has a purpose and a use for man beyond aesthetic pleasure but still linked with it. It is this which leads Frye to say that literature as the art of language exists to serve mankind.

But here Frye's system asks us to remain sophisticated. That the usefulness of art is assumed is no reason to conclude that its use as in the raw material of a cultural refinement program to be devised for the untutored minds of unsuspecting freshmen, or any form of a program of humanistic value to be imposed from without and inculcated into the minds of dullards on the lower slopes of a cultural purgatory. While there is a fundamental sympathy in Frye's theory for the objective aims of Matthew Arnold, there is no room for the doctrine of touchstones which will serve as portable measuring devices of the best that has been thought and said. Such is only an externally applied system of social improvement which can only work on those already sufficiently sensitive to benefit from an exposure to fine art. Neither is there room in Frye's system for the prescriptive tenets of the Babbitt-More New Humanism in which prejudice is allowed to rule over and dismiss a great body of imaginative literature. One sees that Frye's respect for the imagination in whatever form it exhibits itself, and his impatience with any form of directive from criticism to literature would cancel all claims for this kind of misnamed humanism.

Frye's humanism calls rather for a renovation of admiration for the power and the works of the human imagination. When criticism performs its finest task it indicates the structure of literature and the structure of other participants in the verbal universe—psychology, anthropology, theology, law, and all else built out of words. It shows in detail how the imagination works in building these vast structures in the form of myths, not in the sense that they are imaginary, but in the sense that they are imaginative constructs which represent the social and human ideals of man. Criticism in Frye's theory performs the vital function of mediating between the worlds of imaginative creation and knowledge, between art and its counterpart, science, and between myth and concept. Criticism, then, cannot avoid the assertion of value, but as Frye says,

> the question of evaluation in criticism is not . . . a matter of individual appraisal, as one would appraise the value of a diamond or a piece of antique furniture; it is part of a social and moral struggle, of what Ionesco, making an essential distinction that Mr. Wimsatt misses, calls the opposition of archetypes to stereotypes.[42]

Frye looks upon myths, and the verbal institutions which are informed by them, as visions offered by men's imaginations of the total human situation. Quite obviously an exposure to the foundations of society will eventually lead to a greater understanding of its nature and goals. The culture which is assumed by the imaginative vision of art is nothing less than the culture of man, and the nature of that culture is free, classless, and urbane.

We cannot fail to notice that the performance of the imagination lies at the heart of Frye's notion of a cultural revolution. As he says in *The Educated Imagination*, "the fundamental job of the imagination in ordinary life, then, is to produce, out of the society we have to live in, a vision of the society we want to live in."[43] We must realize by now, however, that this is not the job which the imagination "has to" or "must" perform, it is the job which it does perform of its own volition. Frye's critical method found that out by entering into literature with no preconceived notions and no proclivity to judge what it found. In discovering the nature of literature, though, Frye's criticism professes to have discovered that it speaks to man through common ideals whose realization delights the imagination even as it labors to realize them.

In this way Frye's criticism preserves an unwavering dedication to the aesthetic idea of the primacy and the autonomy of the imagination. In the process of examining the works of this imagination the ideal critic must turn off his humanity, don the ascetic and aesthetic robes of the anatomist, and be ruthlessly honest in his quest of what informs those works. When, however, he is forced to conclude that in its ultimate significance art is not concerned, in a sterile relationship, with art alone or artificial beauty, but with the vision of the nature of all-too-human society and the human heart, then the critic must not cower in embarrassed silence, but attempt to graft the ideals of the aesthetic tradition upon the precepts of the humanistic tradition. Then, in the capacity of what we might call an aesthetic humanist, he must be committed to the task of offering his audience a disinterested yet purposive expression of his vision. Exhibiting this hybrid attitude in full flower, Frye says,

> the critic's function is to interpret every work of literature in the light of all the literature he knows, to keep constantly struggling to understand what literature as a whole is about. Literature as a whole is not an aggregate of exhibits with red and blue ribbons attached to them, like a cat show, but the range of articulate human imagination. . . . Literature is a human apocalypse, man's revelation to man, and criticism is not a body of adjudications, but the awareness of that revelation, the last judgment of mankind.[44]

Admittedly such language always leaves us slightly breathless. But Frye has not been merely an Olympian voice speaking from presumed heights; he has been tirelessly willing as well to descend to the workaday world of education and practical criticism. It would be unfair to suggest, as W. K. Wimsatt does, that Frye has been only a visionary critic, and as such far less successful than a visionary poet. For one soon discovers that Northrop Frye's performance as a practical critic of literature and an educator who defends the value of the liberal education has been as impressive as his theoretical work. The pattern of his career is in this way similar to that of Ernst Cassirer who, after the remarkable theoretical explorations of *The Philosophy of Symbolic Forms*, spoke eloquently in defense of liberal education and the cultivation of the imagination in *The Logic of the Humanities.*

Several of Frye's books attest to his energy on the practical level of literary criticism and in the area of educational theory. In *Fables of Identity* Frye has collected a number of his previously published journal articles to form an anthology of practical criticism. The volume gives evidence of Frye's wide-ranging interests and his ability to apply his unique theories to specific literary works. In all these essays Frye's aesthetic sensitivity to the individual character of a given work is quite clear. Moreover, his books of published lectures, such as *The Well-Tempered Critic* and *The Educated Imagination*, contain not only distillations of his theoretical work, but serious practical suggestions relating to the teaching of criticism to students. Here as elsewhere in his writings Frye asserts the crucial importance for the student of literature of an early acquaintance with the aims and methods of literary criticism. And for Northrop Frye it is clear that while the methods of criticism may vary widely, its ultimate aim must be service to man in the form of an intelligible voice which describes what literature, both work by work, and as a coherent whole, is about.

In all these capacities it seems clear that Northrop Frye has worked in the pattern of an aesthetic humanist, which his theory suggests as both the necessary and the ideal blend of attitudes for the literary critic. Northrop Frye has found it necessary to endorse the Horatian notion of the double nature of literature and he has suited his criticism to it. Thus he preserves literature's unique blend of pleasure and human utility in an attitude which, like Aristotle's, recognizes literature as an art of sensuous and beautiful particulars which, in a mysterious way, embody great and moving experiences, and occasionally universal truths.

NOTES

1. Edited with an introductory essay by Murray Krieger, (New York: Columbia University Press, 1966). The volume consists of four critical essays, a reply by Frye himself, and a checklist of writings by and about Frye. Cited hereafter as *NFMC*.
2. Frye, *NFMC*, p. 1.

3. In *Myth and Symbol*, ed. Bernice Slote (Lincoln: University of Nebraska Press, 1963), p. 3.

4. Northrop Frye, *Fearful Symmetry, A Study of William Blake* (Princeton: Princeton University Press, 1947), p. 418. In paperback: Beacon Press, 1962.

5. Ibid., p. 420.

6. Ibid., p. 424.

7. Ibid., p. 418.

8. Northrop Frye, *Fables of Identity, Studies in Poetic Mythology* (New York: Harcourt, Brace & World, 1963), p. 17.

9. Northrop Frye, *Anatomy of Criticism* (Princeton: Princeton University Press, 1957), p. 3. In paperback. New York: Atheneum, 1966). Hereafter cited as *Anatomy.*

10. Frye, *Anatomy*, p. 17.

11. M. H. Abrams, "*Anatomy of Criticism*," *UTQ*, 28 (1958), 190–96.

12. One may justly be disturbed at the discrepancy which exists between Frye's knowledge of, respect for, and use of the work of these men, which is obvious in his notes, and his efficient disavowal of the validity of their work in literary criticism, which is clear in his essays.

13. Frye, *Anatomy*, p. 18.

14. Slote, ed., *Myth and Symbol*, pp. 8–9.

15. Northrop Frye, *The Well-Tempered Critic* (Bloomington: Indiana University Press, 1963), p. 140.

16. Frye, *Anatomy*, p. 28.

17. Frye, *The Well-Tempered Critic*, p. 144.

18. Frye, *Anatomy*, p. 17.

19. Frye, *NFMC*, p. 73.

20. Frye, *Anatomy*, p. 72.

21. See *Anatomy*, p. 92.

22. Ibid., p. 72.

23. Ibid., p. 122.

24. Ibid., p. 119.

25. See his review in *Poetry*, (1957–58), p. 327.

26. Frye, *Anatomy*, p. 134.

27. See *Fables of Identity*, p. 1.

28. Frye, *Anatomy*, p. 162.

29. Frye, *NFMC*, p. 103.

30. Ibid., p. 75.

31. Frye, *Anatomy*, p. 192.

32. Frye, *Fearful Symmetry*, p. 418.

33. *UTQ*, 28 (1958), 196.

34. *MP*, 56 (1958), 70.

35. Robert M. Adams, "Dreadful Symmetry," *Hudson Review*, 10 (1957–58), 618.

36. *An Apologie for Poetrie*, section IIIc in the edition by O. B. Hardison, Jr., in *English Literary Criticism: The Renaissance* (New York, 1963), p. 105.

37. Frye, *NFMC*, pp. 137, 3.

38. Frye, *Anatomy*, p. 361.

39. "The Archetypes of Literature," reprinted in *Fables of Identity*. See p. 12.

40. Frye, *NFMC*, p. 133, 134.

41. Ibid., p. 145.

42. Ibid., p. 143.

43. Northrop Frye, *The Educated Imagination* (Bloomington: Indiana University Press, 1964), p. 140.

44. Ibid., p. 105.

Aesthetic Criticism, Freedom, and the Goals of the Humanities

EUGENE H. FALK
THE UNIVERSITY OF NORTH CAROLINA

I

THE VARIETIES OF AESTHETIC CRITICISM IN THE TWENTIETH CENTURY are as great as the varieties of authors who have contributed to the tradition. The aesthetic stance takes on a didactic coloring in the work of Santayana and Maritain, a political coloring in the work of Sartre, a psychological coloring (actually, the term psychological is inadequate here) in Husserl and Heidegger. What all of these critics and their numerous followers have in common is, first, a conviction that the imagination plays a key role in literary creation; and, second, that to discuss this role and its implications requires a level of sophistication—philosophical as well as artistic—far greater than what is normally found in our journals and polemical debates on "relevance," political involvement, and modernity.

These debates have carried us so far in recent years that the validity of our curricula—indeed, the validity of the profession of letters itself as traditionally understood—has been called into question. A crisis of confidence is evident among scholars, writers, and the public at large which threatens to deprive us not only of our sense of the past but of a balanced, philosophically meaningful sense of the present. This is not the place to attempt a synthesis of the achievements of aesthetic criticism, but it does seem appropriate to remark that the future of the profession of letters, if a future is to exist, lies in the direction of further development of the insights so richly present in the aesthetic tradition. What follows is not an effort at synthesis, but a few notes bringing together elements of the tradition as they bear on the literary work, and, in their implications, on the goals which the humanities pose for themselves.

II

In *Der Ursprung des Kunstwerkes* Martin Heidegger stresses the obvious fact that every work of art uses work material—rock, wood, metal, color, language, tone. He does so to point out one of the basic differences between a tool and a work of art: although both are constructed out of materials, their difference lies in the manner in which these are used. In the case of the tool, the impact of its *usefulness* causes the material to be effaced in the eyes of the beholder; in the case of a work of art, the essential nature of the material is revealed.

This is an important distinction, but its implications need to be examined. To avoid possible confusion, and to remain within the scope of this essay, we shall limit ourselves to literature, however enticing the exploration of parallels among various art forms may be.

The material of literature is language, a coherent structure of words within a given context. Like any other material, language may be used, not only as a tool, but also as material for a work of art. Unlike any other material, language has meaning, and it therefore communicates. When language is used as a tool, its communicative usefulness causes its nature as work material to be effaced, because our awareness is directed toward the object of communication. If a communication is unambiguous, we show no concern for broader implications arising from the manner in which the statement was composed, or from the particular words chosen, and their possible connotations. In this case, we are not induced to "transcend," to go beyond, the communicative meaning of the statement expressed.

If, on the other hand, language is used as material for a work of art, it is still communicative, and therefore, to that extent at least, functional. It is this fact that marks the main difference between language and any other work material used in the creation of an art form. Communication, and therefore functionality, are inherent in language; thus language, in whatever manner or for whatever purpose it may be used, cannot be divorced from its essential characteristic of usefulness. (The reason for this basic differentiating characteristic of language is the fact that it is already a "created" structure, and so communicates a meaning.)

The literary work of art is thus necessarily operative on the functional level, and it is here that it makes a *particular* statement. A statement may be said to be particular in the sense that it pertains to a concretely presented situation (conditions, actions, incidents), regardless of whether or not the situation has a counterpart in existing reality. A statement may be said to have *universality* (in the Aristotelian sense) when it offers the potential for transcending its particularity—that is, for transcending its singular pertinence to the immediately given situation. Thus transcendence on our part is effected by our perception of the allusive force of a statement, of its power to reflect general relevance. (In Aristotelian terms, this general relevance is "that which may happen,—what is possible according to the law of probability or necessity.") It is only by virtue of this quality of revealing the potential as inherent in the actual that a statement may be considered poetic.

What matters in this Aristotelian concept of universality is that it posits as a fundamental principle for the perception of art what we may call a *dual perspective*, as opposed to a specific and exclusive vision. Seen from one focal point, the poetic statement represents an existing, or putative, or desirable reality. From this perspective we direct our vision to the *particular* in the statement—i.e., to the reality which is the object of its communication. If our vision is restricted to this *particular* perspective, if we fail to direct our awareness to the "universal" meaning, we miss the poetic quality of the statement, and therefore the "universal" relevance of the particular situation the statement suggests. With such an exclusive vision we concentrate on the represented reality itself. The material, that is, the language, as well as the structure of the statement, is effaced in our eyes. We are drawn into the experiential world of a particular existence, in which we become involved. We dwell on its inherent qualities: its temporal dimensions, causality, environmental setting, social relations. From this perspective, the statement reveals to us only its immediate function; it becomes a useful key to a world in which we participate emotionally, intellectually, morally, spiritually—but as yet, without reflection or transcendence.

Aristotle ascribes universal quality to a poetic statement when it is composed in such a manner that it presents a unified whole, whose possible reality rests on a cohesion governed by probability or necessity. One of the obvious implications of this primarily aesthetic principle is that a work so composed allows us to focus our vision on a self-contained world, a world quite unlike the agglomeration of disparate units of our empirical, lived reality. We may apprehend not only the concrete existence of this self-contained world, but also its intrinsic relationships and coherences, and even its total cohesion. It is by virtue of this cohesion that we are able to transcend the particularity of this world's concreteness, and behold its universality.

The artist thus offers us a revelation of truth free of the contingencies of time and place. He leads us to focus our perception on the structure of the particulars, so that we may behold the potentiality of the universal. In this process we move from an involvement in the particular to a distanced vision of the universal. The structural principle of cohesion is, however, only a basis for transcendence; without our directed awareness there is no dual perspective, and therefore no eidetic insight. The artist's problem is, then, to induce transcendence, to move the reader from the particular to the universal. He may assume that the cultivated reader will consciously or intuitively effect this transcendence. However, the less cultivated reader may be seduced by the communicative power of language to become involved in the particular representation. In order to combat this tendency toward involvement in the particular, writers in certain literary periods (as, for instance, in French Classicism) have intentionally used subject matter that was divorced from the ordinary experiential world of their readers, and have created characters which were largely depersonalized. By such means they directed their readers to a distanced vision of the work—that is, to a perspective free of emotional involvement—and thereby facilitated their apprehension of universal traits.

However, even the use of such distancing devices on the part of writers proved ineffectual when the sophistication of their reading public declined. Thus traditional literature lost much of its appeal in the course of the eighteenth century in France, because the rising middle class, unprepared as it was to respond to the universal aspects of literature, found classical subject matter too remote from its experience, and therefore of little relevance to its concerns. For these reasons literature was encouraged by the *doctrinaires* to seek its subject matter in topical spheres of interest. Thus literary appeal was no longer to be directed primarily to the intellect, which effects transcendence, but rather to sentiment, which invites involvement. The objective of intellectual transcendence was sacrificed to moralizing. The represented reality was made to appeal to the emotions, and instead of seeking the revelation of universal truth, the public drew the intended moral from an emotionally experienced representation of reality, in which it perceived an example for attitude and conduct.

Literature which reveals the universal differs from literature which offers a moralizing example in that the one affords timeless insights, while the other is primarily concerned with precepts for specific practical application. One represents man in his essential being through particular situations; the other depicts particular situations which may be relevant to men in similar situations. One shows man his human potential regardless of his particular condition; the other shows him his potential within his particular condition. One elicits a dual perspective; the other effects identification through a single specific vision. One is relevant at all times in all places; the other is relevant here and now. One is functional and poetic; the other is primarily functional.

Literature with a moralizing or didactic purpose, tendentious literature of any bias—regardless of whether its primary appeal is to emotion or to intellect—is basically functional. It eschews transcendence and, by emphasizing the particular, it is realistically representational in subject matter. Such literature is concerned with the immediate cause it is intended to serve, and with the temporary dispositions of a public it is supposed to affect. For these reasons it becomes obsolete once its cause has been won or the concerns of the public have changed. Because tendentious literature relies on realism (and often on an emotional appeal) to achieve its purpose, realistic representation has often been falsely identified with characteristics peculiar to tendentious literature. Realism itself has thus frequently been seen as reducing our perspective to the exclusive vision of the particular, limiting our participation to an involvement in the represented objects themselves, and stifling our own potential for transcendence as well as that of the work of art itself.

This endowing of realism with the characteristics of functional literature accounts, at least to a considerable degree, for the various tendencies in the arts to deform, distort, and generally render less recognizable the objects represented. Describing such tendencies, Ortega speaks of the "dehumanization" of art. Whatever the specific historical reasons for this reorientation may have been at different times and in numerous instances, the aesthetic justification for the flight from realism lies in the belief that realism hinders or even precludes eidetic insight.

Yet realistic representation need not have such an effect: it need not restrict the reader's perception of universality simply because it draws its subject matter from daily life. Even naturalistic works, in which subject matter is used primarily for sociological documentation, need not limit the sensitive reader to involvement in particulars alone. Indeed, the best realistic and naturalistic works invite transcendence on the part of an educated and cultivated reader.

However, political necessity, or commitment to a cause, or the desire to reach a wide public, may cause a writer to sacrifice the "poetic" quality of his writing in order to offer useful tools for basic social or spiritual exigencies, or pander to the tastes of a public which seeks in literature messages pertinent to its own concerns. Instead of transcendence, such literature seeks functionality, immediate relevance, or titillation.

Thus we see that, within a realistic representation, particulars may be used primarily to offer stimulating subject matter, opportunity for involvement, examples for behavior, or pleasure derived from a recognition of familiar reality. Even the use of realistic particulars for such purposes necessitates their being grouped into a structure which has at least a rudimentary cohesion. Yet realistic particulars may also be used to create more complex structures which afford a grasp of the universal. Such structures displace the focus of our vision from a concentration on particulars alone and direct it toward the universality which emerges from them. This dual vision, as we have already observed, results in an experience of timelessness which is an attribute of universality. No doubt such an experience accounts for the sense of liberation which accompanies such a vision, a liberation from the transitoriness of particular manifestations and from the insignificance to which they are reduced by passing time. Thus in the course of a vision of universality we transcend not only particulars but time as well, and the universal, set free from time, manifests its significance.

However, our experience of timelessness, resulting from this vision of universality (in the Aristotelian sense), is based on our grasp of only two of the possible coherences within a created structure—that is to say, on the coherences governed by probability and necessity. But there is also another basis for our perception of timelessness in a literary work, and this is our grasp of its total structural cohesion. In the process of this kind of perception, instead of restricting our attention to those coherences that are governed by probability and necessity, we expand the scope of our vision to encompass the various coherences which make up the cohesion of a work's structure. These coherences are woven by the most intricate correlations of word structures, motif structures (i.e., interrelationships of images, actions, incidents, gestures and even silences), and thematic structures (i.e., interrelationships of contextually determined meanings carried by motifs). The whole cohesion of these patterns constitutes what may properly be called the *Gestalt* of the literary work of art, i.e., the totality of its structural features.

In our perception of this total cohesion, as in our perception of universality, we displace the focal point of our vision from an emphasis on the particulars themselves, and in this process we also achieve a sense of timelessness. The experience of timelessness in our perception of a work's universality is derived from our recognition that certain essential features of a particular time- and place-bound situation exhibit an affinity with the essential features of other situations in different times and places. Our sense of timelessness in the perception of a work's *Gestalt*, however, results from our recognition of its uniqueness as a structure. With regard to the universal, timelessness derives from our recognition of the potential recurrence of essential features in the human condition. With regard to the *Gestalt* of a work, timelessness derives from our recognition of its structural uniqueness, a uniqueness which lifts it above the flux of time, by virtue of the significance due to its singularity. Unique thoughts, events, or persons are obliterated by the passage of time unless they are captured within a carefully wrought structure. Even relatively insignificant events or persons assume significance by virtue of our seeing them within a unique world of interrelationships. Emma Bovary, seen within existing reality, would lack all significance, and be condemned to eternal oblivion. Our vision of her as a timeless character is due to our perception of her world in all the complexity of its interrelationships.

Yet even Emma Bovary, ordinary as she might be in existing reality, acquires a unique significance by virtue of her representation as a character. This is true, first of all, because the representation of her as a character is largely determined by the fact that she is a component part of the total structure of a novel. Secondly, this is true because she herself is a representation, and in creating any literary representation, the artist must necessarily select and arrange various features of the object described into a microcosmic *Gestalt* (as distinct from the macrocosmic *Gestalt* of the whole). Thirdly, this is true because, as language is used as a work material to convey both the microcosm of each part of the work and the macrocosm of the whole, the potentiality of language as a work material is fully manifested, and its essential nature is laid bare in its structure. We then see the descriptive potentiality of language, its power to render a reality through contextually arranged words. This reality has no objective existence, and thus it does not become apprehensible until it has achieved its manifest shape through language. This fact may account for Heidegger's assertion that the work of art reveals the very nature of the work material (language), and in the case of literature, we should add, of the raw material (*Stoff*) as well. What is revealed to us as the nature of the raw material is its hidden diversity; and borrowing Heidegger's terms (which he uses in reference to the earth), we may say that the raw material is enclosed within itself, and withdrawn into itself, guarding and hiding its secret, "undisclosed and unexplained." The tension between language and raw material is thus manifested by the former reaching out toward the latter to wrest its secret from it.

One may transcend some material by imagination alone and grasp intuitively the *Gestalt* of certain poems solely from the tension between the words used and the contextual meaning they convey. But in most instances the world of literature does not reveal itself to imagination and intuition alone: an understanding of the spirit of the times and of the spiritual, intellectual, and ethical orientation of the author may also be necessary. Yet it is one thing to behold a literary work of art as a focal point from which a unique world, and an essential vision of it, may be perceived, and it is quite another thing to view a work as a *document* of the spirit of the times in which it was created and of the orientation of a particular author.

In the latter case, we use an iconological approach. No work manifests comprehensively the spirit of the time which determines it; yet neither is any work entirely free of the cultural traits of its period. From an iconological perspective, the work is seen as a "particularized evidence" of its determining forces. In order to discover and interpret these forces, we must be able to approach our task with informed insight and identify the features of a work as relating to a particular cultural tradition. Furthermore, we must be able to recognize an author's particular position within a cultural tradition, his indebtedness as well as his contributions to it, so that we may appreciate the originality of the work in its cultural setting. This approach serves only as a preliminary procedure, but as a factual formulation it is indispensable for an understanding and appreciation of literature. A broad humanistic education is therefore a prerequisite for the reader's attaining the fullest cultural and artistic experience which a literary work of art has to offer.

It is, however, essential to recognize that this preliminary approach focuses upon the work first from what is called the iconographical perspective. To view the work from this perspective is to identify its "factual" and "expressional" meanings, that is, to recognize in the subject matter a representation of what we know from experience to be actually or potentially so. Thus an iconographical approach may be said to be one in which we identify the *particulars*. Such an identification, however, does not serve as a point of departure for our vision of the *universal*, but acts as a basis for our iconological apprehension of cultural determining forces, of which the work is a "particularized evidence." In the first instance (in the vision of the universal), we are concerned with "poetic" insights; in the second instance (in the iconological perspective), we are concerned with scholarly understanding.

When we behold in the work of art a focal point from which we seek to perceive its unique world, we rely on the guiding function of the context established by language and on the unity of the structural patterns of its motifs and themes. The represented reality, as distinct from existing reality, manifests itself of necessity within the *contextual cohesion* imposed on it by language and, at the same time, within a *cohesive structure of meanings*. Every judiciously selected word assumes its special meaning, its *being*, from the context in which it occurs. Hence the being of words is determined by the structure of their interrelationships within the cohesion of the context. Before their use within a context, words merely exist, but they reveal their true being within contextual cohesion.

The same may be said of existing reality: objects, conditions, circumstances, qualities, events, actions, and even silences reveal their being in the world of their interrelationships. There is, however, one important difference between the world of existing reality and that of represented reality. In the former, we normally perceive the being of reality by virtue of our involvement in it and by virtue of its functionality. This implies that we grasp only limited aspects of existing reality and we experience emotionally only those interrelationships to which we are individually predisposed. Represented reality, on the other hand, reveals its being through multiple, comprehensive, and unified thematic interrelationships; and it does so only when we have ceased to search for functionality and involvement, and when we have freed our vision by intentional distancing. We may say, then, that the true b
reality may not be fully apprehended unless it is repre
of art—unless it is freed from restricting actualities a
language and thematic cohesion.

III

In the world of represented reality we behold potentialities which are concealed from us in our confrontation with existing reality; we perceive what reality can be, rather than simply what it is in the restricted world of our daily lives. Art liberates reality through structure and expands our understanding as we perceive what reality truly is, when its potential becomes manifest within the work of art.

It is this which has caused aesthetic critics since Kant to describe both the creation and response to art as an experience of freedom, a release from the bonds of personality and tradition which normally limit our vision; and it is this which has led many educators, since the romantic period, to regard humanistic education, rooted in the experience of literature, music, art, history, and philosophy, as the appropriate center of a system intended to educate human beings for life rather than as cogs in an industrial and economic machine.

Finally, in beholding through structure the unique being of represented reality, as well as its universal aspects, we gain a sense of liberation from the fetters of functional particularity. We transcend existing reality through an eidetic vision, as we recognize in the created structure both its beauty and its true being. Surely, here, if anywhere, we find a goal for the humanities worthy of endorsing. Such a goal is a conquest for the creative spirit, which achieves its own potential as it transcends matter and time in its simultaneous grasp of truth, beauty, and universality; as it captures eternity from fleeting moments of existence, and ordered unity from bewildering chaos.